Zero to Hero in Cryptocurrency Trading

Learn to trade on a centralized exchange, understand trading psychology, and implement a trading algorithm

Bogdan Vaida

BIRMINGHAM—MUMBAI

Zero to Hero in Cryptocurrency Trading

Group Product Manager: Kaustubh Manglurkar
Publishing Product Manager: Apeksha Shetty
Senior Editor: Tazeen Shaikh
Technical Editor: Kavyashree K S
Copy Editor: Safis Editing
Project Coordinator: Farheen Fathima
Proofreader: Safis Editing
Indexer: Manju Arasan
Production Designer: Shankar Kalbhor
Marketing Coordinator: Nivedita Singh

First published: September 2023

Production reference: 1150923

Published by Packt Publishing Ltd.
Grosvenor House
11 St. Paul's Square
Birmingham
B3 1RB, UK.

ISBN 978-1-83763-128-5

www.packtpub.com

Contributors

About the author

Bogdan Vaida is a seasoned private investor who has backed over 300 crypto start-ups. He is a founding member of Iron Capital, a VC company incorporated in Dubai. Eight years ago, he founded his own company and has managed teams at various stages of development. He is an advisor for several blockchain projects, including Gravvity, Blockchain Valley Virtual, Gentlemen Capital, Bountie, MetaVill, and Umay. For fun and profit, he trades daily, having his own trading course and programming his own trading indicators and strategies.

About the reviewer

Ratanlal Mahanta is currently working as a quant trader for a quant firm. He has several years of experience in the modeling and simulation of quantitative trading. Ratanlal holds a master's degree in science in computational finance, and his research areas include quant trading, optimal execution, and high-frequency trading. He has over 10 years of experience in the finance industry and is gifted at solving difficult problems that lie at the intersection of markets, technology, research, and design.

Table of Contents

4

Technical Analysis – Technical Indicators   89

7

Finding Your Edge   161

8

Automated Trading   181

9

What's Next?   209

10

BONUS – One Month of Trading   211

Preface

Trading is like being a seasoned captain navigating the unpredictable sea of the market. You have your vessel, the trading strategy, built with your knowledge and experiences. The instruments at your disposal, the indicators and charts, act as your compass and map. The high and low tides of the sea mirror the volatile market prices.

Weather patterns come and go – storms of market uncertainty, peaceful periods of stable prices, the unpredictable gusts of news events stirring the market – yet, the seasoned captain remains steady, adjusting the sails accordingly.

The goal is not to conquer the sea but to ride its waves, to understand its patterns, to respect its power, and to make it an ally. Success is a journey rather than a destination, and each day brings a new sunrise, a new trading opportunity. Just as the captain learns the sea's moods over time, so does the trader grow in understanding the market's rhythms.

Welcome to a journey through the intricate labyrinth of cryptocurrency trading. This book is your seasoned guide, ready to lead you through the twists and turns and equip you with the knowledge to navigate the market's volatile seas. From debunking market myths to building a unique trading strategy, you'll get the foundations you need to weather even the most formidable market storms. It's not just about theory; it's also about practical, hands-on learning. We explore the understanding of market participants, technical analysis, trading psychology, and money management techniques. This journey is about understanding the ebbs and flows of the market, creating and refining your trading system, and learning to ride the market waves, ever prepared for the next trading opportunity.

Who this book is for

This comprehensive guide is designed to cater to the following audience:

- Trading novices eager to learn the ropes and start their journey into cryptocurrency trading
- Crypto market enthusiasts who want to actively participate in trading rather than just holding
- Traders whose initial attempts haven't been successful and want a structured path to improve their results
- Learners who are interested in trading psychology and money management techniques
- Anyone who wants to develop and automate their own successful trading strategies
- Readers looking for hands-on examples, real-time scenarios, and a wealth of interactive resources to help them navigate the dynamic world of cryptocurrency markets

Dive into structured lessons, learn about trading psychology and money management techniques, and develop and automate your own successful trading strategies. With hands-on examples, real-time scenarios, and a wealth of interactive resources, you'll be well-equipped to navigate the dynamic world of cryptocurrency markets and unleash your potential as a cryptocurrency trader.

What this book covers

Chapter 1, Introduction to Cryptocurrency Trading, sets the stage for the structured learning experience that this book aims to provide. The chapter will share the author's story and process and then debunk market myths and explain why many traders lose money. It will help you understand the pitfalls of information circulating among the trading community and equip you with the practical knowledge needed for your trading journey.

Chapter 2, Understanding the Basics, is designed to help you navigate your emotional responses when trading through a risk assessment questionnaire. You will also take your first steps in studying a chart on various timeframes through a unique candlelight story. The chapter will delve into the trading behaviors of different market participants, helping you comprehend why sudden buy or sell actions occur in the market, even if indicators suggest otherwise. Finally, you'll learn about the three different types of markets.

Chapter 3, Technical Analysis – Candles and Patterns, lays the foundation for your trading career by introducing one of the most powerful charting tools: TradingView. This chapter will guide you to see the "story of the price" on your screen and comprehend the emotions driving small price movements through candlestick patterns. You will explore chart patterns for stronger and long-lasting movements, delve into support and resistance areas, and understand the laws that govern them.

Chapter 4, Technical Analysis – Technical Indicators, introduces the most commonly used indicators in trading, making sure you understand how each works and in which situations you should use them.

Chapter 5, The Centralized Exchange, demystifies the operations of centralized exchanges and trading procedures on these platforms. The chapter also discusses an advanced tool that links to centralized exchanges, making the trading process user-friendly.

Chapter 6, Money Management, dives into crucial aspects of trading strategy management, including loss limitation, position sizing, the advantages of maintaining a trading journal, the essentiality of a precise trading plan, and the choice between trading in stablecoin versus Bitcoin.

Chapter 7, Finding Your Edge, guides you through the extensive process of developing and implementing a successful trading strategy, starting with the basics of a trading system, identifying potential trading patterns, and culminating in defining entry and exit points – crucial elements for risk mitigation and profit securing.

Chapter 8, *Automated Trading*, focuses on the technical aspects of trading strategies, starting with creating a custom indicator in TradingView using Pine Script. It then transitions to coding strategies using an open source bot for cryptocurrency trading. This allows for 24/7 trade execution with accuracy and speed, effectively marrying your trading ideas with technical execution for powerful, automated systems. Why not trade while you sleep?

Chapter 9, *What's Next?*, is a road map for your journey after the book. Having learned sufficient theory and practice and developed a strategy that can be traded manually or automatically, this chapter suggests a recommended path forward.

Bonus Chapter, contains trades I took during one month of trading. Here, you can see me in action: see how I analyze Bitcoin, how I think when entering the trades, and even what I feel regarding consecutive wins and losses (yes, I have those too!).

To get the most out of this book

This book builds your trading knowledge from the ground up. If you are interested in automated trading (found in *Chapter 8*), you will need basic programming knowledge in order to learn the Pine Script language, and basic Python knowledge if you want to use Freqtrade to automate your strategy.

Software/hardware covered in the book	Operating system requirements
Python 3.10 or above	Windows, macOS, or Linux
Pine Script V5	

If you are using the digital version of this book, we advise you to type the code yourself or access the code from the book's GitHub repository (a link is available in the next section). Doing so will help you avoid any potential errors related to the copying and pasting of code. The GitHub repository also includes folders with high-quality images for you to follow, along with templates for indicators, strategies, and a backtesting methodology.

In the event any links in the book expire, kindly drop us an email at errataall@packt.com

Download the example code files

You can download the templates mentioned in this book from GitHub at `https://github.com/PacktPublishing/Zero-to-Hero-in-Cryptocurrency-Trading`. If there's an update to the code, it will be updated in the GitHub repository. You can also find the color images there, in case you want to zoom in on the data presented.

We also have other code bundles from our rich catalog of books and videos available at `https://github.com/PacktPublishing/`. Check them out!

Download the color images

We also provide a PDF file that has color images of the screenshots and diagrams used in this book. You can download it here: https://packt.link/pXrot.

Conventions used

There are a number of text conventions used throughout this book.

Code in text: Indicates code words in text, database table names, folder names, filenames, file extensions, pathnames, dummy URLs, user input, and Twitter handles. Here is an example: "We're using the latest version of the Freqtrade interface, v3. We will use the class name PrivateMACross to call the strategy from the command line."

A block of code is set as follows:

```
class PrivateMACross(IStrategy):
    INTERFACE_VERSION = 3
```

Any command-line input or output is written as follows:

```
docker-compose run --rm freqtrade backtesting --config user_data/
config/config-backtesting-book.json --strategy PrivateMACross
--timerange 20210811-20220812 --timeframe 1d -p BTC/BUSD
```

Bold: Indicates a new term, an important word, or words that you see onscreen. For instance, words in menus or dialog boxes appear in **bold**. Here is an example: "If we run this strategy on BTCBUSD 4H and go to the **Strategy Tester** tab, we'd get a -1% net profit."

> Tips or important notes
> Appear like this.

Get in touch

Feedback from our readers is always welcome.

General feedback: If you have questions about any aspect of this book, email us at customercare@packtpub.com and mention the book title in the subject of your message.

Contact the author: If you are interested in contacting the author, feel free to email him at contact@vaidabogdan.com. Make sure to mention the title of the book in the subject of your email.

Errata: Although we have taken every care to ensure the accuracy of our content, mistakes do happen. If you have found a mistake in this book, we would be grateful if you would report this to us. Please visit www.packtpub.com/support/errata and fill in the form.

Piracy: If you come across any illegal copies of our works in any form on the internet, we would be grateful if you would provide us with the location address or website name. Please contact us at copyright@packt.com with a link to the material.

If you are interested in becoming an author: If there is a topic that you have expertise in and you are interested in either writing or contributing to a book, please visit authors.packtpub.com.

Share Your Thoughts

Once you've read *Zero to Hero in Cryptocurrency Trading*, we'd love to hear your thoughts! Scan the QR code below to go straight to the Amazon review page for this book and share your feedback.

https://packt.link/r/1-837-63128-X

Your review is important to us and the tech community and will help us make sure we're delivering excellent quality content.

Download a free PDF copy of this book

Thanks for purchasing this book!

Do you like to read on the go but are unable to carry your print books everywhere?

Is your eBook purchase not compatible with the device of your choice?

Don't worry, now with every Packt book you get a DRM-free PDF version of that book at no cost.

Read anywhere, any place, on any device. Search, copy, and paste code from your favorite technical books directly into your application.

The perks don't stop there, you can get exclusive access to discounts, newsletters, and great free content in your inbox daily

Follow these simple steps to get the benefits:

1. Scan the QR code or visit the link below

https://packt.link/free-ebook/978-1-83763-128-5

2. Submit your proof of purchase
3. That's it! We'll send your free PDF and other benefits to your email directly

1

Introduction to Cryptocurrency Trading

The main purpose of the book you're holding right now is to provide you with a structured way to learn trading in a way that isn't so theoretical, as it dives right into developing and testing a working strategy that you can ultimately automate and get tangible (and financial) benefits from.

In this first chapter, after I share my story and my process, I'll delve right into market myths and why people lose money in trading. As a heads up, most of the information that you hear from other traders (be it on YouTube or other media) will actually sabotage you unless you are familiar with how the market works. My goal for this chapter is for you to understand the myths that losing traders believe in so that you can circumvent them and get to the practical information that will actually help you in your trading career.

In this chapter, we're going to cover the following main topics:

- Disclaimer
- My journey into trading
- Overview of the book's structure
- Market myths

Disclaimer

If you're reading this book in order to become a super-trader and turn all your hard-earned income into billions, heed my warning: this is not how the world works.

There is always an element of chance, and even by correctly applying a trading technique that statistically provides a profit of 20% a month, you may lose money (and one of the reasons is statistics, which we'll talk about later in the book).

That being said, I truly believe that any reader who puts in the work will achieve a measurable degree of success, but I cannot and will not promise any profits realized due to the methods presented here. I think that what any trader needs (and what the world needs, for that matter) is clarity in the decisions they are going to make and the actions they're going to take.

What I can promise is that I will do everything in my power to help you understand how the market works, how you can identify a way to beat it, and how you can test and automate a system that does that day and night. But the rest is up to you.

You are still going to do all the hard work, from crunching the numbers to learning and applying what you've learned numerous times until you develop a successful method. Such a feat is possible and probable, but only with a lot of work.

Still, once that work is done, success is on the horizon, and once you get a taste of that, you are going to find this work enjoyable and fruitful.

Remember that once you have walked a path, even a hard path, walking it again is easier. You will know the road, the signs, the milestones, and the expected outcome, and in time, your trading techniques and developed strategies will become more efficient at beating the market.

My journey into trading

When I was little, I loved *Indiana Jones* movies. I wanted to travel to unfamiliar places, to have adventures, and to experience unique things.

While growing up, I became that explorer. But more than an explorer of places, I became an explorer of learning. I started coding in the 8th grade, and later, I got a well-paid job at a tech company. Then, I found myself needing to learn to socialize better, so I joined *Toastmasters* and learned the art of public speaking, which got me second place at Toastmasters' national public speaking contest. Next, I started doing trainings and helping others learn and learn how to learn. I broke down difficult theoretical concepts and taught them in an experiential, gamified way. I covered a wide range of topics from time management to online course creation, leadership, and personality typologies, and trained people from varied backgrounds such as business, education, and management. This training extended from my home country to countries such as Iceland, Armenia, and China.

After that, I founded my company in sales trainings together with two co-founders, and during the pandemic, we developed a new direction: we provided live webinars to teachers and helped them teach online. Then, we added three other verticals: a national certified trainer-training program, B2B training, and a non-profit featuring a community of 40,000 teachers, helping them develop their teaching skills and grow as educators.

I started trading in 2004 (right before going to college) and increased my account, the equivalent of today's $500, by 10% in only a trimester. I did it by learning and applying technical and fundamental analysis. During that first year, the account grew even more. However, local politics heavily influenced the local stock market, and trading using insider information (insider trading) was common at that time. I was frustrated at being unable to find the reasons behind price movements long after they had occurred, and after a while, I closed my account to dedicate myself to college.

With crypto, I started with the hype of 2017 just before the market crash (the moment when a lot of people withdrew money from crypto, leaving enthusiasts with cryptocurrencies worth less than what they bought them for). I think most people in crypto start before a crash. I bought some **Bitcoin** (**BTC**) and some **Ethereum** (**ETH**), but suddenly, their values dropped significantly. Still, the technology was unique, and I wanted to play in that market, so I started trading it (and learning everything I could about it).

By learning, I mean delving into everything. When I become fascinated by a project, you can find me devoting 12 hours a day to that project. At that time, my company was successful and running on autopilot, so dedicating 4 months to trading was not out of the question. You will see later in the book how I love creating automated systems of profit.

I was pretty successful at trading; during the bull market, I was outperforming Bitcoin's growth by 15% a month (trading all day), and I was looking into how I could automate my trading to better leverage my time. This is how I started learning **Pine Script**, **TradingView**'s scripting language. Pine Script was used to display indicators on charts on TradingView's platform, and learning it helped me develop better strategies and code alerts that would make my phone ring when a trading opportunity was near.

During that time, I was following an influencer's account (`@EmperorBTC`) and he posted a trading technique that I found interesting. I coded his strategy in Pine Script so that I could check its historical success and get alerts as to when I should enter and exit trades, and I shared the code with him. Next, I found myself added to a private group with other successful traders who were trading at another level. Together with these traders and with EmperorBTC's guidance, we were learning at an accelerated pace and developing great strategies that were beating the market.

I was linking those strategies to bots and automating them, dreaming about owning a Tesla and yachting when the 2021 crash happened.

Suddenly, my money-making strategies were unprofitable. Everything that worked during the bull market was still beating Bitcoin, but Bitcoin was also beating itself.

So, I left my dreams for another day and went back to the drawing board. My learning switched from **Exocharts** and **volume profile** techniques to developing strategies that could work for both markets. I learned about **algorithmic trading**, the `pandas` framework, statistics, and how to better evaluate trading strategies considering **drawdowns**, market crashes, and other (not-so-rare) events.

Since then, I have immersed myself in the world of statistics and developed smaller timescale strategies that run on 5-minute candles (a term I will explain in *Chapter 2*) and provide a smaller but consistent profit through a higher number of trades. That is the place where I found I can best use my analytical mind to identify opportunities to beat the market.

And here I am now, giving you a shorter path to arrive at this place of evidence-based trading—a place from which you can identify, test, and automate profitable strategies.

Overview of the book's structure

I am an avid reader. My *Goodreads* account features over 100 books read per year. That is one every three days, including audiobooks. I mostly read fiction now, but I have read my fair share of personal development books and a whole bunch of trading books. What I found out during my page-turning adventures is that most trading books fail in two respects:

- They aren't clear enough. Basically, they jump from concept to concept, making it hard for you to follow, or they immerse you in stories and don't provide enough useful content.

- They don't provide a step-by-step guide to arrive, together with the author, at the finish line. What they do instead is superficially present concepts, tease you, and promote other programs at the end of the book.

Regarding the second point, I actually know a trading book that is delivered for *free* (minus a shipping and handling fee that actually includes the book's price) and teases the reader with methods of success that they can access by paying for a high-ticket program.

However, throughout this book, I aim to provide you with content that is easy to follow and helps you increase your knowledge in cryptocurrency trading (or fill in the gaps if you've traded before) and, step by step, chapter by chapter, get you to a point where you can develop a successful strategy and automate it.

I've organized the chapters sequentially, but feel free to skim anything that you already know. Note that I recommend *skimming*, not *skipping*. Make sure that you fully understand the sections that you're skimming so that you don't miss important information that you'll need later on.

All the chapters contain detailed explanations of the methods presented, diagrams and screenshots that illustrate the points made there, and exercises that I recommend you do so that you can evaluate yourself and build your confidence in the method.

Do those exercises! They are important, not only from a psychological point but also to identify areas you're not sure about or concepts you haven't fully grasped.

I will also provide some templates you can use when trading. I will refer to them in the book when we arrive at the appropriate sections so that you can jump there and use them.

Aaaaand, of course, GitHub. Together with Packt Publishing, we provide a GitHub link to a repository where you can download all the materials presented in the book, ordered by chapters. Here, you will also find high resolution versions of the images shown in the book, in case you want to zoom in on them. Feel free to access this resource at `https://github.com/PacktPublishing/Zero-to-Hero-in-Cryptocurrency-Trading`.

Note that I will also be providing links to a lot of useful content inside the book. Some of them are harder to type, especially if you're not reading the e-book version, but you'll find all of them aggregated in a file in the GitHub repository for you to point and click.

Market myths

There's a lot of information on the internet regarding how to trade successfully. Yet with all of this information, most people using it fail miserably. A few, though, have incredible success and come to like, comment, and share the videos that helped them succeed. Some might even think that the information works, but they just don't know how to apply it. They too like, comment, and share, mostly because they like the speaker, not because the content actually works.

In this section, we're going to take a closer look at some common market myths and recommendations newbies get from other people, mostly on social media. Next, I'm going to debunk those myths and help you get a critical way of looking at the market—a way that helps you discern random advice from true and tested information.

I will find a successful strategy on YouTube

Here's a screenshot of what a simple search for a trading strategy shows on YouTube. This is what most people who are interested in trading get when they first look for advice:

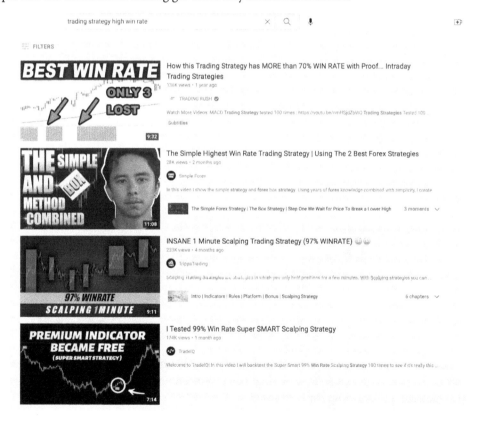

Figure 1.1 – Searching "trading strategy high win rate"

Most of my coaching clients ask me to check one strategy or another that they have found while browsing YouTube. It is either a well-known influencer or a strategy that looks good on screen and that, every time, fails in practice. To prevent that, I tell everyone that I am not looking at a strategy unless it comes with clear instructions and at least 100 trades in a spreadsheet.

I will make money paying for trading signals

Here's another screenshot of what a newbie might look for. The classical get-rich-quick scheme. Over million results later, we see this:

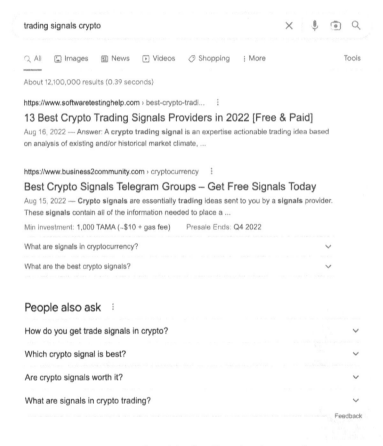

Figure 1.2 – Searching "trading signals crypto"

Trading signals are "*triggers for action.*" After an algorithm (or a human) decides it is the time to enter (or exit) an asset, it sends (or they send) a message to a private group that you subscribe to, where you receive that message and can enter (or exit) a trade.

This can be worse than paying for a winning strategy. When you pay for a strategy, you can test it, understand it, figure out whether it works, and adapt it to the market. With signals, the only thing you can do is record them in a spreadsheet and check their profitability over an extended period (a period during which you are paying for the signal).

Would you trust an estate agent you do not know telling you to buy an apartment? Would you buy it? Even if they are well intentioned and not doing it (only) for the money, even if they are right most of the time, you are still buying only one apartment and might just be unlucky. Also, you are not learning what to look for when buying an apartment; that knowledge is kept secret from you, and you are just told that this is a good apartment.

I will run a successful trading bot

I still remember a phone call from my best friend from high school, enthusiastically telling me that some crypto bots can help me make money. What I need to do is invest in them, and they will trade in my place and give me the profits. He sounded like he'd found the golden goose.

One thing he did not take into consideration was that this was all happening during the bull run. The bot could have just held Bitcoin and it would have made a profit.

And yes—some of those trading bots worked during the bull run, just as in specific market conditions, there are strategies and trading signals that work. But they worked because everyone was investing during that time, and even holding Bitcoin without trading was increasing your assets compared to the dollar. But when you traded, you were actually losing money if you were comparing your portfolio to Bitcoin because Bitcoin was growing faster.

It is not a bad idea to run a trading bot if you know what you are doing. But the bots that most providers offer run based on strategies that if you really test them... do not work!

Yep—you will learn later that **exponential moving average (EMA) intersection** (or any other strategy for that matter) works in theory, and it also works when you plot entries and exits on the chart, but when you crunch the numbers, it does not. That is because the indicator is "repainting" the chart (it's redrawing the lines after the fact) and discounting the lower timeframes. It also does not take fees and slippage into consideration, which can add up quite quickly when trading.

But let's not get into the details just yet. Just promise me you will not pay for crypto bots until you have at least read the whole book. By the end of it, you will not need to pay for any bots, you'll be able to build your own.

I will successfully invest in copy-trading platforms

I am not against copying good investors or traders. On these platforms, you can use filters to find out how profitable (and risky) the traders were during the past years and figure out the ones that made money during both the bull and the bear markets. Then, calculate all the fees that you would incur while doing this (platform fees, traders fees), and see whether you would still be in profit. If so, sure—why not?

The problem is that most of these platforms do not show how the trader performed compared to Bitcoin . It's not particularly relevant if they made profits in dollars ($) during a bull run because you could simply hold Bitcoin and achieve the same result. Next, they do not provide proper statistics, and, for that matter, they do not show how much you would have made minus taxes and fees if you had invested in a particular trader. Also, do the traders have enough of a history? Did they run into the last two bear markets, or have they just recently made an account and have bigger short-term profits just because they risk more? Would you really trust the platform with your money?

Just to name a situation where the charts looked good but the logic was flawed: copy traders were investing only in the Terra stablecoin, which had a 10% staking yield. They were beating the dollar by 10% and the charts looked amazing. However, the portfolio was not diversified, and when the ecosystem collapsed, all the traders, copy traders, investors, and other involved parties lost their money. If you were to check current traders on the platform, you would see that they are not successful traders (their total results are poor). However, if you had looked at them before the Terra crash, they would have been at the top, and you would have probably invested in them. Here's a link to what happened to Terra: `https://www.forbes.com/sites/qai/2022/09/20/what-really-happened-to-luna-crypto`.

And why do these strategies, signals, and bots fail?

In this section, I will bust the myths we went through in the previous sections. However, since I will be providing examples that might not be that clear to understand if you are new to trading, feel free to skim through this part and come back to it after reading *Chapter 3* and *Chapter 4*.

Reason #1 – A high win rate does not mean a high profit

From the following options, which would you choose?

A.   A 75%-win-rate strategy where you win $1 75% of the time and lose $10 25% of the time

B.   A 20%-win-rate strategy where you win $10 20% of the time and you lose $1 80% of the time

"Market-mathics" would say that with option A, over a long time, you would win $1 for trades out of and lose $10 on a fourth one. That means -$1,750, a big loss for a 75%-win-rate strategy over 1,000 trades. For option B, you would win $10 for trade out of five and lose $1 for the rest. That means a $1,200 profit for a 20% win rate strategy over 1,000 trades.

If you don't believe my calculations, you can always ask ChatGPT:

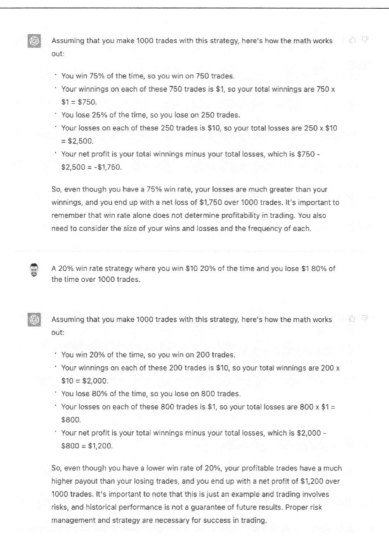

Assuming that you make 1000 trades with this strategy, here's how the math works out:

· You win 75% of the time, so you win on 750 trades.
· Your winnings on each of these 750 trades is $1, so your total winnings are 750 x $1 = $750.
· You lose 25% of the time, so you lose on 250 trades.
· Your losses on each of these 250 trades is $10, so your total losses are 250 x $10 = $2,500.
· Your net profit is your total winnings minus your total losses, which is $750 - $2,500 = -$1,750.

So, even though you have a 75% win rate, your losses are much greater than your winnings, and you end up with a net loss of $1,750 over 1000 trades. It's important to remember that win rate alone does not determine profitability in trading. You also need to consider the size of your wins and losses and the frequency of each.

A 20% win rate strategy where you win $10 20% of the time and you lose $1 80% of the time over 1000 trades.

Assuming that you make 1000 trades with this strategy, here's how the math works out:

· You win 20% of the time, so you win on 200 trades.
· Your winnings on each of these 200 trades is $10, so your total winnings are 200 x $10 = $2,000.
· You lose 80% of the time, so you lose on 800 trades.
· Your losses on each of these 800 trades is $1, so your total losses are 800 x $1 = $800.
· Your net profit is your total winnings minus your total losses, which is $2,000 - $800 = $1,200.

So, even though you have a lower win rate of 20%, your profitable trades have a much higher payout than your losing trades, and you end up with a net profit of $1,200 over 1000 trades. It's important to note that this is just an example and trading involves risks, and historical performance is not a guarantee of future results. Proper risk management and strategy are necessary for success in trading.

Figure 1.3 – ChatGPT's math works

But note that I have said, *"over a long time."* If you toss a coin, there's a 50-50 chance to get heads or tails. When tossing, you can get heads four, five, and even six times in a row. So, even though you would choose option B for higher profitability, you might not be as profitable as option A in the first few trades.

Reason #2 – Community and echo chambers

When a famous influencer posts a strategy on YouTube, you will see a lot of positive reactions. You will read about how some people had quite a successful run with that strategy and how grateful they are, and, right next to them, how other people want to better understand it and need additional explanations.

Now, imagine a bell curve. Or better yet, look at it:

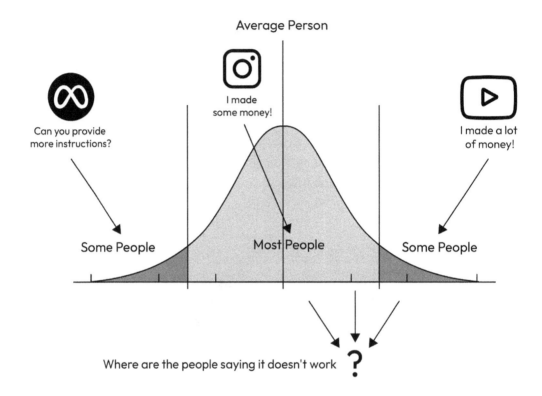

Figure 1.4 – A bell curve

Imagine a strategy that is profitable. Even though most people applying the strategy will turn a profit, statistics show us that a small percentage of people will not profit (and another smaller percentage will profit a lot).

That is all reasonable, right?

Well, imagine an influencer posts a trading strategy without testing it. Even though most people will not profit, the bell curve shows us that, even then, a small percentage will still profit (yes—even with an unprofitable strategy).

OK—but then, wouldn't the number of comments saying that the strategy does not work overflow the comments saying that it does?

Well, not quite. Because you are on an influencer's platform and their following already believes in them. Welcome to... the echo chambers!

An echo chamber refers to situations in which beliefs are amplified or reinforced by communication and repetition inside a closed system and insulated from rebuttal. By participating in an echo chamber, people are able to seek out information that reinforces their existing views without encountering opposing views, potentially resulting in an unintended exercise in confirmation bias. Echo chambers may increase social and political polarization and extremism. On social media, it is thought that echo chambers limit exposure to diverse perspectives, and favor and reinforce presupposed narratives and ideologies. (Echo chamber (media). (2023, August 29). On Wikipedia: `https://en.wikipedia.org/wiki/Echo_chamber_(media)`).

An influencer runs their own echo chamber where the community will support them (and believe in them) even though they might be wrong.

When people are writing about the technique's success, the vast majority for which the technique did not work will think that it is their fault and that they do not know how to use it and will either skip to the next video or ask for more details on how to use that technique.

Basically, the echo chamber will echo the influencer's beliefs and propagate a feeling of success on the platform (and yes—some people will have success using that trading technique).

Reason #3 – The strategy was not tested properly

To check whether a strategy provides an advantage over the market, that strategy needs to be tested correctly. But what does "correctly" actually mean? Here are a few questions you can ask yourself before you apply the strategy:

- Did the trader test it over 30 trades? 100? 10,000?

- Was it tested during the bull market? During a bear market?

- Was it backward tested over a sufficient period? Did it take into consideration tokens that were unlisted from the exchange or tokens that were dumped? Market switching direction? New tokens listings? Does it need new tokens to age in the market before trading?

- Was it forward tested? Was it paper traded? Was it tested live? For how long?

- Does it work on all token pairs or only on large-cap/mid-cap/small-cap/blockchains/volatile assets and so on?

- Does it take into consideration lower timeframes, intra-candle movement, repainting, slippage, fees, and drawdown?

- Can somebody else reproduce the results by following the exact same steps?

- Was it tested automatically or manually?

- Is it well defined or is it discretionary? Can it be coded into clear rules? Is the risk mentioned? Or the drawdown?

- If it will be traded manually (for example, discretionary strategies), does it mention the time availability needed for those results?

- Were delays such as market delays, API delays, overfitting, and underfitting taken into consideration?

- Was it detrended or is it biased toward a market direction?

- Does it work in the current market? Does it work in crypto?

And the list goes on...

In *Chapter 5*, we will talk more about what you must watch out for when testing a strategy and how to do that, but for now, understand that there is more to testing a strategy than looking for 5 minutes over a chart and pinpointing places to successfully trade it.

Reason #4 – Past performance is no guarantee for future results

Even if the strategy was tested successfully and it works, **markets change, and past performance cannot guarantee future results**. Do not expect your strategy to work until the dawn of crypto. Understand the necessity of fine-tuning it from time to time and even changing it in favor of other strategies better suited to the markets you will find yourself in.

Reason #5 – The outcome of any single trade has a random outcome

No matter how successful a trade is, you cannot take into account all the factors that go into that particular trade. By random, I do not mean 50-50 randomness; even a trade that has a 99% success rate will, over time, fail in 1 out of 100 situations. So, any one single trade that you take can be that trade that has a 1% chance of failing.

Extrapolate this into a situation where an influencer is showing how a strategy is successfully applied in five consecutive situations. That is irrelevant statistically, but it sure looks good in a video.

Reason #6 – Cognitive biases

According to *Wikipedia, "A cognitive bias is a systematic pattern of deviation from norm or rationality in judgment. Individuals create their own "subjective reality" from their perception of the input. An individual's construction of reality, not the objective input, may dictate their behavior in the world. Thus, cognitive biases may sometimes lead to perceptual distortion, inaccurate judgment, illogical interpretation, or what is broadly called irrationality."*

And here's a list of biases, on the same page: `https://en.wikipedia.org/wiki/Cognitive_bias#List_of_biases`.

Here are some biases that can affect an influencer, you, or any trader, for that matter:

- **Confirmation bias** (`https://en.wikipedia.org/wiki/Confirmation_bias`) is the tendency to search for, interpret, favor, and recall information in a way that confirms or supports one's prior beliefs or values. "*Look at how I correctly predicted the market. This indicator also proves my view.*"

- **Attribution bias** (https://en.wikipedia.org/wiki/Attribution_bias) is a cognitive bias that refers to systematic errors made when people evaluate or try to find reasons for their own and others' behaviors. "*I succeeded in that particular trade because of my technique, not because of random market movements.*"

- **Illusion of control** (https://en.wikipedia.org/wiki/Illusion_of_control) is the tendency for people to overestimate their ability to control events. "*My small modification to this indicator is what makes the strategy work (not the small sample size where I overfitted).*"

- **The overconfidence effect** (https://en.wikipedia.org/wiki/Overconfidence_effect) is a well-established bias in which a person's subjective confidence in their judgments is reliably greater than the objective accuracy of those judgments, especially when confidence is relatively high. "*After 10 trades, I can tell you that the strategy works correctly!*"

- **Optimism bias (or the optimistic bias)** (https://en.wikipedia.org/wiki/Optimism_bias) is a cognitive bias that causes someone to believe that they are less likely to experience a negative event. "*I won't test this strategy over a larger time range because I know it will work; my first trades were pretty successful.*"

- **Selection bias** (https://en.wikipedia.org/wiki/Selection_bias) is the bias introduced by the selection of individuals, groups, or data for analysis in such a way that proper randomization is not achieved, thereby failing to ensure that the sample obtained is representative of the population intended to be analyzed. "*My strategy works because I have tested it well, not because I tested it in a favorable market.*"

- **Hindsight bias** (https://en.wikipedia.org/wiki/Hindsight_bias), also known as the **knew-it-all-along phenomenon** or **creeping determinism**, is the common tendency for people to perceive past events as having been more predictable than they actually were. People often believe that after an event has occurred, they would have predicted or perhaps even known with a high degree of certainty what the outcome of the event would have been before the event occurred. "*You can see how many times we can apply the strategy on the chart. Look here, here, and here.*"

- **Illusory correlation** (https://en.wikipedia.org/wiki/Illusory_correlation) is the phenomenon of perceiving a relationship between variables (typically people, events, or behaviors) even when no such relationship exists. "*Bitcoin always goes down before the halving, so the next time it goes down, it will be because of this.*"

- **The representativeness heuristic** (https://en.wikipedia.org/wiki/Representativeness_heuristic) is used when making judgments about the probability of an event under uncertainty. We use heuristics to create shortcuts in our decision-making, but when something is more representative to a group, it doesn't mean it is also more likely to happen. "*When these two indicators show buy, the price goes up. You can see this happening here, here, and here. So, these are correlated.*"

- **Insensitivity to sample size** (https://en.wikipedia.org/wiki/Insensitivity_to_sample_size) is a cognitive bias that occurs when people judge the probability of obtaining a sample statistic without respect to the sample size. *"Based on the last 50 trades, I can assure you this strategy works."*

- **Random reinforcement** (https://www.investopedia.com/articles/trading/09/random-reinforcement-why-most-traders-fail.asp) occurs when a trader misattributes a random outcome to their own skill or lack of skill. The market sometimes rewards bad players too and, statistically, some bad traders get rewarded more than others, giving them the illusion that they are skilled. *"I'm a successful trader because I have good trading skills, not because I was lucky."*

All these biases are hard to detect because they come naturally to us in our day-to-day lives. So, imagine how easy it is to fall for one of these biases (and there are more). Developing a strategy is not that simple, and even good strategies have a lot of conditions when they do not work.

What I want to say here is that we, as human beings, will fall into these traps. And it is all right—we do not have to solve all our problems to trade successfully. Still, if we want to shake the hand of success, we will need to work on the psychological factors that prevent us from being successful, as well as on the technical factors. And we should stop, while reading this book at least, following influencers and instantly believing what they say about trading techniques, even (and especially) if they have a large following. Before believing in something, understand what is behind it, check the assumptions, verify the results yourself, and then, if everything checks, believe in it. This is how you become profitable.

Don't take extreme examples of success, such as Bill Gates and Steve Jobs. They were very successful, but their success also contained an element of luck, maybe even an extreme version of it. Instead, think of the moderately successful people. That's your realistic target. **Venture capital** (**VC**) companies lose a lot in the majority of their investments, but they recuperate everything and come out on profit from their top 3-4% investments. Also, take into account the element of time. Disney created a lot of cartoons before it had their success with *Snow White and the Seven Dwarfs*. And consider the element of personalization. You can get some information when searching the internet for the symptoms of your particular medical condition, but when you go to an expert, the treatment is tailored to you.

Summary

In this chapter, I have told you my story and presented you with the book's structure.

Then, we went right into market myths and the reasons people believe in them. We finished with cognitive biases and how they can impact your trading, and now, we are ready to jump right into the basics.

My goal for this chapter was for you to understand the myths that losing traders believe in and to understand why get-rich-quick schemes don't work.

The next chapter is great for new traders who will get a grasp on what happens psychologically when they trade, what mistakes they usually make, and why people lose money. Then, we are going to talk about how to read a chart and who are the market participants trading that chart.

Exercises

1. *"A father and son were involved in a car accident in which the father was killed and the son was seriously injured. The father was pronounced dead at the scene of the accident and his body was taken to a local morgue. The son was taken by ambulance to a nearby hospital and was immediately wheeled into an emergency operating room. A surgeon was called. Upon arrival and seeing the patient, the attending surgeon exclaimed, "Oh my God, it's my son! Can you explain this?"* (Story adapted from the Father/Son activity found in *Pendry, Driscoll*, and *Field* (*2007*).)

2. Try to remember how many times you were afraid of being wrong. Now, imagine that you're presenting a trading technique. Would you make sure that you are presenting it in the best light possible? Would you choose a chart where you have 10 successes and 2 failures or a chart where you have 7 failures and 3 successes? Some people would say they would present both, but when you have hundreds of thousands of people following you, the title of your video refers to a successful strategy, and you can only present one of the charts; which would you choose?

3. Do you remember any "I told you so" instances happening after breakups? Maybe those people have not "told you so" before, just after. What about situations where your favorite football team plays against another good team? Before the game, you are asking yourself, "Will they win?" After the game, you are telling yourself, "I knew they'd win!"

Explanations follow next.

Answers to the exercises

1. The surgeon is the boy's mother. Most readers miss this answer and try to elaborate complex stories regarding paternity and priesthood. This is related to stereotyping.

2. This is related to confirmation bias. You are presenting the information in a way that confirms your beliefs.

3. This point is related to hindsight bias. It is easy for us to think we know the answer to a situation that has already passed, but we can't actually predict the outcome when the situation is in the future.

2
Understanding the Basics

In this chapter, you're going to take a risk assessment questionnaire so that you can better understand yourself and be able to handle the emotions you'll encounter when trading. Next, I'm going to share with you a candlestick story so that you'll take your first steps in studying a chart on various timeframes. After that, I'm going to share with you how different market participants trade so that you can better understand the market environment and why suddenly one of them buys a token, even if all the indicators show it should be sold. Finally, you'll learn about the three types of markets and what makes them different.

My goal for this chapter is for you to get to know your risk level and to find out more about the entities that trade alongside you.

Here are the topics we're going to talk about:

- A trader's psychology
- Understanding risks
- Cryptocurrencies as an asset class
- A candlestick story
- Timeframes
- Market participants
- Types of markets

A trader's psychology

In this section, you'll complete a risk assessment questionnaire and learn about the three types of traders to determine which category you fall into. Based on your responses, you'll gain insight into potential risks you may encounter while trading and how to address them.

Risk assessment questionnaire

Answer questions 1 to 10 by choosing the answer that's most related to your current situation (or what you're most likely to do in the situation provided). Ignore what you think you've learned after reading the question (what you *should* do) and focus on what you would do:

1. How would you be characterized by your best friend?

   A. Gambler

   B. Willing to take some risks

   C. Cautious

2. Choose your prize:

   A. $1,000 cash

   B. 50% chance of winning $5,000

   C. 10% chance of winning $15,000

3. The price declines by 50%. What's the percentage it needs to increase to arrive at the same level as before?

   A. 50%

   B. 75%

   C. 100%

4. What win rate do you need to break even (getting $0 in profit) for trades with a risk-reward ratio of 4:1 (for every trade you risk $1 to win $4)?

   A. 20%

   B. 25%

   C. 33%

5. What does *risk* mean for you?

   A. Prejudice

   B. Thrill

   C. Possibility

6. What would you do with $1,000?

    A. Invest all of it in a fast-growing crypto asset

    B. Invest 25% of it in a fast-growing asset, 25% in a stable asset, 25% in a risky asset, and keep 25% for other opportunities

    C. Keep it in cash for better opportunities

7. If you had $10,000 to invest for 10 years, which option would you choose?

    A. Low risk, low return

    B. Medium risk, medium return

    C. High risk, high return

8. When the market goes down, what would you do?

    A. Do nothing

    B. Double down

    C. Sell riskier assets and buy safer ones

9. If you left $1,000 in a deposit with a 2% interest rate per year and inflation was 2% per year, after 1 year, how much would you be able to buy with the money in the account (without taxes)?

    A. More than today

    B. Less than today

    C. Exactly as much as today

10. When making a trade with a strategy that has an 80% win rate, if you're at a minus of 10%, what would you do?

    A. Consider exiting the trade

    B. Double down—the strategy has a high win rate

    C. Set a stop-loss lower, just in case it falls even further

Here are the scores for the answers to these questions:

Q	a	b	c
1	3	2	1
2	1	2	3
3	1	3	2
4	2	1	3
5	1	3	2
6	3	2	1
7	1	2	3
8*	1	3	2
9	3	1	2
10	2	3	1

Figure 2.1 – Scoring table for the answers to the questionnaire

For question 8*, it's logic versus psychology. Doing nothing is what a low-risk investor would do, even though financially speaking, selling riskier assets and buying safer ones is what a low-risk investor *should* do. In my test, I'm biased toward psychological accuracy.

The gambler (score < 17)

What is life without a touch of risk?

You are a gambler at your core, and you actually know it. When you trade, your emotions run high, and you're there, into the trade, living every high of it and dreading every low. When you win, you win. You smile and you think of all the future earnings that you'll receive. And when you lose, you sure lose. You've already doubled down, and every loss hurts.

In my coaching business, I have a lot of gamblers who come and want me to teach them how to win when trading. When they see the work it takes, they ask for the best strategy or daily signals. And when I show them what's the work behind creating and managing such a strategy, they have a choice to make. Either slow down hard or risk losing money before actual learning occurs.

The best advice I have for the gambler is to better understand their counterpart, *the cautious trader*. I invite you to do swing trading that is not micromanaged, to set trades that enter at a certain price and that exit at specific prices, be it at a loss or a win. Before each trade, you need to have a hypothesis (reasons for entering the trade and for exiting the trade at your chosen levels). Then, after the trade has run its course, you need to revisit your hypothesis and update it with the result.

In time, this will help the gambler in you create a distance between your emotions and the trades you are taking so that you can follow a strategy to its success.

And to also have a release for those emotions, you can either use another account or just mark your trades as **#spontaneous** and do those trades with a lower amount of money.

The cautious trader (score > 23)

I want to protect my money before I win anything.

You value your hard-earned money, and you know you're not here for the easy win. Maybe you've already started studying the classics of investment literature; if not, you're surely planning to and you are ready to put that money into some fruitful investments. You are a bit scared of losing them, especially in the cryptocurrency world where you've heard that there are big fluctuations, but you're here to stay and to ride those waves for the win.

I don't have a lot of cautious traders as clients, but when I do, I identify them instantly. From the first few minutes, they are telling me what's important to them (variations of *not losing money*), and they are also making sure my credentials are intact (*How much did you win? What types of strategies do you use? What's the success rate of your clients?*). They are trying to make sure that they've made the correct choice.

My top advice for (fellow) cautious traders is to dedicate money to losses. Not to risk, but to lose. Trading is an emotional game, and when you switch from paper trading to money-based trading, a lot of emotions will circle around you, waiting for that chink in your armor. In paper trading, it's easy to start a trade and then wait for it to finish. In real trading, you're enticed to always watch the charts and to make sure that your trade is working... So, what happens if the price starts falling? Should you exit early or wait for it to touch the price you've set as a stop-loss?

Here, the cautious trader's brain freezes. There are too many variables, and they can look at reasons for the trade to end in profit, but they can also find reasons that the trade will fail.

In order to overcome all of those emotions, they need to accept risk as part of their trading career and learn to manage it rationally and predictably.

The balanced trader (score between 18 and 23)

Winning is a slow and steady process.

You have lived a life full of experiences. You know that winning involves risk, and you're ready to put some money where your desires are. Yet you have a financial reserve that you will not touch, and that is there just in case you realize trading is not for you. You're willing to give it all but also to analyze your results after a time and to decide if this is for you or not.

I have quite a few balanced traders as clients, and they are the easiest to work with. That's because I can put the psychologist in me to sleep and focus on the mechanics of trading with them. Some catch the mechanics pretty quickly, some a bit later, and most of them leave when they have a few techniques that they can trade and when they understand that trading is like chess—easy to learn, hard to master. Sometimes, they come back when they need a technique automated or when they have some really advanced questions.

My advice for the balanced trader is to continue what you are doing. If you've got this score, your emotions won't impede your trading that much, and you will be able to grasp the concepts and learn at the pace needed to keep your motivation and start getting results. And after you've got the results, everything else is just scaling.

Some final thoughts on risk assessment

Every type of person can fit in the trading space, but some have more challenges than others. Maybe a cautious trader progresses slower, but they also lose less money. During this time, the gambler might get some early wins, enough to push their motivation to learn the difference between trading and gambling. But they might also get enough early losses to make them leave the markets for good. And in all this time, the balanced trader progresses slowly and steadily, still wondering how all those people win so much. Each personality has its own set of questions and emotions that help or impede them when trading and its own battles on the money battlefield. All you can do is prepare yourself to the best of your abilities and then live your life as you want to live it.

We've identified what type of trader you are, and next, I'm going to show you who the other market participants are and how they behave in specific market types.

But first, let's start with an answer to the following question: *What exactly are currencies?*

Cryptocurrencies as an asset class

A cryptocurrency is a digital currency, secured by a cryptographic algorithm that prevents double-spending and counterfeiting. Most of today's currencies work on computer networks independent of central authorities such as governments or banks, eliminating the need for traditional middlemen and facilitating true ownership of funds and quick (almost instantaneous) transactions.

Even though they are named cryptocurrencies, they are not considered to be currencies in the traditional sense (though they are classified as commodities, securities, or even currencies). They are usually viewed as a distinct **asset class** and are theoretically immune to government financial manipulation.

By asset class, we are referring to the ability of the asset to hold value and have true use cases. The first cryptocurrency, Bitcoin, defined in a white paper that was published on October 31, 2008, has already proven its value-holding potential; its returns for the last 10 years have been positive, even with its high volatility. Its main use case can be considered fast and cheap transfers (through the Lightning Network) that work between any parties having a Bitcoin wallet, 24/7.

In this section, you will hear a candlestick story, followed by an overview of the different timeframes that traders use. We will also discuss the various market participants and how their trading affects the market, creating different types of markets, each with its own unique characteristics and trading style.

A candlestick story

Hey Siri, play "The Candlelight Story" by Tony Chen.

The God of Markets, Munehisa Honma, is said to be the creator of candlestick charts. He was a rice merchant from Sakata, Japan, who traded the Dojima Rice Market in Osaka, during the Edo shogunate. Stories are told about when he created a personal *postal service* (men spread every 6 kilometers over 600 kilometers) to get the market prices in time. In 1755, he wrote the first book on market psychology, *San-en Kinsen Hiroku*, or *The Fountain of Gold – The Three Monkey Record of Money*, in which he talks about traders' emotions and how they influence prices.

In 1991, the candlestick appeared in the Western world in a book called *Japanese Candlestick Charting Techniques*, written by Steve Nison, who says that, according to his research, it is unlikely that Honma used candlestick charts.

So, the initial story might actually be the first trading urban legend in Japan.

But what is a candlestick chart?

Well... let's first start with a candle...stick!

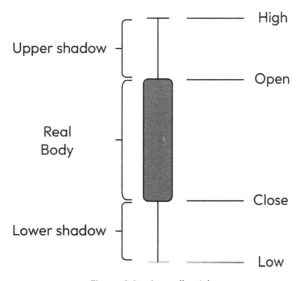

Figure 2.2 – A candlestick

A candlestick chart is a financial chart that shows the price movements of securities, derivates, or (crypto)currencies. It is also called a Japanese candlestick chart or a K-line chart. Each candlestick there represents four essential pieces of information: the price at opening time, the price at closing time, and the lowest and highest price of that timeframe. They are usually colored white or green for rising prices (*Close* > *Open*) and black or red for falling prices (*Open* > *Close*).

> **Note**
> All images in this book are in grayscale, so there may be a slight adjustment period when you view the colored candles on **TradingView**.

So, with just one look, you can see if the price is rising or falling, by how much, and even what were the highest and lowest points it traded during that timeframe.

Here's how it looks on a chart:

Figure 2.3 – A candlestick chart

This chart is also called an **open-high-low-close (OHLC)** chart (because you can see these values for each candle on the chart). To make it easier, we're going to use the short forms for **Open**, **High**, **Low**, and **Close** (**O**, **H**, **L**, and **C**).

Here, you can see how the white candles (or green candles) show rising prices ($C > O$, meaning that the close price is greater than the open price; basically, it closes "*higher*") and the black candles (or red candles) show falling prices ($O > C$).

Each candle on this chart represents 1 hour of price movement, and we'll find out in the next section what exactly these timeframes are.

Timeframes

We know what a candlestick is and what a candlestick chart looks like, and now it's time to understand how to represent price movements over large (or small) periods. Have a look at the graph shown in *Figure 2.4*:

Figure 2.4 – The Bitcoin Liquid Index (BLX); each candle is 1 month (logarithmic display)

In stocks, you can have gaps between candles because markets can open at different prices than when they've closed, but this doesn't normally happen in crypto. Here, the market trades 24/7, so when you trade you can expect the close of one candle to be the price the next candle opens with.

Then, if a candlestick shows the OHLC values, the distance between the opening of one candle and the next opening is the time length of the candle. Based on how we configure the chart, we can have anywhere from 1-second candles to 1-month candles (and more).

A 1-hour candle starts at :00 (minute zero) and ends at :59 (minute 59), and these candles are displayed on the hourly timeframe (also called the 1-hour timeframe or 1H). A 1-day candle starts at 00:00 and ends at 23:59 and is displayed on the 1D timeframe.

So, 1 candle on 1D equals 24 candles on 1H because there are 24 hours in a day.

Let's check this out:

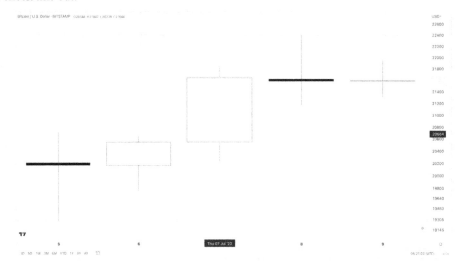

Figure 2.5 – A daily candle

The candle in the middle represents the price for BTC on July 7, 2022, in the BTCUSD market on **Bitstamp**. Its values are O **20546**, H **21847**, L **20238**, and C **21644** (as explained in the section titled *A candlestick story*).

Let's look at this candle in the 4-hour timeframe:

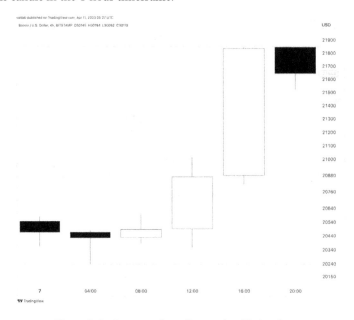

Figure 2.6 – A range of candles on the 4H timeframe

Here, the vertical bars show the start of each day. Starting from July 7, 2022, we have 6 4-hour candles until the next day. The last candle (black) is at 20:00, signifying the range 20:00-23:59.

The opening of the 1D candle is the O of the first 4H candle, at **20546**.

The L of the 1D candle (**20238**) can be found as the lowest point in the range, at the L of the second black candle.

The 1D H (**21847**) and 1D C (**21644**) are both in the last candle of the 4H range.

If we draw a 1D candle over its 4H range, the result looks like this:

Figure 2.7 – The indicator used was HTF Candles by Prosum Solutions (author prosum_solutions)

Now, it's time for you to play with TradingView and make sure you understand the different timeframes and how a **higher timeframe (HTF)** candle is composed of smaller **lower timeframe (LTF)** candles. In the next section, we're going to talk about identifying the three types of markets that drive the *cryptoconomy*.

Market participants

All right. We have basic knowledge regarding timeframes now. But how does that help us trade?

Let's consider the following types of key market participants:

- **Commercials—insurance funds, pension funds, hedge funds, and institutions**: Their main goal is protecting their capital using a portfolio profile, and for this, they can go where the market goes. The current price doesn't matter that much (for example, they need to have a percentage of their portfolio in Bitcoin by the end of the quarter, no matter what happens to BTC). And their entries influence the price of the cryptocurrency being traded.

- **Speculators—(manual) traders, algorithmic traders**: The price matters; they consider the risk of their entries and trade market anomalies. Their entries don't usually influence the price.

- **High-frequency traders—bots and other automations**: They do 90% of the trading, having well-defined entries and exits so that they can get the highest profit with the least risk. These entries influence the speculators because they both have the same short-term objectives.

The following are the types of traders:

- **Scalpers**: Scalpers trade quickly, based on order flow. Trades can take seconds or minutes.

- **Day traders**: They start and finish the day without an open position, trading based on technical analysis and order flows. They don't care about the fundamentals of the cryptocurrencies they trade because they exit quickly. The trades take minutes or hours.

- **Short-term traders**: These traders use technical analysis, followed by some fundamental analysis, and their trades last for 3 to 5 days (for instance, they trade breakouts).

- **Intermediate traders/swing traders**: They use a combination of fundamental analysis and technical analysis to trade. Their trades take days, weeks, or even months.

- **(Big) Long-term investors**: They use fundamental analysis, and usually, filling their orders takes time (days even). Their moves influence the market, and they start and stop trends with their entries and exits. They stay in trades for years.

In order to simplify the mentality we should have when trading, let's imagine we have a smart opponent that we're trading against. When we win, they lose; when we lose, they win. They can wear different hats at different times—sometimes the hat of a commercial; another time the hat of a day trader.

The question we should always be asking ourselves is this: *Which of the hats are they wearing in the current market conditions?* Now, I'm going to give a few examples, but if you're new to trading, feel free to skip them now and come back later, after reading the book.

Here are some examples of situations, but remember that any interpretation is relative to the truth:

- If we see a big upper wick on a 1-second timeframe on a specific exchange (and not on other exchanges), we can consider this to be a big one-time exit that reflects the needs of a commercial and doesn't necessarily reflect a trend in the market. Basically, someone sold a lot of currency there, and then the market participants corrected that move by buying the orders back. But if we see multiple wicks, we can presume someone is continuously selling at that price a very large order by splitting it into small orders. There, we can expect more selling pressure than when a single wick forms. Here's an example:

Figure 2.8 – Big upper wick

- If a cryptocurrency continuously trades in a price range, moving to the top, falling back, rinse, and repeat, that might be a situation where automatic algorithms are feeding themselves in a loop. If we spot these in time, we can enter longs (long trades) when the price is low, sell at the top of the range, and enter shorts (going short or shorting) until the price comes back down. Here is an example (but a low volume one) with an 8% increase and decrease in price, with each candle being 1 hour. Just imagine trading that:

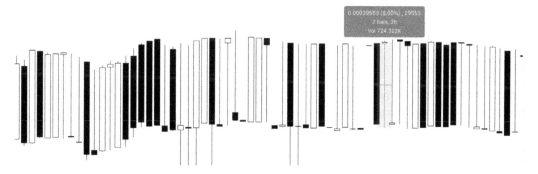

Figure 2.9 – Steady price range

- Key news announcements in crypto create market volatility. A lot of speculators are trading at that point to profit from the volatility, specifically commercials that want to execute big orders. They are trying to find the liquidity that they need to sell their orders to:

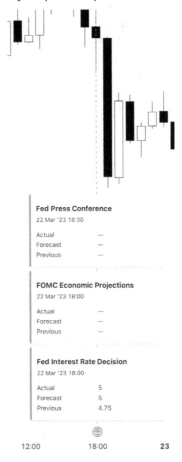

Figure 2.10 – Fed press conference impact

All of these moves are influencing the trend, making the markets go up, down, or sideways. Let's see how that looks in the next section.

Types of markets

Markets can go up or down or they can stay in a range. We call these markets a bull market, a bear market, and a sideways (or ranging) market.

Here's what they look like:

Figure 2.11 – A bull market

A **bull market** represents a period (months or years) when the price of an asset appreciates over its historical value. If the period is smaller than a few months, it is named a **bullish trend**.

A bull market is characterized by the following:

- Positive news (called bullish news)
- A lot of big investments
- Money is thrown around (even in mediocre businesses)

You can't usually identify the start of a bull market until you're already in it.

Most people start trading during bull markets because that is the time when everybody is bombarded by optimistic news and the economy is strong enough that everybody has some money left to invest. But the problem is that latecomers are joining in right at the peak (or end) of the bull market.

And then, the bear market comes. Here's how it looks:

Figure 2.12 – A bear market

A **bear market** represents a period (usually years) when the price of an asset depreciates over its historical value. And, if the period is shorter, we can call it a **bearish trend**.

A bear market is characterized by the following:

- Negative news (called bearish news)
- Few investments
- No money in the market or long periods without any big activity

After starting, newcomers are usually faced with a bear market where all the techniques that they've used to make money suddenly stop working. This is the point where they usually lose money and, after a while, leave the market.

When the new bull market comes, you will hear from them *it's all a lie, you're gonna lose money*, and other such things.

A **sideways market**, also called a **lateral market** or a **ranging market**, is a period when the price stays within a certain range. If the period is lower than a few months, we can call it a **sideways trend**. Here's a sideways market on the chart:

Figure 2.13 – A sideways market

People don't usually talk about sideways markets, and that is mostly because there is either no particular activity there or because the news is polarized, creating uncertainty. You can also see sideways trends during long bear markets where a lot of market participants have left the field.

But why do we call them bull markets and bear markets? Imagine how these animals attack their opponents. The bull thrusts its horns up, throwing its opponent in the air, while the bear swipes its paws down, pushing its opponent to the ground. Here's a depiction of this:

Figure 2.14 – Bulls versus bears

If there's an uptrend, we say that the bulls are in control, and when the prices are falling (there's a downtrend), we say that the bears have taken control.

There are tips and tricks to trade each market, but for now, let's focus on learning how to identify them. At the end of the chapter, there will be some exercises to help you do this.

Summary

In this chapter, I helped you identify your risk level and taught you about other market participants and how they behave in the market. We also discussed a bit about cryptocurrencies and timeframes and started reading a chart.

My goal was for you to get to know your risk level and to find out more about the entities that trade alongside you.

In the next chapter, we're going deep—right into technical analysis, talking about TradingView, candle patterns, **moving averages (MAs)**, the **Relative Strength Index (RSI)**, and much, much more.

Exercises

1. After taking the risk assessment questionnaire, ask yourself (and write down) three things you're doing to keep your emotions in check in real life. I know a couple that say that when they want to fight, they speak in pirate English. Think: "Ye be mighty pushy! Belay that!" ... or just use *The Pirate Translator* here: `https://pirate.monkeyness.com/translate`.

2. Identify 3 daily candles in TradingView, then go to the 4-hour and 1-hour timeframe and look at the candles that formed them. See how the low of the bigger candle was formed using the low of the lowest candle in the group, how the high was formed, and so on. How does the price move inside that big candle? Is it going directly to the close? Is it pushing toward the high, then dropping to the low, then jumping to the close?

3. Identify a big news event in crypto (which happened at a specific hour, on a specific day). *Tip*: You can look for big Fed announcements or a black swan event (such as the crash of FTX). Check on the chart how the price reacted to the news and for how long. Imagine the market participants getting fueled by the news and trading during those times. Which market participants were involved? What was their thought process?

4. Go to TradingView and open the daily chart for BTCUSD. First, try to identify the periods I've shown you in the screenshots about the bear market and the bull market, and then, go to a lower timeframe (4 hours or 1 hour) and identify 2 bullish trends, 2 bearish trends, and 2 sideways trends.

3

Technical Analysis – Candles and Patterns

In this chapter, you'll lay the foundation for your career in trading. We'll begin by introducing you to one of the most effective charting tools available: TradingView. With this tool, you'll be able to see on your screen what I like to call the "story of the price." Next, we'll delve into candlestick patterns, which will help you understand the emotions driving small price movements. After that, we'll cover chart patterns for stronger and longer-lasting movements. Finally, we'll explore support and resistance areas and the laws that govern them. All of this will provide you with a solid understanding of the fundamentals you need to succeed in your training career.

My goal for this chapter is for you to understand how to view the story and the emotions battling behind a price movement.

Here are the topics that we'll be covering:

- TradingView
- Market patterns
- Candlestick patterns
- Chart patterns
- Supply and demand
- Support and resistance

Let's begin!

TradingView

"*Check what the price is telling you*" is something I so often tell my students. The price always has a story to tell—a story of enthusiasm, one of disappointment, or one of indecision. That story is written in the chart, and it's called **price action**.

Wikipedia tells us, "*At its most simplistic, it attempts to describe the human thought processes invoked by experienced, non-disciplinary traders as they observe and trade their markets. Price action is simply how prices change - the action of price. It is most noticeable in markets with high liquidity and price volatility, but anything that is traded freely (in price) in a market will per se demonstrate price action.*" (`https://en.wikipedia.org/wiki/Price_action_trading`)

However, before we can fully understand the story, we need to learn the alphabet and how to read it from its canvas, **TradingView**.

TradingView defines itself as follows: "*Where the world charts, chats, and trades markets. We're a supercharged super-charting platform and social network for traders and investors.*"

In essence, it's a tool used for tracking prices that also has a social network feature. This allows you to follow other traders to learn about their ideas, strategies, and indicators.

Here's how it looks at first glance:

Figure 3.1 – TradingView at a glance

You probably know the saying "*A picture is worth a thousand words.*" Well, let's put it into practice. In this section, I'm going to show you the basics of TradingView and, later in the book, you'll learn how to use it to chart price action and develop trading strategies with it.

In the upper-left section of the chart (*Figure 3.2*), you have the current market, **Bitcoin / U.S. Dollar**, the current time frame, **D** (meaning daily), the exchange, **BINANCE**, and information regarding the current candle pinpointed by the mouse cursor, its **Open, High, Low, Close (OHLC)** data:

Bitcoin / U.S. Dollar · BINANCE   O 30340.17 H 30482.60 L 29962.49 C 30099.74

Figure 3.2 – Upper-left section

As you can see in *Figure 3.3*, right under the chart, we have the time scale, which now shows dates from 2023 to April 16. If we zoom out, it will also show the months, and if we zoom in, the hours or seconds:

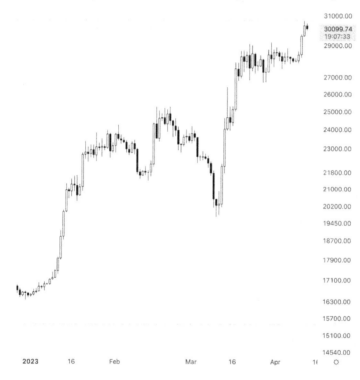

Figure 3.3 – Lower-right section

If we right-click on the time scale, we can change the time zone. My recommendation is to set it to **UTC** as most traders are using that, so you will instantly see the correct time on your chart when watching a video on the internet. Also, when explaining a trade to someone, you need to make sure they are using UTC too, or you'll have different hours at which the trade occurred.

In the same screenshot, on the right of the chart, we can see the price scale now ranging from 14,540 to 26,000. The box at 30,099.74 shows the current price. The number under the 30,099.74 box shows how much time is left until the current candle ends: 19 hours, 7 minutes, and 33 seconds.

If you right-click on the price scale, you have the option to set it to **Auto** (to fit the current data on the screen), to change from price to percentage or logarithmic, to disable some labels or lines, and much more. Try it!

Following that, we have the top-left part of the screen, as seen in the following screenshot:

Figure 3.4 – Top-left section

Here, in the top-left section, you have the menu (represented by your profile image), the symbol search, which is now set to the **Bitcoin / U.S. Dollar** trading market (appearing as **BTCUSD** in the image), followed by the compare or add symbol (the plus sign), which allows you to add another market over the current one so that you can compare them.

After that there's the **Time Interval** (or time frame) button, currently set to **D** (each candle represents one day now), then the **Candles** button through which you can change the current candle format to **Candles, Lines, Bars, Heikin Ashi**, or others.

After that, the **Indicators, Metrics & Strategies** symbol is the place from which you can add indicators, metrics, or strategies to your chart.

The **Indicators Templates** symbol (four squares) allows you to save a combination of indicators on a symbol at a specific interval so that you can change your view of the chart (and current strategy) at the click of a button. The **B** and **D** symbols to its right are two of the templates I've created.

The **Create Alert** button allows you to add alerts that will trigger once certain conditions are met (the price reaches a certain point, the indicator gives a signal, a value is in a certain range, and so on). Alerts can pop up on the phone app or in a browser notification; they can be sent via email, or they can be connected via API to various services.

Bar Replay shows you how a chart looked at a certain point in time, simulating how the market (and the indicators) behaved in the past. It's a great tool for backtesting a strategy but it also has its flaws, which we will be talking about in a later chapter on backtesting.

The left and right arrows allow you to undo and redo certain actions that you've made on a chart (such as drawing a line).

The following screenshot shows the top-right section:

Figure 3.5 – Top-right section

It starts with the **Select Layout** icon (the square), which allows you to load different window positions (you can have four charts up at the same time or one chart on different time frames). **Programming** is the name of my current layout (I also have a **Trading** layout and a **BTC High Timeframe Analysis** layout).

When you click on the layout's name, it saves it, or if you push the down arrow next to it, you'll have some options such as **Save, Autosave, Rename, Make a copy, Load layout, Share layout**, or **Export data**.

The quick search tool is shown as a magnifying glass, and it allows you to search for drawings, functions, and settings. I use it to quickly find a setting to turn on/off.

After that, we have the chart settings icon (the gear), which allows you to configure how a chart looks and behaves in various situations. Here you can change the timezone or remove information that you don't use, such as **Open market status** (used in stocks) or maybe **Bid and ask price**, and you can also save the settings as a template to use later.

Then, we have the fullscreen mode button (the interrupted square), followed by the *take a snapshot* button (the camera icon), which allows you to copy, share, download, or tweet the current chart image.

There's also a **Publish** button on the right of the camera from where you can publish an idea you might have (your chart and a description under it) or record a video of that idea.

Let's look at the left menu bar now. It shows quite a lot of icons; most of them are used to interact with charts (drawing, measuring, zooming):

Figure 3.6 – Left section

Let's go through the icon list in detail:

- The first icon is the cursors icon (the mouse pointer), which you can change from a cross to a dot, an arrow, or an eraser (that removes drawings).

- The second is the trend line tools icon (the vertical line), showing a lot of tools that can be used to draw on a chart. From there, I mainly use **Trend Line**, **Horizontal Line**, **Horizontal Ray**, **Vertical Line**, and **Parallel Channel**. I suggest you add them to your favorites by clicking on the star symbol to the right of the tool's name.

- The third is the Gann and Fibonacci tools icon. From there, I mostly use **Fib Retracement**.

- The fourth is the geometric shapes icon. I use **Brush**, **Rectangle**, **Ellipse**, **Curve**, **Triangle**, and **Rotated Rectangle**.

- The fifth is the annotation tools icon. I use **Text, Signpost, Callout, Arrow Mark Up**, and **Arrow Mark Down** from there.

- The sixth is the patterns icon. Though I've played with **Elliot Waves** in the past, **Triangle** and **Head and Shoulders** are the most common patterns I use. I haven't added anything to my favorites, but feel free to experiment once you learn more about them.

- The seventh is the prediction and measurement tools icon. I use **Long Position, Short Position, Date and Price Range, Ghost Feed**, and **Fixed Range Volume Profile**.

- The eighth is the symbol (smiley face) for icons. You will find a variety of symbols and smileys to choose from that you can add to your chart for some fun and profit. I don't use them that much.

- The ninth is the measure tool (symbol: a ruler), which is used to measure bars, volume, percentage, and price modifications.

- Under it is the zoom tool, which is used to zoom in (and, after you zoom in, to zoom out) on a chart.

- The magnet symbol can be used to make the drawings stick better to certain points on a chart.

- The stay in drawing mode symbol (pencil and lock) is used to be able to draw with the same tool after you do a drawing (by default, it switches to the cursor).

- Lock all drawing tools (the lock symbol) will allow you to use the mouse on a chart without fearing you'll move a drawing by mistake (something that happens more often than you think, though you can always use the **Undo** arrow in the top bar on the right to undo a move).

- Hide all drawings (the eye symbol) well... hides all drawings, all indicators, or positions that you've put on a chart.

- And then, we have the trash icon, which I only use when I want to completely clean a chart. Beware of this button, and use undo if you've pressed it by mistake.

- On the lower-left side, we also have a star symbol that will gather all your favorite items (the ones you've marked with a star) into a floating bar on your chart. That is the bar I use when drawing; I rarely use the left menu.

Here's how my favorites look on the floating bar:

Figure 3.7 – Favorites

And now, we've arrived at the bottom-left part of the chart:

Figure 3.8 – Bottom-left section

Let's learn more about the icons present in the preceding screenshot:

- The **1D**, **5D**, and other time interval buttons allow you to quickly switch between different chart views, showing the price action over the course of 1 day, 5 days, and even the entire time the token has been listed on the exchange.

- The "go to" button (represented by a calendar icon) lets you select a specific time range to display on the chart.

- Under it, you have **Stock Screener**, which you can change to **Crypto Pairs Screener** (as seen in *Figure 3.8*) by clicking on the down arrow to its right. With it, you can quickly filter tokens by percentual rises in price, volume, and specific indicators, helping you quickly find out which tokens have the proper setup for your strategy.

- At its right, **Pine Editor** allows you to code your own strategy in Pine Script. Before moving to Python, I developed quite a few strategies in Pine Script, and I recommend you learn the language if you want to automate your trading strategy, connect it to various bots, or just get alerts when specific conditions happen.

- The **Strategy Tester** to its right shows the performance of any strategy added to the chart.

- The last tool is the **Trading Panel**, which allows TradingView to connect to brokers so that you can trade directly on TradingView. Here, you can also select **Paper Trading**, which allows you to simulate your trades. As part of my coaching sessions, I strongly advise my clients to only trade with real money once they have successfully completed a paper trading period of at least 3 consecutive months. This approach allows them to test their strategies and gain confidence in their trading abilities without risking any actual capital. By mastering paper trading first, they can minimize their losses and maximize their chances of success when they begin trading with real money.

In the bottom-right corner, we have the clock and the **Timezone**. Make sure it's set to **UTC** so that you can correlate all the moves you'll see on YouTube, Telegram, or Discord with your chart:

Figure 3.9 – Bottom-right section

At its right, the **auto** symbol can be changed in order to display the chart and price percentual, logarithmical, or automatically (which is the default setting and includes an autofit feature that optimizes the chart for your display).

On the right side, we have another toolbar:

Figure 3.10 – Right section

Let's look closely at each icon in *Figure 3.10*:

- The first symbol is the **Watchlist, details and news** icon, from where you can follow specific tokens and organize them into lists. I have a list named after each strategy I use, and once I see a setup on a chart, I add that token to that strategy's list. After I exit the trade, I remove it. This way, I can see all the tokens that fit a specific strategy at a glance. I also have lists of tokens that

I trade daily or that I trade with bots. News helps me quickly find out why a token crashed or spiked, but I find that the news on TradingView arrives too late for me to react to it. Currently, I'm using the **CryptoPanic iOS** app to quickly get the news. You can also use the following website: `https://cryptopanic.com/`.

- The **Alerts** symbol (the alarm clock) allows you to see which alerts you have on your charts at a glance, and you can pause/stop/start them quickly.

- **Data Window** is great when you code an indicator or when you want to quickly find out the values of a certain candle (including the values the indicators throw).

- **Hotlists** and the **Calendar** are mostly used in stocks, so we'll skip them.

- **My Ideas** (symbol: lightbulb) contains ideas you've published on TradingView using the **Publish** button on the top right.

- **Minds** is a social media-like feed for discussing the token you are currently trading. I don't use it. Same for **Chats**; the information there is too random and I prefer to stay focused on my own analysis and strategies. I do have my own private groups where I know the traders and can trust their expertise, but I would never trade on information I get from strangers. In **Chats**, you also have **Private** chats, which contain messages people send to you.

- **Ideas Stream** (the ringing lightbulb symbol) is used to check what other authors you like have published. I don't usually post on social media, but if you want to follow my ideas and my scripts, here's the link: `https://www.tradingview.com/u/vaidab/`.

- I don't use **Streams** for the same reason as public chats: too much noise, too much emotion. There, you can check videos of people you follow, but I prefer to take a step back from all this information and have a clear head when entering trades.

- **Notifications** will show you the latest notifications that you have.

Next, we have the bottom-right corner with two little icons. The object tree shows all of the drawings that you've made on the chart (which you can organize into folders, showing or hiding them based on folders). I love this part. Basically, you can have multiple analyses of a token or trades on different time frames, and you can hide and lock them (so that you don't accidentally erase them).

And finally, the **Help Center**, where you can find information that you might need:

Figure 3.11 – Bottom-right corner

Activities

1. I encourage you to experiment with all of the drawing tools available on TradingView. Don't be afraid to make drawings on a chart; take note of how they look, and double-click on the drawings to explore the various options you can change. By familiarizing yourself with all of the features and functions available on TradingView, you'll be able to chart much more efficiently and accurately. So, don't hesitate to take some time to play around with the platform and make the most of its powerful tools.

2. Go to `https://www.sandwich.finance/` | **Binance** | **BUSD markets**, download the file, and import it into TradingView. (*Tip: The import option is found in the* **Watchlist, details and news** *panel.*) You've just imported Binance's listed tokens in a TradingView list, so you can easily check them one by one (and you can do this with other exchanges, too).

3. Create a watchlist of tokens you want to follow.

4. Go to `https://www.tradingview.com/` | **Trade Ideas** | **Crypto** and read a few ideas from traders. Then, click on the trader's ID and **Follow** them. Also, check the **Educational Ideas** area on the main page.

5. Go to `https://www.tradingview.com/` | **Community** | **Scripts** | **Popular scripts**. Read about one and, if you like it, add it to your favorite indicators.

6. Add two indicators on the **BTCBUSD 15M** chart and save the layout.

7. Go to the **Indicators** button (top-left section), search for `Hull Suite by InSilico`, hover over it, click on the star to the left of the name (to add it to your **Favorites** tab), and click on it to add it to your chart. Play with it, with its settings, and then remove it from your chart.

Market patterns

Traders develop trading techniques by identifying patterns in the market. After rigorous backtesting, the trader watches for those patterns that indicate the potential for a specific price movement and enters a trade before the movement happens.

In the following sections, I'm going to present some of the basic patterns that most traders use, but before I do that, let me present you with…

The five pattern commandments:

I. The story of the pattern is more important than the pattern.

II. The story changes as the pattern develops.

III. Every pattern instance has a random outcome.

IV. Seek confluence, not certainty.

V. There's always a pattern you haven't noticed.

I. The story of the pattern is more important than the pattern

The price tells a story. When it rises, it's because there are more buyers than there are sellers, and we say that the buyers are pushing the price up. And when it falls, the sellers are pushing the price down (or the buyers are losing the fight, or the bears are in control, or any other metaphor):

Figure 3.12 – Market-cycle psychology

When looking at the patterns, I want you to think of the story the price is trying to tell you. It isn't about the specifics of the pattern, but the story behind it. Some patterns might tell a story of hope, others of euphoria, some of anxiety, and even of betrayal and panic. It's not about the specific candle that has a High identical to the Close; it's about the optimism it evokes. And when three candles are doing that, one after another, the *"three white soldiers"* pattern is formed and the emotion behind the chart changes from depression to hope, or even to belief in good times ahead.

II. The story changes as the pattern develops

The *RMS Titanic* was hailed as a marvel of engineering and an *"unsinkable"* ship during its construction and maiden voyage in 1912. Passengers and crew alike were optimistic about the luxurious and seemingly safe journey ahead. However, after the ship struck an iceberg and began to sink, that optimism rapidly transformed into panic as people realized the gravity of the situation and struggled to find a place on the limited number of lifeboats. The disaster serves as a reminder of the potential consequences of overconfidence.

The same things can happen in trading where emotions change together with (or maybe in anticipation of) price movements. Occasionally, optimism and faith in better times transform into anxiety, denial, and panic during difficult periods. The situation is not fixed, and one must observe its progression, fully aware that the price may move in the opposite direction.

III. Every pattern instance has a random outcome

Every trade is random. Yes—repeat after me: *every trade is random*.

That is because you can never take into consideration everything that goes into it. There's always a piece of news, some inside information being traded, or a big venture capital fund that did something that you couldn't have expected. So, even if the pattern that you've traded got you a profit, that one specific trade had a random outcome. The pattern is profitable because of statistics; that is because, in time, trading it will be profitable, not because this one trade you're doing using the pattern is profitable.

IV. Seek confluence, not certainty

Since we've already established at *III* that every pattern instance has a random outcome, you can eliminate certainty from your vocabulary. Sometimes I play a game with my clients where I go into the past and replay the candles from a random period and trade on the spot. I'm mostly successful doing this exercise, but there's always a day when most of my trades fail. That's not because the entries weren't good enough; it's usually because of market randomness.

What do we do against a random market when we have a profitable trade technique? We trade through the losses knowing that, on average, we'll be profitable.

What do we do when we have a profitable chart pattern? We seek confluence with another pattern or with an indicator so that we increase our chances of profit.

I usually seek four points of confluence when trading, and there's always one point against taking that trade.

V. There's always a pattern you haven't noticed

Looking back on a chart, it is very easy to spot patterns. There's always a bullish flag that you haven't noticed or a parallel channel that you could have traded. But if you use **Bar Replay** to go to the point in time when a pattern forms, you'll see that it's pretty easy to ignore its early stages or to find another pattern that, at that point, is as valid as the one that formed after. I'm going to show you an example at the end of the *Chart patterns* section.

Next, you're going to learn about the most common candlestick and chart patterns that I use when trading.

Candlestick patterns

A chart is (usually) formed by Japanese candlesticks; each candlestick represents the price movement during the chosen time frame. On a 4-hour **BTCUSD** chart, each candlestick represents the price movement during a 4-hour period.

The way the price moves inside that candlestick (or that candlestick, and a few more) can generate a pattern that we can use in trading.

> Warnings
>
> **First warning**—Don't trade by one candlestick pattern! Trade using a confluence of patterns and indicators so that your chances of success are increased.
>
> **Second warning**—It's extremely hard to test the patterns presented. Some, such as Thomas N. Bulkowski, have tried doing this for stocks, but still, even with the statistics at hand, the right moment to enter and exit is, again, debatable.
>
> **My recommendation**—Look at the market's emotion, at the story behind the price. And yes—I know I'm repeating myself, but I'm doing it for your own good. Don't take a pattern that was presented as bullish in a book about stocks 5+ years ago and think that it still applies now, in the crypto market. Test everything before taking it into consideration.

Hammer (bullish) versus Shooting Star (bearish)

A **Hammer** found in a downtrend is a bullish reversal candlestick pattern:

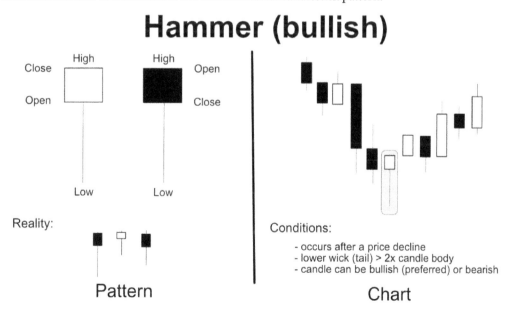

Figure 3.13 – Hammer

Why is this?

Well, consider this: the price has been moving downward, as seen in the previous candles, with the bears firmly in control. However, after a string of candles where the sellers dominated, the bulls are now starting to buy, and they're buying in sufficient quantity to drive the price up and close to the high (and the open) of the day. If the wick is long, it signifies an extended struggle (which indicates a stronger signal). This is especially true if the trading volume increased significantly, meaning that even more market participants were involved in the conflict when the reversal occurred. The pattern is considered valid when the wick is at least two times greater than the body. Indeed, charting can be seen as a battlefield.

When examining the following diagram, you can see how a Hammer is actually formed on a lower time frame. For instance, if you look at the Hammer pattern on a daily chart, it consists of 3 candles on an 8-hour chart. The pattern might begin with two bearish candles followed by a bullish one. Alternatively, it could have a different configuration, altering the narrative somewhat. Even when we identify a candlestick pattern on a particular time frame, we shouldn't rely solely on this information for trading. We can either zoom in to gain a clearer understanding or consider additional information before forming a conclusion:

How a Hammer is formed

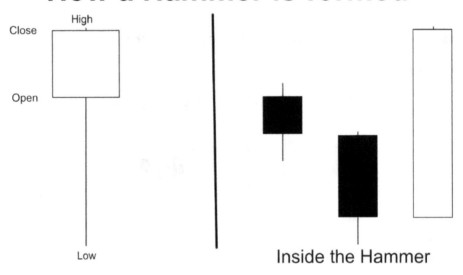

Figure 3.14 – How a Hammer is formed

Shooting Star is the same pattern, in reverse, and it is found in an uptrend:

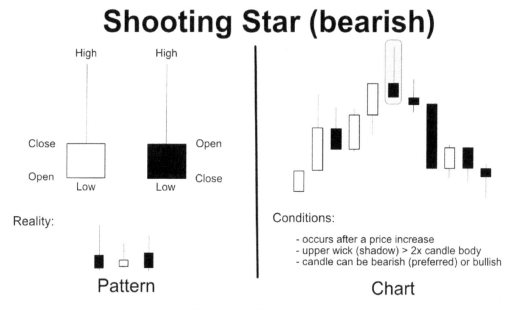

Figure 3.15 – Shooting Star

Basically, the wick shoots for the stars but the sellers are driving the price down, ideally on a high volume and on a long road (long wick).

When this happens after an uptrend, it's a sign of weakness, of a trend reversal.

> **Warning**
>
> When examining these patterns on a chart, it's apparent that even when a hammer is identified in a downtrend, the price can still continue to decline. The same applies to other patterns. These patterns only reveal one aspect of the situation (for instance, the forces were driven out of a particular area), but the battle persists, and there may be numerous other factors leading to the conquest of that region shortly after. To increase the reliability of these patterns, use them in conjunction with at least three other confluence points (which should be of a different type, as we'll discuss later).

Inverted Hammer (bullish) versus Hanging Man (bearish)

An **Inverted Hammer** found in a downtrend is a bullish reversal pattern:

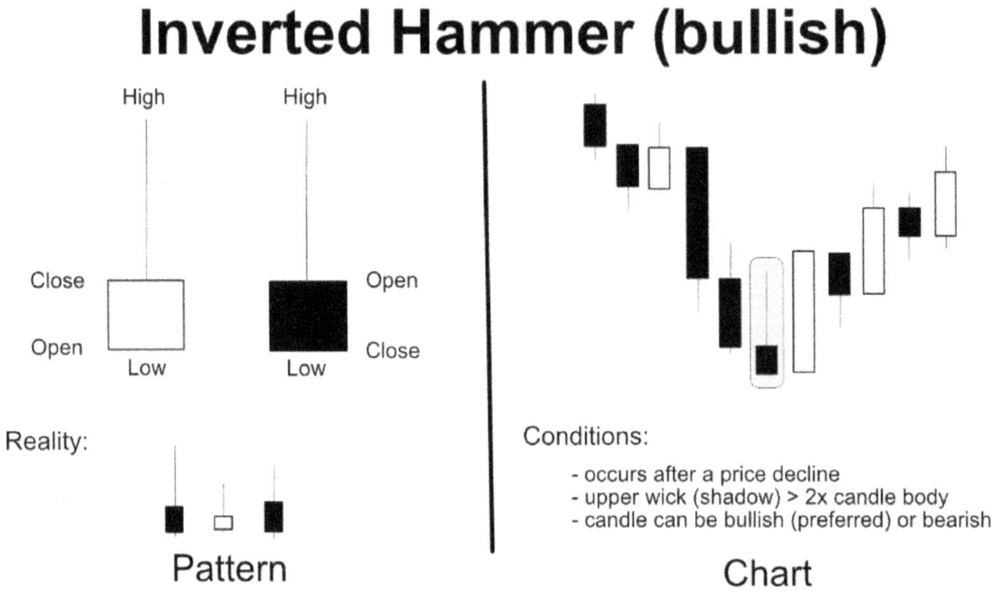

Figure 3.16 – Inverted Hammer

You might wonder why a wick pointing upward or downward would indicate a reversal. The explanation lies in the shifting balance of power between bulls and bears.

In the case of an Inverted Hammer, the bulls push the price up, but then the bears drive it back down. Did the bears win? Temporarily, yes. However, in the previous candles, the bears encountered no resistance; now, the Inverted Hammer signifies that the bulls have entered the fray and started fighting.

The Hammer illustrates a similar dynamic, with the bulls battling the bears and driving the price back up. In both cases—whether it's a Hammer or an Inverted Hammer—the presence of the bulls in the struggle is the crucial factor. These patterns reveal that the bulls are taking action: they've tried to push the price upward, and although the bears have fought back, the balance of power is beginning to shift, potentially signaling a reversal in the trend.

The **Hanging Man**, illustrated in the following diagram, represents the opposite scenario, indicating that after a clear uptrend, a sudden bearish action emerges in the candles, suggesting a bearish reversal:

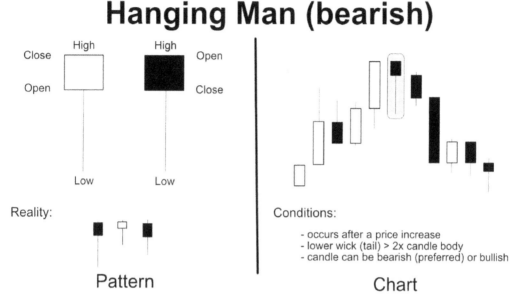

Figure 3.17 – Hanging Man

It has a lower wick (ideally at least two times greater than the body) and a short body.

Doji (neutral)

The **Doji** is a neutral pattern formed when the Open and the Close prices are very close to one another. It provides little information, suggesting an indecision in the direction of the price. The word comes from the Japanese phrase meaning "*the same thing*."

Multiple Dojis after a strong trend might indicate a trend reversal:

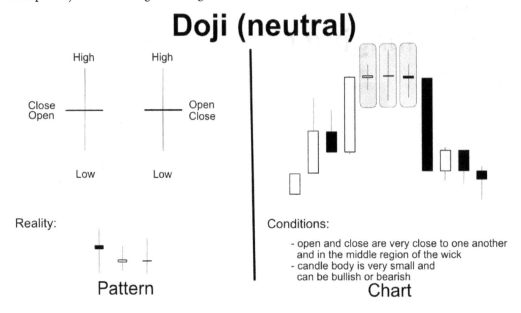

Figure 3.18 – Doji

Spinning Top (neutral)

A **Spinning Top** is a type of candlestick pattern with a small body and long upper and lower shadows, indicating a neutral market sentiment. This pattern is similar to a Doji, with a similar story, the only difference being in a more significant body:

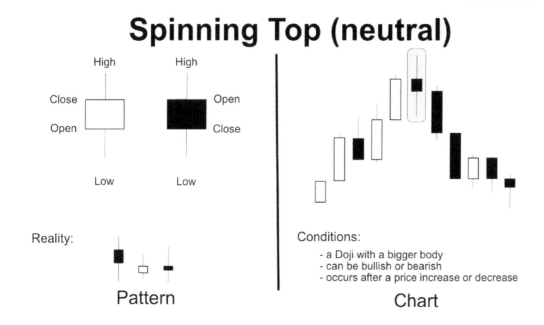

Figure 3.19 – Spinning Top

A Spinning Top pattern forms when bears push the price lower than the opening price; a spinning top appears, and then the bulls push it back up (a slight bullish signal), or when bulls push the price higher than the opening price, then a spinning top appears, and bears push it back down (a slight bearish signal).

Dragonfly Doji (bullish) versus Gravestone Doji (bearish)

Dragonfly Doji is just a Hammer where the bulls had a stronger comeback, bringing the close price near to the open price (as shown in the following diagram):

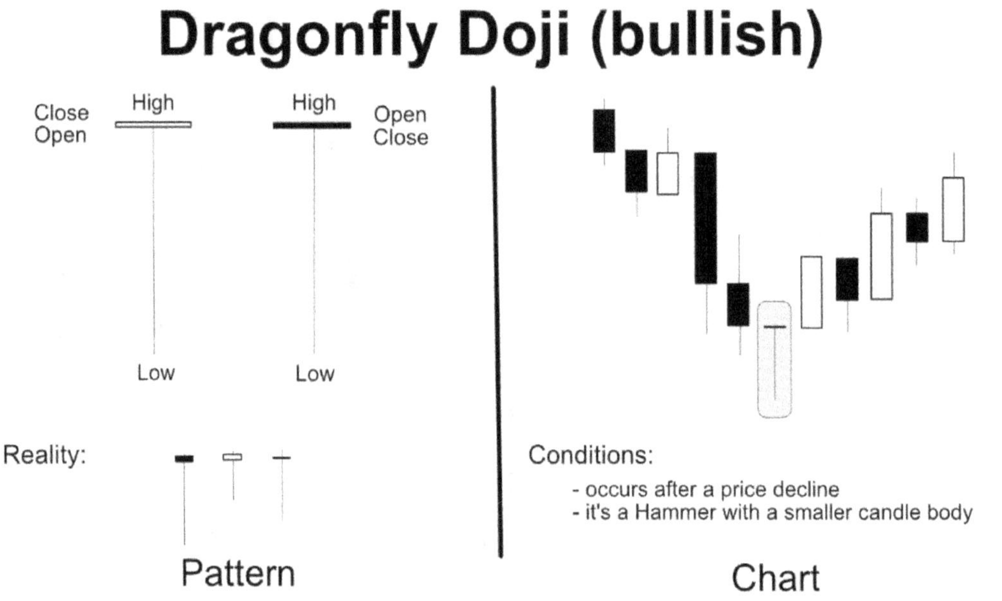

Dragonfly Doji (bullish)

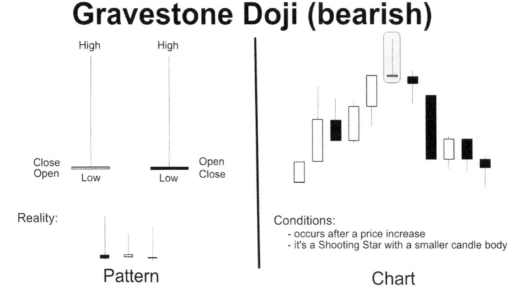

Figure 3.20 – Dragonfly Doji

The same goes for the **Gravestone Doji** where we have a Shooting Star that was brought back near its beginning (illustrated as follows):

Gravestone Doji (bearish)

Figure 3.21 – Gravestone Doji

They are considered to be a bit more powerful than the Hammer and the Shooting Star patterns.

Morning (Doji) Star (bullish) versus Evening (Doji) Star (bearish)

The **Morning (Doji) Star** is a bullish reversal candlestick pattern that occurs after a downtrend. This three-candle pattern signals the potential end of a bearish trend and the beginning of a new bullish trend.

This diagram illustrates the situation:

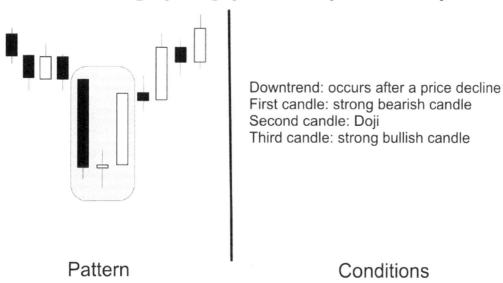

Morning (Doji) Star (bullish)

Downtrend: occurs after a price decline
First candle: strong bearish candle
Second candle: Doji
Third candle: strong bullish candle

Pattern   Conditions

Figure 3.22 – Morning (Doji) Star

The first candle in the pattern is a long bearish candle, indicating a continuation of the downtrend. The second candle is a Doji, suggesting indecision in the market and potential weakening of the downtrend. The third candle is a bullish candle that should close above the midpoint of the first candle, confirming a reversal in sentiment and a shift from bearish to bullish. It is even more powerful if it's accompanied by strong trading volume (indicating that the fight was bigger).

The **Evening (Doji) Star** works in reverse, using the same principles:

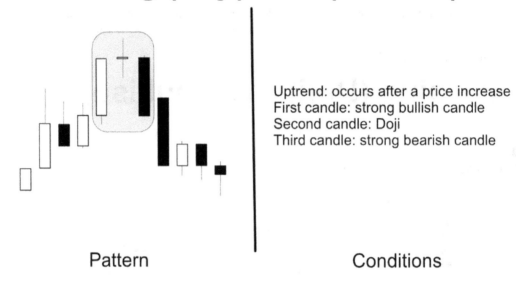

Evening (Doji) Star (bearish)

Uptrend: occurs after a price increase
First candle: strong bullish candle
Second candle: Doji
Third candle: strong bearish candle

Pattern   Conditions

Figure 3.23 – Evening (Doji) Star

Note that instead of the Doji, there might be another indecision pattern such as a Spinning Top.

Also, it's funny when we say the pattern occurs "at the top of the trend" as we don't usually know where the trend's top is until it changes direction. What we see is the first candle as part of the previous trend, the Doji as an indecision, and the third candle as a trend reversal. So, again, I refer to the story of the price here. When you see a Morning (Doji) Star after the price goes down, it indicates a potential trend reversal. Same for when you see an Evening (Doji) Star after the price goes up. They don't promise change; they only suggest it.

Bullish Engulfing versus Bearish Engulfing

These patterns are formed with two candles. Actually, even if the previous patterns contain only one candle, they are valid only because of the context (an Inverted Hammer is only valid in a downtrend), so we are always taking into consideration what happens before the pattern.

Bullish Engulfing is a pattern in which the bullish candle engulfs (contains) the bearish candle. The story is that the bears tried to take the price down and then the bulls reacted powerfully, getting the price well above the point where the bears started fighting for it:

Bullish Engulfing Pattern (bullish)

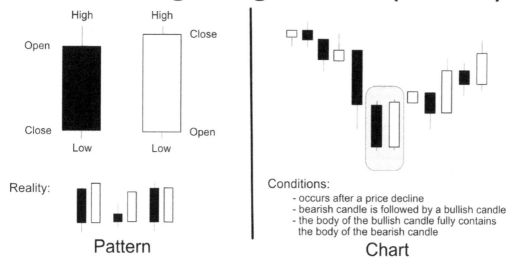

Figure 3.24 – Bullish Engulfing

The same applies (in reverse) to the **Bearish Engulfing** pattern, in which the bears successfully displayed a show of force, bringing the price from the bullish close lower, under the body of the bulls' candle:

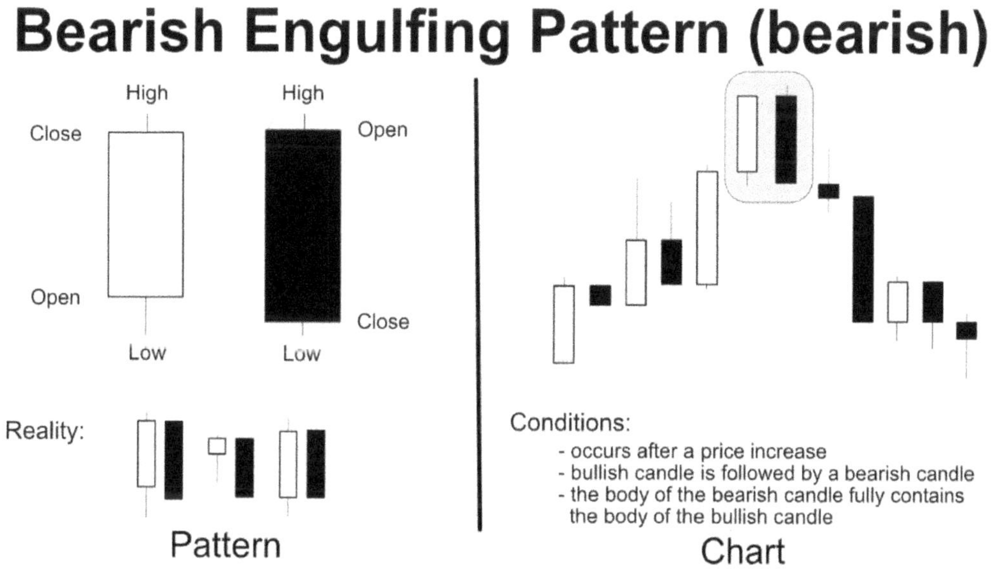

Bearish Engulfing Pattern (bearish)

High   High
Close   Open

Open   Close
Low   Low

Reality: Pattern

Conditions:
- occurs after a price increase
- bullish candle is followed by a bearish candle
- the body of the bearish candle fully contains the body of the bullish candle

Chart

Figure 3.25 – Bearish Engulfing pattern

Bullish Harami versus Bearish Harami

A weaker bullish pattern, the **Bullish Harami**, comes in a downtrend signifying that the trend might be reversing. It's generally displayed as a bearish candle followed by a smaller bullish candle that's contained in it. It looks like a reverse Bearish Engulfing pattern:

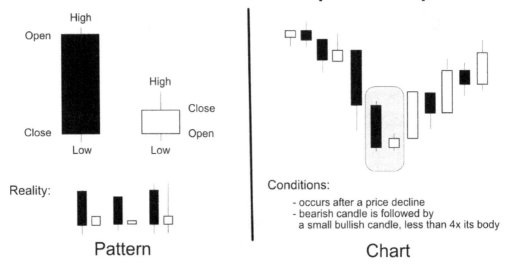

Figure 3.26 – Bullish Harami

Bearish Harami shows the same pattern, in reverse, in an uptrend:

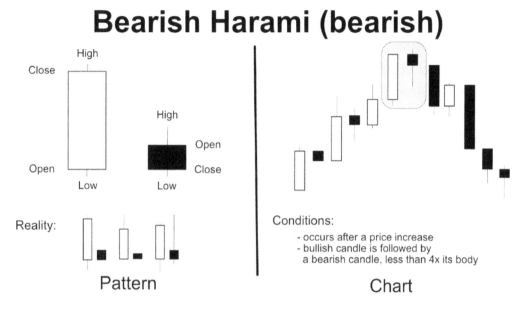

Figure 3.27 – Bearish Harami

I consider these weaker patterns as they might just point to a retracement on a lower time frame. Basically, the second candle might be a temporary price reversal, and the price might form a trend following a pattern on a lower time frame. In stock trading, there is also a gap where the second candle *"jumps"* from the close of the first candle, which in crypto we don't usually see (and which would strengthen the pattern a bit).

Three White Soldiers (bullish) versus Three Black Crows (bearish)

The **Three White Soldiers (TWS)** indicates strong upward momentum while the **Three Black Crows (TBC)** indicates strong downward momentum:

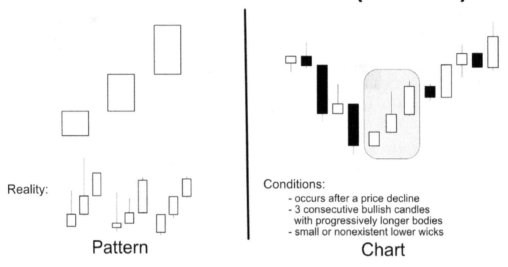

Figure 3.28 – TWS

The TWS pattern occurs after a downtrend and consists of three consecutive long-bodied bullish candles, each with a higher closing price than the previous one. It shows the ongoing dominance of buyers over sellers during the formation of the pattern. Even if you see a short retracement after the TWS, the bulls are in power there, and after the retracement, the price will probably continue in its ascension.

The reverse is also true for the TBC, where the bears are strongly dominating the chart, as seen here:

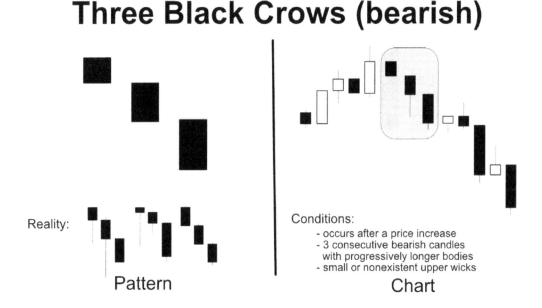

Figure 3.29 – TBC

Marubozu (bullish or bearish)

Marubozu is a strong pattern in which the price, after a downtrend, goes up without any wick (clear bullish run) or, after an uptrend, goes down without any wick (clear bearish win). Basically, it's a strong push in a direction:

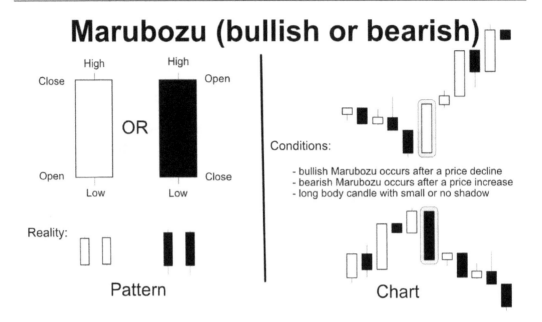

Figure 3.30 – Marubozu

Candlestick patterns questions

The patterns may appear simple to recognize while examining the diagrams; however, when you start using them in trading, you'll likely find yourself asking questions such as the following:

- Is it considered a Hammer if it has a small wick, or is it just another candle that could potentially form TWS?

- Does a Gravestone Doji at the end of an uptrend count or I should wait for another confirmation? Do two Dojis count?

- Does a Bullish Engulfing followed by an Evening (Doji) Star suggests a bullish or a bearish trend?

- Why do I see so many patterns that don't work? (*Tip: A 51% success pattern is successful, but that doesn't mean you won't see 10 continuous situations where it won't work.*)

- Why do patterns never work when I'm trading but always work when I'm charting? (*Tip: There is other information you're missing but, for the time being, it's important just to identify them on the chart.*)

Activities

1. Open **BTCBUSD on 15 Minutes** in TradingView and identify all of the patterns mentioned. If you can't find a particular pattern, try to identify it on another time frame.

2. For each pattern identified, check the story on a lower time frame. For example, How does the **4H** Doji candle look on **1H**? How does it look on **15m**? Add to your chart the following indicators: *HTF Candles by Prosum Solutions* by *prosum_solutions* (`https://www.tradingview.com/script/wmkhSkqq-HTF-Candles-by-Prosum-Solutions/`) and *Candlesticks Patterns Identified* by *repo32* (`https://www.tradingview.com/script/BK4lEoKq-Candlesticks-Patterns-Identified/`). Use them to quickly pinpoint particular candles and see how they are formed on lower time frames.

3. Use **Bar Replay** to go back in time and press **Play** at an appropriate speed so that you can follow the candles. Try to identify the patterns once they form.

4. Use **Bar Replay** to make bets with yourself: Will the price rise on this particular pattern that you've found or not?

Chart patterns

Chart patterns represent a collection of candlesticks that form the potential of a trend. Basically, they suggest what the price will do next.

You can find most chart patterns in the *Encyclopedia of Candle Patterns, 3rd Edition* by Thomas N. Bulkowski (`https://www.wiley.com/en-us/Encyclopedia+of+Chart+Patterns,+3rd+Edition-p-9781119739685`). Thomas is a successful investor with 35 years of experience trading stocks, and he is considered the leading expert on chart patterns. Note the "*stocks*" keyword.

In his book, you'll find what the best patterns are for stocks in various conditions, but if you want to see if they apply to crypto, you'll need to do the tests for yourself. I'm not telling you this to dissuade you from applying them, or to demoralize you about crypto trading; I'm telling it as a warning to not take anything for granted. There's no pattern with a 68% win rate, and whoever tells you there is, ask them for the spreadsheet file with the test conditions, and, due to this book, you'll be able to pinpoint the issues that they've neglected when testing.

But patterns that indicate trend reversal or trend continuation do exist; it's just that they need to be taken in the context they are identified.

Next, I'm going to show you the most common chart patterns and the story they whisper. Don't believe in that story blindly; think of it as your grandpa's war story: it's probably true, but embellished for sure.

Double Bottom (bullish) versus Double Top (bearish)

Double Bottom and **Triple Bottom** signify a bullish trend reversal:

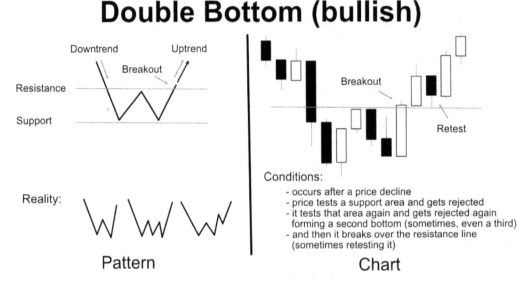

Figure 3.31 – Double Bottom

The price hit a strong support area and bounced from it and then it hit it again, bouncing from it again. This signifies strong support and strong price reactions in that area. The trick with the **Double Bottom** is that even if you bet the price will go up, it might test the support area again, forming a **Triple Bottom** before doing so. The pattern resembles the letter *W*. **Double Top** and **Triple Top** signify a bearish trend reversal for the same reasons—the price hits a strong resistance, bouncing from it. The pattern resembles the letter *M*:

Double Top (bearish)

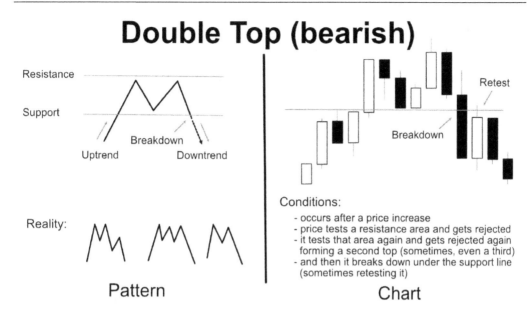

Resistance

Support

Breakdown

Uptrend   Downtrend

Retest

Breakdown

Reality:

Conditions:
- occurs after a price increase
- price tests a resistance area and gets rejected
- it tests that area again and gets rejected again
  forming a second top (sometimes, even a third)
- and then it breaks down under the support line
  (sometimes retesting it)

Pattern   Chart

Figure 3.32 – Double Top

Note that the two peaks occur at approximately the same price level, but it's up to you to judge what "*approximately*" means. After hundreds of trades and thousands of charts, you'll get a feeling regarding how big that area is. The support line is also called the neckline, and it will become a resistance line once the price breaks through it.

Think of it like this: when the enemy conquers a strategic area, it becomes their strategic area. We say that once the price breaks a resistance line, that line becomes the new support, or, once the price falls through a support line, that support becomes the new resistance. And when we say support "*line*," we actually refer to an area around the line that we're drawing, not the specific line.

Inverse Head and Shoulders (bullish) versus Head and Shoulders (bearish)

The **Inverse Head and Shoulders (iH&S)** pattern is a bullish chart pattern in technical analysis that signals a potential trend reversal from a downtrend to an uptrend. It resembles an upside-down human silhouette with a central trough (the *"head"*) flanked by two higher troughs (the *"shoulders"*). The pattern is confirmed when the price breaks above the neckline, a resistance level connecting the highs between the shoulders and the head, after the formation of the right shoulder:

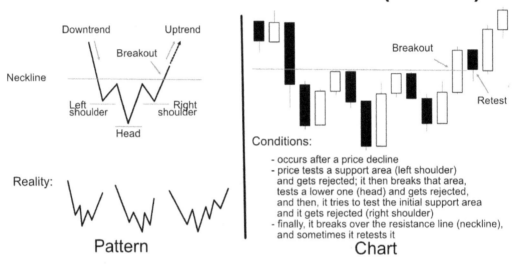

Figure 3.33 – iH&S

How it works: After a price decline that hits a support line, the price moves up, creating a *"left shoulder"*; it hits a resistance line, *"the neckline,"* and then there's a strong bounce that passes under the left shoulder's *"support"* forming a lower support line, *"the head."* After that, it moves up again and hits the neckline, but now the reversal is weaker and the price forms a *"right shoulder"* around the same area where it had its left shoulder. When it bounces from that area, it does a stronger bounce, breaking out over the neckline.

The story here is that the price tried to get up, fell, tried again, fell but not that hard, and the third time it succeeded, and the effort was rewarded.

The **Head and Shoulders** (**H&S**) pattern is confirmed when the price breaks below the neckline, a support level connecting the lows between the shoulders and the head, after the formation of a right shoulder:

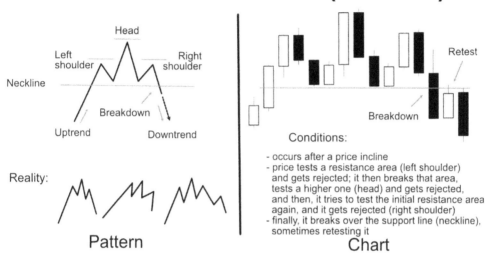

Figure 3.34 – H&S

Note that most H&S patterns can also be identified diagonally; they are not always straight.

Bull Flag (bullish) versus Bear Flag (bearish)

These patterns signify trend continuation. Essentially, the price follows a direction, retraces within a channel-like region, and then the trend resumes. On higher time frames, it appears as a bullish trend accompanied by one or two bearish candles, after which the trend persists. On lower time frames, these candles create a parallel channel:

Bull Flag (bullish)

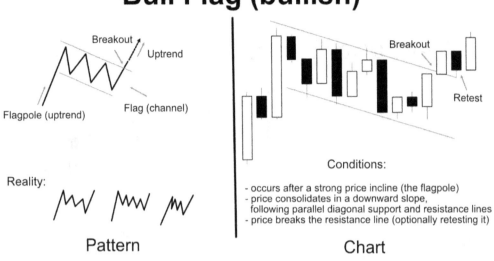

Breakout

Uptrend

Flagpole (uptrend)

Flag (channel)

Breakout

Retest

Reality:

Pattern

Chart

Conditions:

- occurs after a strong price incline (the flagpole)
- price consolidates in a downward slope,
  following parallel diagonal support and resistance lines
- price breaks the resistance line (optionally retesting it)

Figure 3.35 – Bull Flag

As you can see from the preceding diagram, a **Bull Flag** continues an upward trend while a **Bear Flag**, as shown next, continues a downward trend:

Bear Flag (bearish)

Flagpole (downtrend)

Flag (channel)

Breakout

Downtrend

Retest

Breakdown

Reality:

Pattern

Chart

Conditions:

- occurs after a strong price decline (the flagpole)
- price consolidates in an upward slope,
  following parallel diagonal support and resistance lines
- price breaks the support line (optionally retesting it)

Figure 3.36 – Bear Flag

Cup and Handle (bullish) versus Inverted Cup and Handle (bearish)

A **Cup and Handle** (**C&H**) is a bullish pattern in which the price falls and rises in a rounded fashion, forming a cup, and then it falls and rises again in a smaller version of the cup, forming a handle. After forming a cup-like formation, the price encounters resistance through which it passes after at least another try that looks like a cup's handle.

The story here is that the price didn't encounter any support line when falling, up to the bottom, and no resistance line when rising, up to the top. Basically, it tried to go down, but it didn't stay there because there was no interest for it to be there (no fight), so it went back up, and there it had a small battle that it victoriously won, and now, it follows its path. The round form suggests visiting behavior, not war-like behavior:

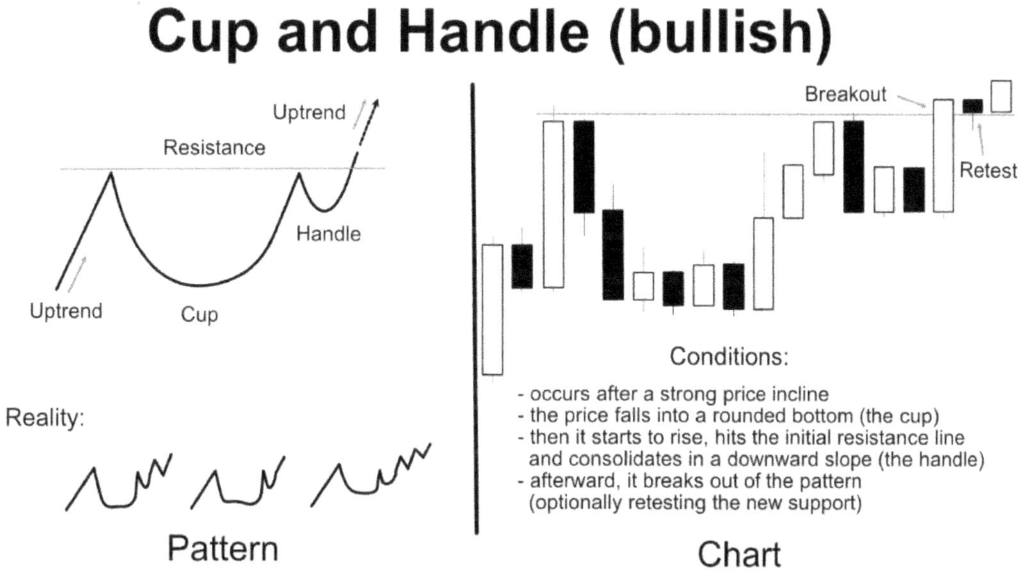

Figure 3.37 – C&H

In **Inverted C&H** (**iC&H**), we see the same story in which the price slowly (roundly) visits the top, hits the support line, slowly does another rounded rise, falls again on the support line, passes through it, and continues its journey:

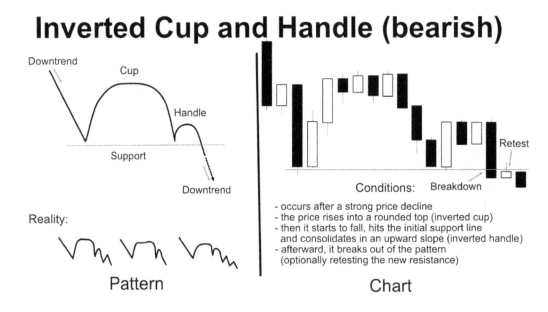

Figure 3.38 – iC&H

Descending, ascending, symmetrical, and expanding triangles

When the price rises and then hits a strong resistance line, hitting it again and again but from higher and higher bounce areas, we call this an **Ascending Triangle**. What it shows is that even though the support line is strong, the battle still moves closer to it, building momentum. The move from that area is usually upward.

A **Descending Triangle** does the same thing when the price falls, hitting a strong support line, bouncing, and arriving closer and closer to it. After it wins the fight, it continues its trend.

A **Symmetrical Triangle** usually continues the previous trend of the price, but it's not as strong as the previous patterns.

An **Expanding Triangle** is an inverse version of the triangle. We call a **Bearish Expanding Triangle** one in which the price rises, then, instead of a retracement and an upward movement, or instead of a flag, the price tries to go up, comes down, tries to go even further but falls with a much bigger force, and on and on. Basically, the more it tries to rise, the further it falls. When it realizes it won't succeed, it will fall drastically in a trend reversal.

The reverse is true for a **Bullish Expanding Triangle**, and, of course, don't forget about the **Symmetrical Expanding Triangle**:

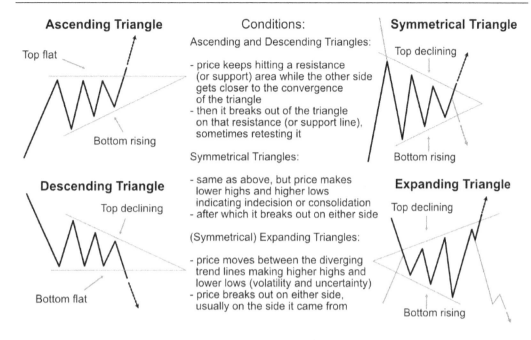

Figure 3.39 – Triangles

Here's how an Ascending Triangle looks on a chart:

Ascending Triangle (bullish)

Figure 3.40 – Ascending Triangle

Should an Ascending Triangle contain another, smaller Ascending Triangle near its apex (typically on a lower time frame), it can serve as confirmation and potentially provide a head start for the breakout. Keep in mind that a triangle can include many more candles than those depicted in the diagram. The presence of the pattern is what matters, not the number of candles involved.

Falling Wedge (bullish) versus Rising Wedge (bearish)

Look at the Ascending Triangle diagram again. And now, look at the following **Rising Wedge** diagram:

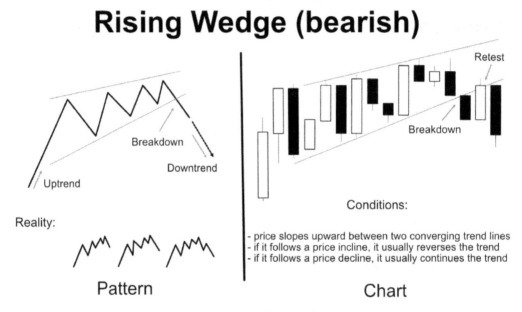

Figure 3.41 – Rising Wedge

Why are the outcomes of these patterns so different?

The Ascending Triangle hits the resistance line with more and more force and from a closer and closer angle. It's like an army pushing more and more against an adversary that tries to hold its position. And momentum is built—a momentum that will explode, usually in the direction of the pushers.

In a Rising Wedge, the army falls back a little when it is pushed, and when it is pushed again, it falls back again (a little), regrouping. Though the pushers are able to push the army back, they don't break past it, nor do they hit the same area creating momentum. Actually, the opposite happens: the pushers' power deflates when they see they can push but never push hard enough. The price doesn't rise enough because of all of these pushes, so it does the opposite—it falls.

Now, imagine the **Falling Wedge** and picture the opposite story of what happened with the Rising Wedge. Picture the price consolidating and converging downward, with the support and resistance lines getting closer together as they slope downward. When the Falling Wedge pattern is recognized, the breakout usually happens in the opposite direction of the downward trend, signaling a potential reversal of the trend to the upside:

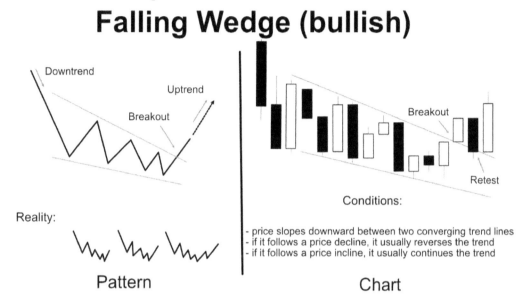

Figure 3.42 – Falling Wedge

Ascending, Descending, and Horizontal (Parallel) Channels (or Rectangles)

If you search for chart patterns on the internet, you'll rarely see parallel channels. These (and the wedges) are my favorite patterns to trade, and I have no idea why no one else talks about them:

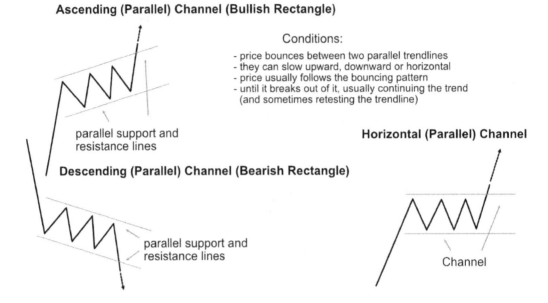

Figure 3.43 – Channels

When we have three points of contact, near strong support and resistance lines, we can draw a parallel channel using those points and enter longs when the price hits the bottom and shorts when the price hits the top. We'll be always right until the channel ends, when we'll have one bad trade. Of course, we won't catch all the entries as sometimes the price starts rising before it hits the floor, and other times, it's falling only to the middle of the channel and then it returns, but trading channels is a skill I always teach my students as I find it's pretty easy to grasp and it's easy to get your first wins from.

We do the same things with **Ascending** and **Descending Channels**, but they are not as strong as the **Horizontal Channel**.

Buildup, Breakout, and Breakdown

The **Buildup** (**Long Buildup** if it's near a resistance line or **Short Buildup** if it's near a support line) is another chart pattern you'll rarely find on the internet:

Descending Rectangle + Buildup + Breakdown

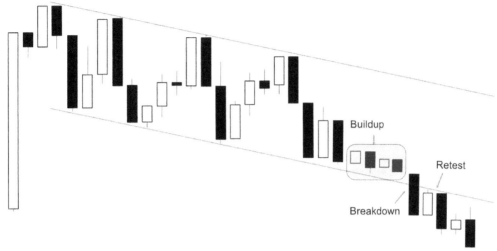

Figure 3.44 – Descending Rectangle + Buildup + Breakdown

The Buildup is a metaphor for when the price crunches through a support or a resistance. It eats at the orders placed there until it finds no order left, and then it continues its descent or ascent. Compared to the **Descending Rectangle**, it doesn't bounce from that support; it stays close to it, eating hungrily. Compared to the Ascending Triangle, it doesn't get closer to the resistance; it's already close.

When you see price gathering near a resistance, there's a fight there and the direction is probably up, and we call that a **Breakout**. And when the fight happens near the support, the direction is probably down, and we call it a **Breakdown**.

Note that they look like the **Bullish Rectangle** and the **Bearish Rectangle**. The difference is that these are smaller compared to the price movement before. Basically, the price gathers at the very top or very bottom; it doesn't form a big pattern.

The Retest and the Fakeout (trend confirmation)

The **Bounce** (also called the **Retest**) is another pattern that's not directly shown or explained in images about chart patterns, though it is usually mentioned in the text. The bounce is a confirmation of a movement.

The story here is that the price followed the pattern correctly, and now it broke into the expected direction. In order to make sure that it follows its intent, we wait for a short bounce on the resistance (or support) line that got broken. We call this a retest of that line, and, if the line holds, we say that the previous resistance line became the new support line (or vice versa).

Risky traders trade the exit of the pattern, medium-risk traders trade the bounce, and the safest traders trade when the price bounces over its local top (the place where it fell from for the bounce):

Horizontal Channel + Buildup

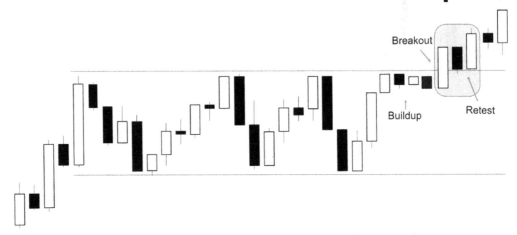

Figure 3.45 – The Retest

We refer to them as **Breakouts** or **Breakdowns** when the price escapes from previously established momentum. However, sometimes the momentum isn't sufficient and the price feigns an escape, falling back down or possibly even reversing the trend, as depicted in the next diagram. This can occur within the same candle that crossed the line, in subsequent candles, or during a retest of the line. We call this phenomenon a **Fakeout**, as the price deceives by appearing to exit. Consequently, most traders wait for a retest of the support or resistance lines:

Ascending Triangle+ Fakeout + Breakdown

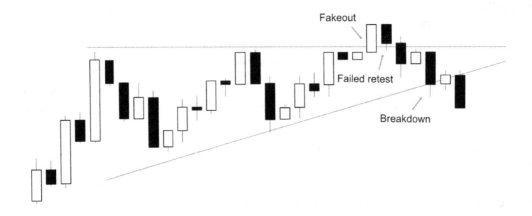

Figure 3.46 – Ascending Triangle + Fakeout + Breakdown

Differences between candlestick patterns and chart patterns

There are some differences between candlestick patterns and chart patterns that you should know:

- Candlestick patterns occur in one or just a few candlesticks. Chart patterns occur over a lot more candles, a group of them creating a pattern.

- Candlestick patterns form quickly, candle by candle, while chart patterns take longer to form.

- Candlestick patterns provide a shorter trend bias than chart patterns.

- Candlestick patterns provide quick entries and exits while chart patterns provide longer entries and exits.

Chart pattern questions

Chart patterns are a bit harder to identify compared to candlestick patterns, and often they can be misinterpreted. Here are some questions you might face when you start trading them:

- Do I take wicks into consideration? Is it a Double Top if one wick rises way further than the second one (the Highs are at a distance)? (*Tip: Look at the story; the patterns will never form perfectly, and a trader will always say there wasn't a pattern there... after the fact. The pattern forms around the story; the story is what matters.*)

- Do I trade the Double Top or wait for the Triple Top? How do I know the pattern is fully formed? (*Tip: It takes time and experience to trade with better accuracy. For now, do your trades, learn from your mistakes, and, in time, you'll develop an intuitive feeling on when you need to wait and when you need to go in. If the perfect time for entering a trade could be identified, everyone would win.*)

- Why do I see so many patterns that don't work? (*Tip: As I said in the previous section, a 51% success pattern is successful, but that doesn't mean you won't see 10 continuous situations where it won't work.*)

- Why do patterns never work when I'm trading but always work when I'm charting? (*Tip: There is other information you're missing but, for the time being, it's important just to identify them on the chart.*)

We discussed in *Chapter 1* the **hindsight bias**, also known as the **knew-it-all-along phenomenon**.

Let me give you a situation and let's see what happens:

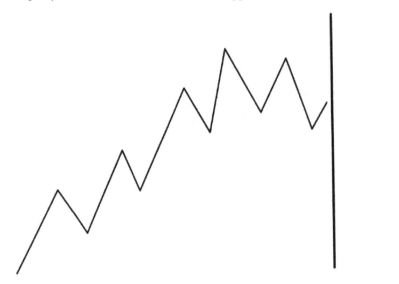

Figure 3.47 – What's the story there?

Is it a plane? Is it a fly? Is it a... famous chart pattern?

Which chart pattern is it?

Go back to the *Chart patterns* section and make sure you know before turning the page.

As you can see in the diagram... it's a Bull Flag. And the price continues to rise after the short retracement:

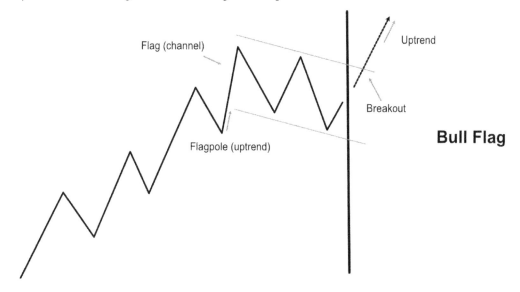

Figure 3.48 – It's a Bull Flag!

Well, I was actually mistaken. This is the H&S pattern! Of course it's the H&S pattern; how could I have missed it?

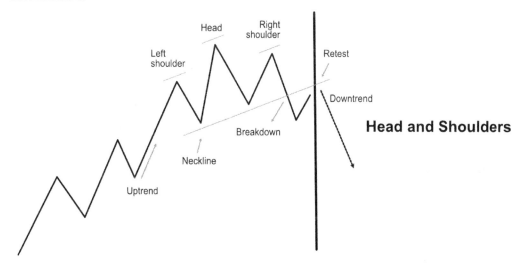

Figure 3.49 – It's a H&S pattern!

So... which pattern is it? And where will the price go?

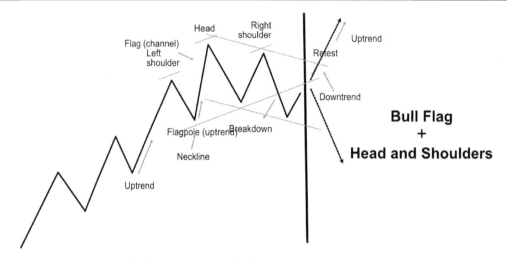

Figure 3.50 – It's the hindsight bias!!! (images intentionally overlapping)

If I look at the price movement for the H&S pattern, I will clearly see how wrong I was in thinking it was a Bull Flag. And if I look at the diagram with the Bull Flag pattern, I will clearly see how I was wrong thinking of the H&S pattern. But the reality is that both patterns were there and the hindsight bias sabotaged me into thinking I was wrong.

The point here is that charting is not a clearly defined process. There's always ambiguity and patterns that you'll miss. You're human, as am I. We'll miss dozens of patterns in each analysis, and this shouldn't bother us as long as we trade with a net positive outcome.

Activities

1. Open **BTCBUSD on 4 Hours** in TradingView and identify all of the patterns mentioned. If you can't find a particular pattern, try to identify it on another time frame.

2. For each pattern identified, check the story on a lower time frame. For example, how does the Descending Triangle look on 1H? How does it look on 15m?

3. You can search for indicators such as C&H, but there's a lot of relativity with chart patterns, and they will miss patterns because of the parameters encoded. Instead, for chart patterns I definitely recommend you identify them without indicators. Still, you can add indicators just to see if they notice patterns you didn't.

4. Use **Bar Replay** to go back in time and press **Play** at an appropriate speed so that you can follow the candles. Try to identify the patterns once they form.

5. Use **Bar Replay** to make bets with yourself: Will the price rise on this particular pattern that you've found or not?

Supply and demand

To understand all those fancy lines on the chart that, when drawn, the price reacts to them, you must first understand the laws of supply and demand.

The law of demand

There is an inverse relationship between the price and the quantity demanded.

For example, if a company sells a 4K TV at half the usual market price, all other specs being the same, the demand for it will grow. When the price increases, the demand for it will fall.

There are three reasons for the law of demand:

1. **The substitution effect**:

   When the price of a 4K TV grows too much, an 8K one becomes affordable and vice versa.

2. **The income effect**:

   When the price rises, fewer people can afford the item; when it falls, more people can afford the item.

3. **Law of diminishing marginal utility**:

   You don't necessarily need a second 4K TV, but if the price falls low enough, you could buy another one for the other room.

There are five shifters of demand:

1. **Preferences**:

   There are a lot of articles about 8K TVs, so people buy fewer 4K TVs.

2. **Number of buyers**:

   More consumers versus fewer consumers.

3. **Price of related goods**:

   The price of substitutes (8K TVs, 1080p TVs, computer screens) is cheaper, so people buy more of these instead of 4K TVs or vice versa.

4. **Income**:

   When income goes up, people buy fewer inferior goods (1080p TVs) and more superior ones (4K TVs). Vice versa when income goes down.

5. **Expectations**:

   If you think Black Friday will lower the price, you might wait for it to lower the demand in the weeks previous to Black Friday.

The law of supply

There's a direct (and positive) relationship between the price and the quantity supplied.

When item X becomes expensive, if you supply more item Xs, you make more money.

For instance, there are five shifters of supply:

1. **Price of resources**:

    If the price of the microchips used in 4K TVs goes up, the price of TVs will follow.

2. **Technology**:

    If 4K TVs can be produced cheaper, faster, or simpler, the price will reflect that.

3. **Government involvement**:

    If the government involves itself by reducing taxes for them or creating some specific regulations, offering subsidies, and so on, the price will follow.

4. **Number of sellers**:

    If there are more sellers, the price will decrease (some will compete against the price); if there are fewer, the price will increase.

5. **Expectations**:

    If producers are betting the 4K TVs' price will go up in the future, they might hold up the supply now so that they can have a bigger stock then.

The market-clearing price

When the lines of supply and demand intersect, we have equilibrium, and we call this the market clearing price. That is the price where the demand equals the supply.

A change in the price of 4K TVs will impact both the demand and the supply.

This is called **disequilibrium**, and it manifests like this:

*   If the price is too low, there's too little supply for too much demand. It's called a shortage, not enough product for the need, and the price is forced to increase.

*   If the price is too high, there's too much supply for too little demand. It's called a surplus, too much product for the need, and the price is forced to decrease.

*   In a free market, the price will reach equilibrium.

Note that supply and demand do not respond to price movements in proportion to those movements. There's a degree of change called price elasticity, which explains the fluctuations you will see.

Again, take the story from these explanations, understand the forces, and do the activities. These laws are helpful to investors because they can predict the macro conditions.

Activities

1. Imagine there's a shortage of microchips for 4K TVs due to, let's say, the main manufacturer having financial troubles. What happens to the supply, to the demand, and to the price now?

2. Research comes out stating watching TV leads to depression. The research is confirmed, and most governments increase taxes on TVs and streaming services while promoting outdoor activities. What happens to the supply, to the demand, and to the price?

3. You're a financial investor and know that technology changes. How do you view the future of 4K TVs in the next 3 years, 5 years, or 10 years?

4. Now, replace the 4K TV with one Bitcoin and see how the law of demand and supply impacts the purchase of Bitcoin. How is the clearing price set? Which forces impact it, and which don't?

Support and resistance

When the laws of supply and demand meet on a chart, they generate reactions that we can use when trading.

When there's too much demand and too little supply, that area is oversold, or we call it having support against a potential price decrease, which helps the price increase. Price in that area becomes very attractive for buyers, so orders there are getting filled. Think of support as an area where buyers want to buy, an area where the forces of demand overwhelm the forces of supply.

Even though the support line promotes a price increase, if it is broken, the forces that created the supply and demand move to the lower level, the previous support line becoming the new resistance line.

When there's too much supply and too little demand, we can call the area overbought or having resistance to a potential price increase, which entices the price to fall.

The price there is too expensive for market participants to buy, so the sellers are setting orders to sell at a lower price to be able to fill their orders.

Who determines when the prices are too high? Well... the market does. The price is attractive for buyers; they buy so the orders that were put at that level are filled, so they buy orders at a higher level (higher price) until suddenly the price is too high for buyers to be willing to buy.

When we identify these areas of support and resistance, we can exploit them in our orders, buying when the price enters a support area and selling when it reaches a resistance area, for example.

This will be much clearer in the further chapters when we talk about how orders are placed in the order book, but for now, what's important here are the following points:

- Support areas are places where the price finds a concentration of demand and a lack of supply.

- Resistance areas are places where the price finds a concentration of supply and a lack of demand.

- If these areas hold, they become stronger (more market participants know that they exist, they trade by them, and they enforce them).

- When an area is broken, it becomes the opposite (old resistance becomes the new support, and old support becomes the new resistance).

- We can find support and resistance on all time frames, but the higher the time frame, the stronger they are.

- If the price reacted to previous areas of support and resistance, those areas become stronger. (The more times the price touches a level, reacting to it in the same pattern, the stronger the level becomes.)

Support and resistance areas can be identified by the following criteria:

- Horizontal lines (the most common and the strongest areas)

- Round numbers (another strong area)

- Trendlines

- Moving averages

- Fibonacci retracements

- Other indicators

We'll talk more about them in the following chapters.

Let's speak in pictures

The following diagram shows a horizontal support line through which the price broke, becoming a resistance line, broke again, becoming support, and in the end, broke another time, becoming resistance:

Figure 3.51 – Horizontal support and resistance line

Round numbers also represent strong support/resistance areas, as seen here:

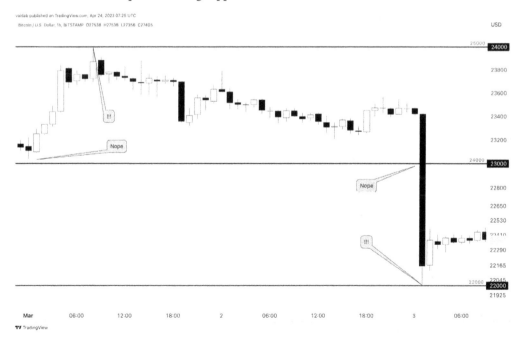

Figure 3.52 – Round numbers: horizontal lines

Note that the middle line, at 23,000, isn't respected by the price. There are always instances where a support or resistance line is ignored, and that is fine. As I mentioned earlier, there's an element of randomness combined with a lack of information in the mix:

Figure 3.53 – Trendlines

A trendline illustrates a consistent pattern in which one side is continually losing by approximately the same degree.

A game of randomness

Do you remember when I said that any one trade is random?

Let me show you how this applies to support and resistance lines:

1. Go to **BTCUSD** on TradingView, the last price in the 5-minute time frame.

2. Now, go far to the right, where you don't see the price, and move up and down randomly to get to a position on your screen where you don't see anything. Don't look at the price scale (so that you're not influenced by previous knowledge of price ranges).

3. Now, add horizontal lines randomly on the screen. Zoom out, add some more, move up, move down, and add again. Add around 10 lines. They need to be at a sufficient distance to differentiate themselves on the screen.

4. Go to the 1-hour time frame and see how those random lines indicate *"support"* and *"resistance."* It seems like magic, but you'll see how the price reacts to them.

5. Think long and hard. Why do some random lines drawn on the chart show places where the price reacts to them?

As I mentioned before, markets are random, and in any one particular place, price reacts randomly. Due to this, its *"fuzziness"* on the chart makes it bounce from various imaginary lines of support and resistance.

So, how can we differentiate between imaginary lines and real lines?

By knowing the theory and making sure it applies to our market.

Yes—you can always find a random line where the price seems to react. But is this confirmed by the theory? For example, is there a particularly round number that has an emotional impact on buyers and sellers? Is there a trendline that is sustained there or a moving average to which the market has reacted in the past?

Note that I've made statistical tests using the `pandas` framework to identify the best intersection for moving averages on the **BTCUSD** market on various time frames, and I found numbers never mentioned on any YouTube channel. Why was that? Because, in my tests, I took into account the exchange trading fees, not how the chart looked visually (where it is actually rounded). So, my numbers, though correct, didn't reflect visually on the chart. What this means for you: Use any indicator that makes sense when charting, but double-test everything when trading; you might be surprised by small differences that make a big impact.

Summary

In this chapter, I walked you through my favorite tool for charting and helped you identify various candlestick and chart patterns, and we finished it with support and resistance and the laws that move them.

My goal was for you to understand the story of the price so that you're able to predict it. Imagine the price as an old grandparent who stays by the fire, telling you stories. At first, you don't know the stories and you listen attentively to them. Then, you begin to understand where they are going, what they are trying to illustrate, and how they portray themselves in the story. And finally, when you really know them, you begin to predict what they'll say from their first few words.

In the next chapter, I'm going to put you in the middle of those stories, learning about indicators and how to combine them to create a profitable (and unique) strategy that beats the market.

4

Technical Analysis – Technical Indicators

In this chapter, I'm going to show you the indicators most traders use when trading. They are the most common, and they are so often used because they work. I've split them into categories so that you don't use multiple indicators that look at the situation from the same angle (thus not giving you enough information), and I made sure you have enough examples to understand how they work.

My goal for this chapter is for you to understand the story of the price that's being told through these indicators.

Just as when we looked at candlestick and chart patterns, these indicators add information to the same story but from different angles. Understand them, and you'll be able to begin predicting price directions and trade them accordingly.

Here are the topics we're going to talk about:

- Technical indicator categories
- Trend indicators, moving averages
- Momentum indicators, relative strength index
- Volatility, average true range
- Volume, market volume
- Trend analysis, divergences

Technical indicator categories

Everybody and their uncle categorizes indicators in different ways. You might go to a YouTuber and get a list of indicators that they use, you might read a book and get a list of *tested* indicators (though the author probably doesn't quite specify how they were tested), you might go to Investopedia and get a somewhat better list or just Google it and get an infographic with yet another way of doing things.

You can do all that, and it will get pretty confusing. In my opinion, the best way to categorize indicators is to split indicators into categories that don't influence each other that much. If you manage that, you're basically predicting price movement from multiple angles.

For example, if we have two indicators that have different names but are interpreting the same part of the ticker data, using both is almost the same as using only one. An extreme example would be an indicator that tells you to buy every time the volume rises suddenly and another indicator that tells you to buy every time the volume has risen over a period of time. Of course, they are different indicators, but they use the same portion of data to make their predictions. They might ignore that there's a resistance line just above the current price level or that the price is in a downward trend.

If instead we use an indicator that's based on one part of the ticker data and another that's based on another part, for example, an indicator based on trend and another based on volatility, we will have done our prediction from two different angles, which gets us more information.

Here are some examples of my proposed categories for technical indicators:

- Trend analysis:

  - **Candlestick patterns**

  - **Chart patterns**

  - **Support and resistance**

  - **Indicator divergences**

  - **Fibonacci extensions and retracements**

  - **Pivot points**

  - Elliot waves

  - Zig zag

  - Ichimoku cloud

- Trend indicators:

  - **Moving averages**

  - **Moving average convergence divergence**

  - **Parabolic SAR**

  - Linear regression

  - KAMA

- Momentum indicators:

  - **Relative strength index**

  - **Stochastic**

  - **Stochastic RSI**

  - Average directional index

  - Chande momentum oscillator

  - Commodity channel index

  - Momentum indicator

  - Awesome oscillator

  - Williams %R

- Volatility:

  - **Keltner channels**

  - **Bollinger bands**

  - **Average true range**

  - Standard deviation

  - Volatility channels indicator

  - Rate of change

  - Donchian channels

- Volume:

  - **Market volume**

  - **On-balance volume**

  - **Open interest**

  - **Volume-weighted average price**

  - Money flow index

  - Ease of movement

When trading, I usually confirm my prediction using information from at least three of these categories. The indicators in bold are the ones I've been using during the past year, but I love to experiment and, as long as the backtests hold, I might use a totally different indicator or technique. For example, during the last two months, I've traded token unlocks, meaning that I put on my calendar the times when tokens worth $1 million or more were released by their smart contracts, and, if the market structure was ready for a short, I shorted those releases. That would be called *trading the news*.

In the following section, I'm going to present a few indicators that I use when trading and make sure that you understand them through a list of activities I propose for each. Make sure to go through the activities and do the work or you'll have a hard time understanding the charts later on.

Trend indicators - moving averages

The **moving average** (**MA**) calculates the average price of a token over a period of time.

Let's say we have three candles: C1's closing price is 2, C2's is 4, and C3's is 6.

The MA3 (MA calculated over the last three candles) is calculated as $(C1+C2+C3)/3 = 12/3 = 4$.

Now C4 is being formed. The timeframe is four hours and we're only 30 minutes in, so for now, C4's price is 8.

MA3 is now $(C2+C3+C4)/3 = (4+6+8)/3 = 6$.

On a chart, we'd draw a line from C3's MA3 4 value (where our MA3 starts) to C4's MA3 6 value, forming a line. That line would continue as each new candle is formed. Note that we can't calculate MA3 for the first two candles because we need three candles to get that information (MA3). Here's what it looks like:

Moving Averages

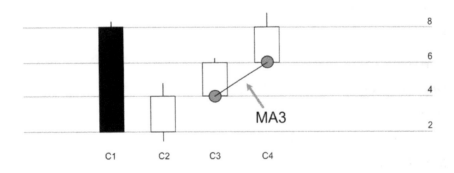

Figure 4.1 – Moving average (MA3)

Every YouTuber and his cousin are talking about specific moving averages that, once the price touches them, create a bounce that can be traded. The truth is, they are wrong!

And here's what it looks like in TradingView:

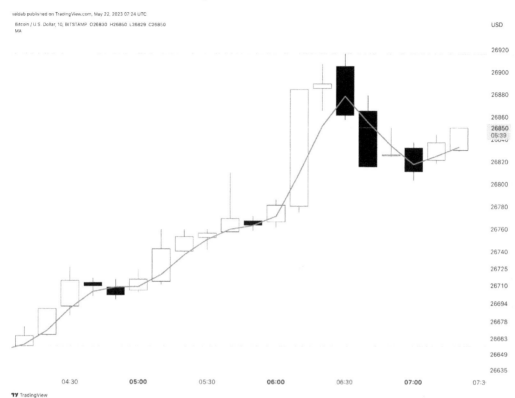

Figure 4.2 – TradingView's moving average (MA3)

The TradingView indicator additionally incorporates smoothing techniques to the lines, preventing abrupt transitions between numerical values. It removes noise from a signal, which in this context is an indicator. It makes the data clearer and easier to interpret. That's why you don't see sudden jumps from one number to the other.

Next, I'm going to present two of the issues that you might encounter when trading MAs

Repainting

Remember our MA3, calculated as $(C2+C3+C4)/3 = (4+6+8)/3 = 6$? It was calculated after 30 minutes on a four-hour time frame, so the C4 value still had time to change.

What happens if, at the end of C4, C4's price drops to 2?

MA3 would be $(C2+C3+C4')/3 = (4+6+2)/3 = 4$.

So the line would be repainted at another value. Basically, during the whole four hours, our indicator will give different values each time we're checking it.

There are two reasons why we call the MA a **lagging indicator**:

- It's based solely on past price information
- It needs to wait for the current candle to close to show the correct value

The longer the MA is (for example, MA250), the more it lags because it uses more information from the past. This is not necessarily bad as it can be used to predict big market movements and ignore smaller ones.

Indicators don't actually display the final value if we take the last candle into account. Some indicators might even use the last candle to compute something for previous candles, thus displaying incorrect information for previous candles too.

Think of it this way: an indicator that will give a buy signal once MA3 is >= 6.

During C4, after 30 minutes, when C4's value is 8, MA3 is 6, so there's a buy signal given. But at the end of C4, the actual value for C4 is 2, and MA3 is 4. So, the buy signal disappears from the chart. When you look at this indicator in the past, you'll see only the signals that it has given at candle close and not in real time. Basically, the indicator *steals information from the future* in each candle. So, when you calculate its profitability, you are actually incorrect.

We need to take all of this into consideration when using indicators that we don't yet understand. And it's always important to know if our indicator is being repainted or not. If it doesn't redraw information on the chart, we say that it's not repainting.

Fees

I'm not going to talk much about fees here, but I'm going to mention their impact on your indicator.

Fees in trading vary from exchange to exchange, but let's give a range of 0.1% to 1% of the amount you're trading. What this means is that when you put an order of $100, $0.1 to $1 are going to the exchange. This might not seem like much, but when you're doing high-frequency trading with take-profit orders at a 1% profit, a 0.1% fee is taking 20% out of your profit. Why 20%? Because the fee applies when you place an order to buy a token and when you place an order to sell your token. It doubles. So, you need to beat the market by quite a lot to be profitable, even with a fee that looks small.

When we plot an MA, we're not taking this into account. So, even if the price is hitting our MA and we take repainting into consideration, entering a trade might give us a smaller profit than we estimate just by looking at the chart.

Activities

1. Go to https://www.investopedia.com/ and search for Simple Moving Average.

2. Read all about it.

3. Understand the mathematical formula behind it.

4. In TradingView, add the MA technical indicator on BTCUSD 4H.

5. Double-click on it and set its length to 5 (calculating for the past five candles).

6. Open the **Data Window** tab on the right-hand bar to see the indicator values.

7. Apply the formula for the last five candles and verify the results with the indicator.

8. Follow the indicator for three more candles and see how the MA line is constructed.

9. Play with the other settings there, and understand **Offset**, **Smoothing**, **Source**, and the **Style** and **Visibility** sections.

> **Tip**
> Visibility makes the indicator visible on specific timeframes.

10. Read about the **exponential moving average**, which is a type of moving average that puts more weight on the last candles and acts faster to the market.

My philosophy is that you learn better when learning the same subject from two to three sources. The explanations might be different, but the examples provided and the repetition may force the learning to happen. We also can't cover each and every option that you can toggle in an indicator, and playing with it will help you get a better understanding of how it works.

Here's the full link:

https://www.investopedia.com/ask/answers/071414/whats-difference-between-moving-average-and-weighted-moving-average.asp

Momentum indicators - relative strength index

As the name says, the **relative strength index (RSI)** shows the relative strength of the price and, along with the exponential moving average, it's one of the top indicators used in trading.

The RSI is displayed as an oscillator ranging from 0 to 100, and it was developed by J. Welles Wilder Jr. in 1978.

It shows bullish and bearish price momentum. Typically, when the RSI is < 30, it's considered oversold and when it is > 70, it's considered overbought. Traders typically buy when the RSI is oversold (usually in confluence with other indicators) and sell when the RSI is overbought. We will get back to these values later on when studying their formula.

Here's what it looks like in a diagram:

Figure 4.3 – Relative strength index

And here's what it looks like in TradingView:

Figure 4.4 – RSI in TradingView

It looks easy to trade, right? You just buy when the indicator tells you to.

Hmm...

So what about here? Take a look:

Figure 4.5 – RSI loss

Here, you would typically enter on an oversold signal on the left of the chart and wait for the RSI to become overbought in order to sell. Well, you'd be pretty disappointed. The price went against you and, after waiting a long time you ended up at a loss.

That's why we need that confluence and the backtesting that we've been mentioning since the beginning of the book.

In the following sections, I'm going to explain how the RSI formula works and why those 30 and 70 values are important.

RSI formula

RSI is a momentum oscillator that measures the speed and change of price movements. This is the formula:

```
RSI = 100 - [100 / (1 + ((Prev AvgGain x Period) + CrtGain) / ((Prev AvgLoss x Period) + CrtLoss))]
```

Here's some additional information to be more specific:

- `Prev AvgGain`: The average gain of the previous periods.
- `Period`: The number of periods used for calculation. The typical choice is 14 periods (candles).
- `CrtGain`: The current gain (0 if the current change in price is negative or zero).
- `Prev AvgLoss`: The average loss of the previous periods.
- `CrtLoss`: The current loss (0 if the current change in price is positive or zero).

The first `RSI = 100 - [100 / (1 + AvgGain / AvgLoss)]`.

If `AvgGain` is 0, `RSI` is set to 0. If `AvgLoss` is 0, `RSI` is set to `100`.

What this formula tells us is that if too many people have bought a token (`AvgGain` and `CrtGain` are high, resulting in an `RSI > 70`), the token is overbought, and it is bound to be sold. If too many people have sold the token (`AvgLoss` and `CrtLoss` are higher, resulting in an `RSI < 30`), the token is oversold, and it has the potential to rise again.

You can find the whole method for calculating the RSI on Investopedia at https://www.investopedia.com/terms/r/rsi.asp, and you can go to StockCharts for an example: https://school.stockcharts.com/doku.php?id=technical_indicators:relative_strength_index_rsi.

As previously suggested, I recommend you go through these resources so that you really understand the intricacies of the indicator. This will also help you understand other indicators that are displayed as an oscillator.

> **Note**
>
> I'm not going to delve into mathematics here as some of the formulas can get quite complex, and it would detract us from the trading part. When I started out, I did my homework, and I recommend you do the same. You'll have to choose one or two indicators from each category and learn them well. If you know them well enough, you'll be able to use them to enter profitable trades. But the choice of which indicators you're going to learn is up to you. My job here is to show you a few angles and to let you choose which ones suit you best.

Activities

1. Go to `https://www.investopedia.com/` and search for `RSI`.

2. Read all about it.

3. Understand the mathematical formula behind it.

4. Next, add the RSI indicator to your chart.

5. Check what happens to the price in relation to the RSI.

6. Does the price react when RSI is > 70 or < 30? How?

Volatility - average true range

The **average true range** (**ATR**) is another indicator developed by J. Welles Wilder Jr. in *New Concepts in Technical Trading Systems*.

The indicator is useful in estimating how volatile the market is. I mainly use it to set proper stop losses so that the volatility doesn't take my stop loss before my trade gains traction.

Now, how about that formula?

ATR formula

```
ATR = (PrevATR * (n - 1) + TR) / n
```

Here's what it means:

- `PrevATR`: The ATR of the previous period.

- n: The period of time over which the ATR is calculated. Typically, this is set to 14 periods.

- TR: The *true range* for the current period. It's the greatest of the following values:

  - The current high (H) minus the current low (L)

  - The absolute value of the current H minus the previous close (C)

  - The absolute value of the current L minus the previous C

Here are the three methods for calculating TR:

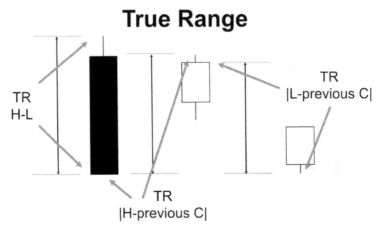

Figure 4.6 – The three ways to calculate true range

Note that when you have volatility and a 24-hour trading exchange, you won't need to calculate the last two situations for TR because the previous C is the current open (O), basically already between H and L. So, if you're trading on Binance, the TR formula is H - L.

The first `ATR = (1/n) * Σ(TRi) for i = 1 to n.`

You can find the whole method for calculating the ATR on Investopedia at `https://www.investopedia.com/terms/a/atr.asp`, and you can go to StockCharts for an example: `https://school.stockcharts.com/doku.php?id=technical_indicators:average_true_range_atr`.

As previously suggested, I recommend you go through these resources so that you really understand the intricacies of the indicator. In short, *ATR is the average of the highs minus the lows* but smoothed so that it gives more importance to recent values. Additionally, it shows the fluctuation between those two. Imagine a trading rule where you exit the trade at a loss whenever the price falls below the entry point by twice the average true range. This is called setting a stop at 2 ATRs, and it is a technique used by traders when exiting a trade.

In the following figure, I've added two indicators: the default ATR indicator (the red line in the lower part of the screen), and **ATR trailing stops colored by HPotter**, an indicator that applies the ATR values on the main chart, showing you where a stop loss could be placed based on ATR multiples:

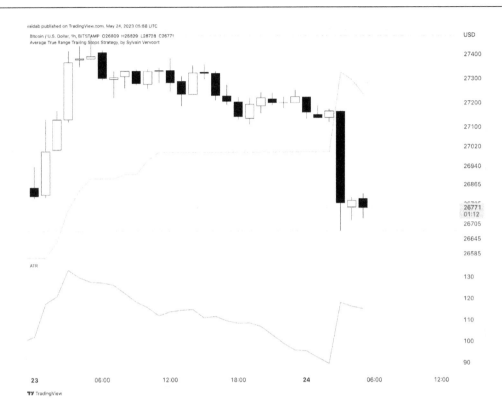

Figure 4.7 – TradingView's average true range

Activities

1. Go to https://www.investopedia.com/ and search for Average True Range.
2. Read all about it.
3. Understand the mathematical formula behind it.
4. Add the ATR indicator on TradingView on BTCUSD 1m.
5. Set the indicator length to 3.
6. Calculate the ATR for the last three candles.
7. Set the **Smoothing** setting to **SMA** and check the result again. Notice how **Smoothing** impacts the formula and remember this for when you use an external ATR indicator (using Python libraries), where you won't apply **Smoothing** to the result.
8. Let the price run for 10 more minutes (10 candles) and see how the ATR evolves.
9. Imagine drawing a line at 2.5 ATRs under the price. How often would that line be touched? Does the ATR help protect your trade from normal price fluctuations?

Volume - market volume

The market volume, also called the trading volume, the volume, or the volume indicator, measures how much the token has traded during each candle.

The higher the volume was, the more intense the battle in that candle was.

A high volume on a big white (or green) candle means that the battle was intense, yet the bulls had a clear win. It also means that during that period, the token was very interesting for the traders and that there was high liquidity in play there. This means that there are both buyers and sellers in play, so it's easy to trade the token.

When the volume rises together with the price, we say that the price is sustained. This means that even when the battle is fierce (high volume), the token rises in price (bulls win). It's considered a healthy rise. Here's what it looks like on a chart:

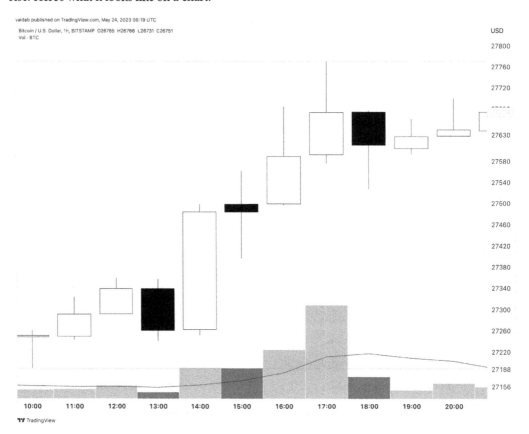

Figure 4.8 – Volume rising with price

When the volume falls while the price rises, the rise is not supported by the volume. Even though the token rises (bulls win), there's not that much interest (not many bears have entered the fight), so, when they enter, the outcome might be different. It's considered an unhealthy rise:

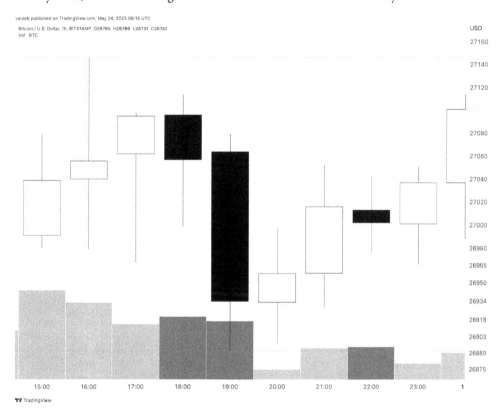

Figure 4.9 – Volume decreasing as prices rise

I'm curious if you've noticed a difference between the two charts in the way the volume indicator is displayed. If you haven't, stop right here and check the images again.

Maybe you noticed the MA line moving on the volume chart in the first image, which didn't exist in the second. I usually use MA30 when checking the volume so that I have information regarding the historical direction of the volume rather than just the last few candles.

The purpose of this brief exercise is to illustrate a scenario in which a trader may advocate for a specific trading technique. However, without using the precise settings that the trader has adjusted on their particular indicator, replicating the same results becomes unfeasible. In this case, I'm also taking into account the direction of MA30 when trading the volume. This example underscores the importance of understanding not only the trading method but also the precise configuration of the tools being utilized.

When the volume rises while the price falls again, the volume sustains the price and the bears are winning:

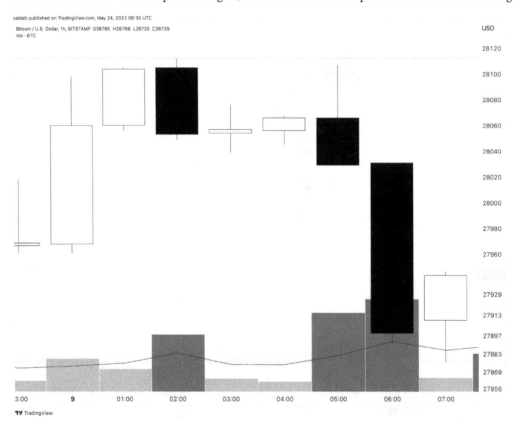

Figure 4.10 – The volume rises while the price decreases

And when the volume falls while the price falls, the fall is not supported because the bulls were not there for the fight:

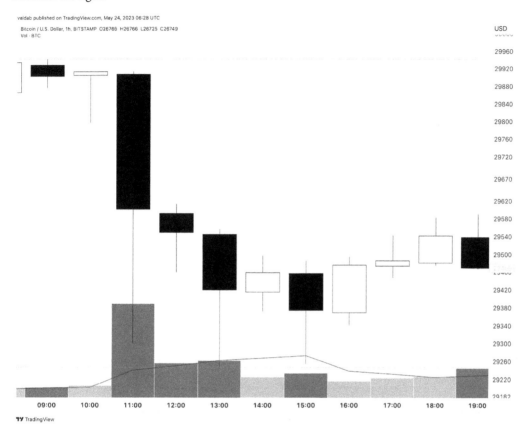

Figure 4.11 – The volume decreases while the price decreases

When the price reaches a new (local) high or low on decreasing volume, a reversal might be expected. You can see in *Figure 4.11* how the low was touched on decreasing volume at *13:00*, then again at *15:00*, and then it reversed on increasing volume.

Here's an image that summarizes how volume usually works:

Price Volume Relationship

Price	Volume	Conclusion
Increases	Increases	Uptrend is supported by volume
Increases	Decreases	Uptrend is not supported by volume
Decreases	Increases	Downtrend is supported by volume
Decreases	Decreases	Downtrend is not supported by volume

Figure 4.12 – The relationship between price and volume

There are more things to notice with volume. Various chart patterns can be confirmed with this indicator, and price stories can be explained. Let me outline a few situations:

- **Trend confirmation**: I've mentioned a few examples in which a price rise supported by a rise in volume is bullish, while a fall in volume during a price rise would be an unsupported rise (indicative of a trend reversal) and vice versa. When volume is low, the signal is weak. Pullbacks (short-term drops in price) are confirmed when they have a lower volume. Otherwise, they might turn into trend reversals (more permanent changes in the trend).

- **Pattern confirmations**: Chart patterns can have their structure confirmed by volume. Imagine a triangle pattern where a breakout occurs on a high volume. The volume means there is an increase in trading happening there, so there is more potential for the move. The same thing happening on a low volume means no one is looking. When they look, a reversal may occur.

- **Exhaustion moves**: When the market rises and you see a sudden sharp rise in both volume and price, it might mean that the trend is ending and there's potential for a reversal. That's because everyone joined in the move (afraid of missing out), and now there are not that many buyers left. This also applies to a market drop.

- **Liquidity potential**: Where there is volume, big orders can be taken. With a lot of trading in the area, banks, funds, and other big players can add their bigger orders.

- **Volume history**: Don't look at one volume bar. Look at the local range of bars. This is why I've added MA30 to the volume indicator. Was the volume high 20 candles ago and now it's very low? It seems that the pattern we've identified is not yet interesting for the traders. Is the volume starting to rise, compared to the last period, on a bearish pattern? We might see a market decline.

I use volume mostly in manual trading and ignore it in automatic trading. That is because I prefer very clear numbers and conditions in automatic trading, which I don't usually get from volume. I recommend you read *A Complete Guide To Volume Price Analysis: Read the book then read the market* by Anna Coulling to know more about how to trade based on volume.

Activities

1. Go to `https://www.investopedia.com/` and search for `Volume`.

2. Read all about it.

3. Understand the mathematical formula behind it.

4. Add the volume indicator in TradingView on BTCUSD 1H.

5. In the indicator configuration, set the **MA** length to **30** and check **Volume MA** in **Style**.

6. Identify three chart patterns and see how the volume confirms or invalidates them.

7. Go to `https://www.investopedia.com/` and search for `On-Balance Volume` (OBV).

8. Read all about it, add it as an indicator, and play with it a bit. Understand the differences between OBV and volume. OBV is my second go-to indicator in the volume category, and I would definitely recommend you add it to your repertoire.

Trend analysis - divergences

Divergences are among the most powerful tools in trading, but they are often misunderstood. Most traders trade with them, but when they try to automate the trading, the process becomes elusive.

A divergence can be considered an imbalance between what the price chart shows us and what an indicator shows, with the presumption that this will lead to a trend reversal. The indicator is usually an oscillator, as they are particularly suited to showing overbought or oversold conditions, but they can also be other types of indicators, such as OBV.

Let's consider the four divergences in the following figure:

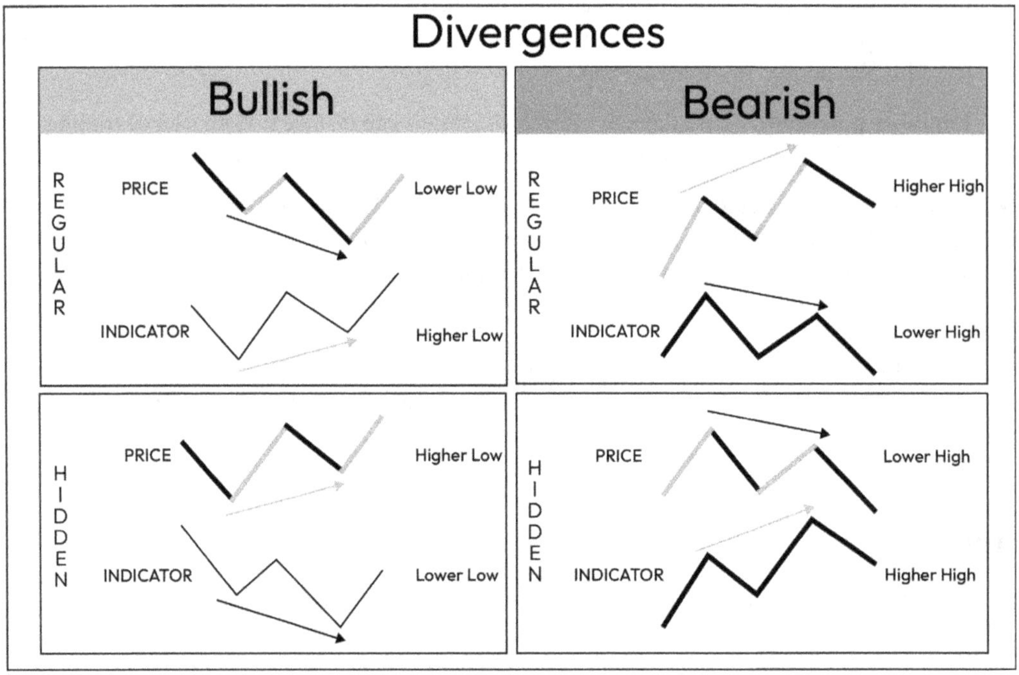

Figure 4.13 – Class A divergences

In *Figure 4.13*, we have the following:

- **Regular bullish divergence**: The price has lower lows, and the oscillator has higher lows
- **Hidden bullish divergence**: The price has higher lows, and the oscillator has lower lows
- **Regular bearish divergence**: The price has higher highs, and the oscillator has lower highs
- **Hidden bullish divergence**: The price has lower highs, and the oscillator has higher highs

These are called *Class A* (*Strong*) divergences. *Class B* (*Medium*) divergences have the price at a resistance line (bullish, think double-top) or support line (bearish, like in a double-bottom), and *Class C* divergences have the oscillator at a resistance line (bullish) or support line (bearish). They are weaker, and I don't usually trade with them, but it's better to notice them on the chart when they happen:

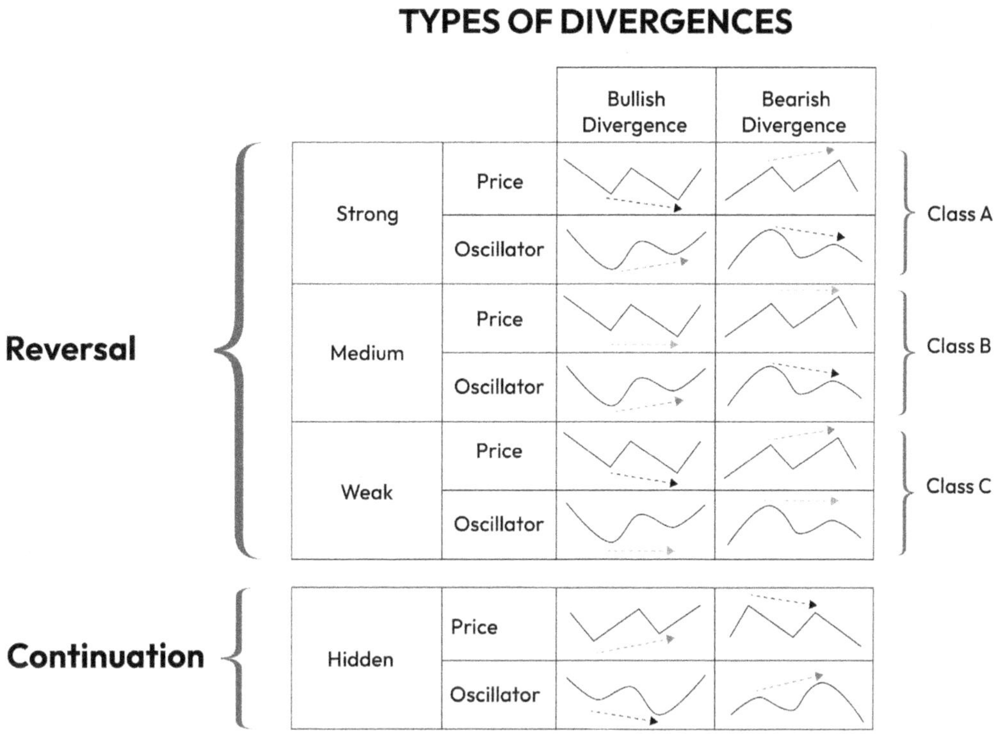

TYPES OF DIVERGENCES

Figure 4.14 – Divergence types

Also, here's an easy way to remember divergences: look at the lows for bullish divergences and look at the highs for the bearish divergences.

Regular divergences are reverse signals, with the bearish one pointing to a local top and the bullish one to a local bottom. Hidden divergences are continuation signals, and they occur during an existing trend (usually when a pullback has finished inside that trend).

Divergences have an advantage over other indicators out there in that they are predictive in nature. They are basically **leading indicators** (the opposite of the common lagging indicators traders usually use).

Their disadvantage is that you don't actually know how long it takes for the price to do what the divergence suggests.

To make it easy, we'll look at the RSI divergences, since we've already covered the RSI indicator.

If you look at the four following diagrams, you'll notice that *Figure 4.15* is a regular bullish divergence, suggesting a price reversal. But in *Figure 4.16*, the price continues to fall, providing an extended divergence. Then it continues again, in *Figure 4.17*, at which point the price rises (shown in *Figure 4.18*):

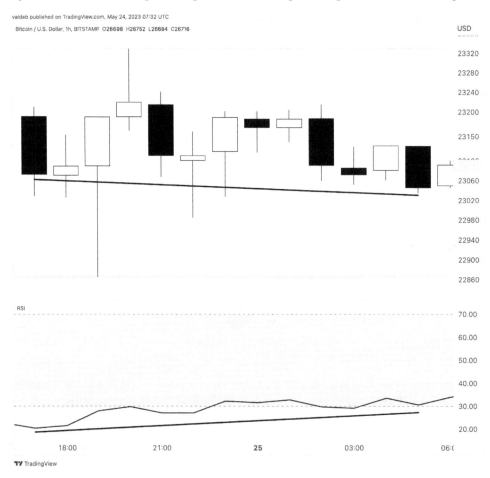

Figure 4.15 – Divergence

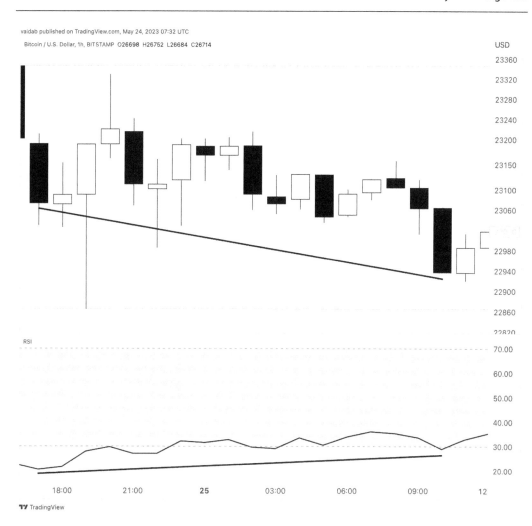

Figure 4.16 – Divergence (extension)

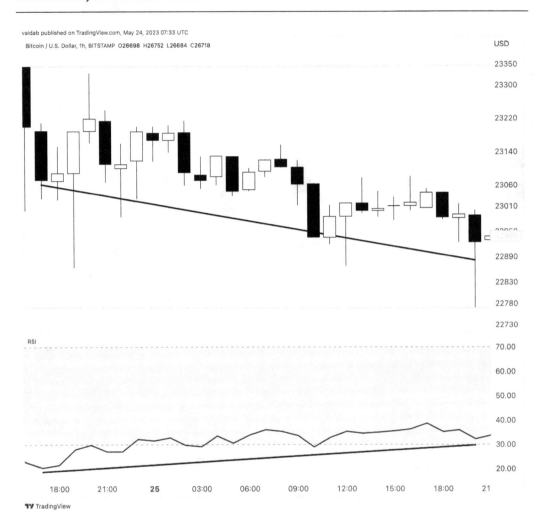

Figure 4.17 – Divergence (still extending)

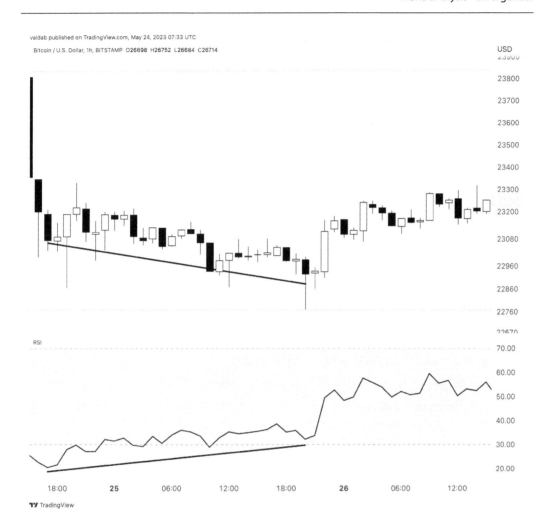

Figure 4.18 – And finally, the bullish trend reversal I was expecting

So how do we know when the price follows the prediction? We can't just wait for it indefinitely.

Let's define a trend by the general direction over a sufficiently long period of time and momentum as a short-term burst that can happen against the current trend.

Since RSI is a momentum oscillator, and it's, by default, based on the last 14 candles, its memory is quite short. So, we can expect it to work in the range of 15 to 30 candles. We can't call it an RSI divergence if it started 50 candles ago on a 14-candle RSI momentum oscillator, but we can modify the indicator to use more historical candles and see what's there. I personally know a trader who trades a longer RSI thinking it will get him ahead of the general population of traders. I haven't looked over his tests, so I don't know how well he puts everything into practice, but my personal opinion is that modifying indicators to better suit you is a good direction. In this way, you're frontrunning a lot of bots and newbie traders.

Professional traders also use the **rate of change** (**RoC**) indicator to pinpoint when the momentum will change direction. I recommend you learn more at `https://www.investopedia.com/terms/r/rateofchange.asp`.

Activities

1. Go to `https://www.investopedia.com/` and search for `Divergences`.

2. Read all about them. There are multiple articles, but here are three I recommend: `https://www.investopedia.com/articles/trading/04/012804.asp`, `https://www.investopedia.com/terms/d/divergence.asp`, `https://www.investopedia.com/articles/forex/07/divergence.asp`

3. Understand the advantages and drawbacks of using them.

4. Add the **Divergence** indicator in TradingView on **ETHUSD 4H**. You can also use one from **Community Scripts**. Also, add the RSI oscillator to your chart.

5. Identify all of the divergences mentioned, including types B and C. You can change the time frame to find more opportunities.

6. When you notice a divergence, try to identify the point at which you would have entered the market if you had not known the outcome in advance. Then, determine whether the price moved in the anticipated direction or whether the divergence continued. Count the candles, and if it extends over too many, change the indicator length/history to take more candles into account. See how it behaves then.

7. Go to `https://www.investopedia.com/` and search for `Rate of Change`.

8. Read all about it, add it as an indicator, and play with it a bit. Use it with the divergences indicator and see if it helps or hinders.

9. (Advanced) Now remove all indicators from TradingView and try to spot the divergences without the indicator. How do you do it? You know that the RSI formula tells you that the indicator drops when the price loses its power. Check for good upward momentum in an uptrend followed by a peak and then weak upward momentum. If you add the indicator, you'll notice that the weak upward momentum (after the strong momentum) creates a divergence. Understand this well and you won't need the oscillator to spot the RSI divergences.

10. (Advanced) Tell the story of these elements that generate the divergences: fear, greed, momentum, oscillator, and price. What are they telling you right before the divergence happens?

Moving averages, the relative strength index, the average true range, the market volume, and divergences are the basic tools every trader should know. By learning them and understanding how they work, you're actually getting ahead of all the traders who add an indicator to the chart and expect it to just point to the winning trade. Make sure you go through all of the activities mentioned and ask ChatGPT to explain the terms of the mathematics that you are still struggling with.

A template is available on GitHub, which features 36 indicators broken down into the aforementioned five categories. This template comes with my suggested settings and includes a sheet dedicated to testing purposes.

Summary

I hope I haven't scared you with all of the mathematics and other extra information. I'd like to balance it by promising you that, by the end of the book, you'll also get a tool that takes into account all of this (fees, repainting, intra-day candles) when doing the backtesting and forward testing for your strategy. But, in order for you to use it, you need to understand what you're trying to accomplish and why you need to take all of this into consideration.

My goal in this chapter was for you to understand the story of the price told through indicators and to start seeing through the different lenses the indicators provide so that you'll be able to use them to predict the direction of the price.

In the next chapter, we're going to talk about the centralized exchange and how we can trade there.

5

The Centralized Exchange

In this chapter, I'm going to present how the **centralized exchange** (**CEX**) works and how to trade there, as well as discuss a tool that connects to these CEXs and allows you to trade with an easier-to-understand yet more advanced interface.

My goal for this chapter is for you to understand the types of orders you can issue on an exchange, how they behave there, and what actually happens when they get executed.

One of the main differences between good traders and bad ones is that good traders know in detail what they are doing and base their trades on a good analysis while bad traders trade emotionally, hoping the price will increase because of *<insert any invalid reason here!>*.

Here are the topics we'll cover:

- The CEX
- Long versus short
- Types of orders
- Spot versus futures
- Leverage and liquidation
- The order book, market depth, commissions, spreads, and slippage
- A metaphor for it all – 3Commas

What is the CEX?

CEXs are platforms that act as an intermediary to facilitate the buying and selling of cryptocurrencies (and other assets). They are also custodians of your funds and wallets.

The term *centralized* refers to the fact that there's an entity controlling these exchanges and, by trading there, you are placing a lot of trust in that entity, including trusting it with your money.

In crypto, we also have **decentralized exchanges** (**DEXs**) that use peer-to-peer systems to facilitate exchanges without the user ceding a lot of control to the entity.

A list of CEXs can be found here: `https://coinmarketcap.com/rankings/exchanges/`, with Binance being currently at the top. There's also a list of DEXs, though we won't use them for trading just yet: `https://coinmarketcap.com/rankings/exchanges/dex/`.

As you can see in the first list, Binance is at the top, so I'm going to use screenshots from this exchange in this section of the book. Here's how the main page looks:

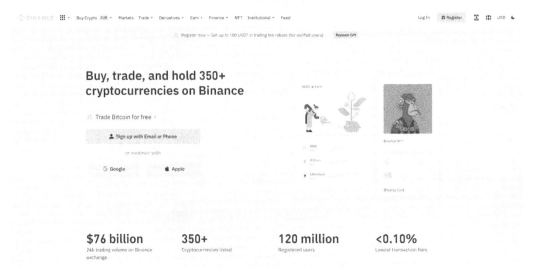

Figure 5.1 – A first look at Binance

I also recommend you check Binance's FAQ, which includes a guide on how to best use the exchange (as well as video and text guides for most of its functions, including trading): `https://www.binance.com/en/support/faq/`. There's also **Binance Academy** and **Binance Learn & Earn** found in the menu (the nine dots in the top left), where you can learn more about the various features available and more about crypto in general.

For the purpose of this book, I'm going to focus on the relevant section of the exchange, and I won't bother you with tools such as NFTs, farming, earning, and the launchpad.

Depositing money

Depositing money on Binance (and other CEXs) is quite simple:

1. You create an account there (on Binance, you do this by clicking on the yellow **Register** button). If you're from the US, use `https://www.binance.us`. Otherwise, please use `https://www.binance.com`.

2. Choose **Buy Crypto** from the top menu via **Bank Deposit** (usually the most advantageous in terms of fees, but not the quickest), **Credit/Debit Card** (usually the quickest but with some additional fees), or the other alternatives.

3. The next steps are pretty straightforward. You select the currency you want to deposit and send it to their bank account (read everything they show you as you might need to add a specific keyword in the bank transfer details field). If you've chosen to deposit via credit or debit card, you just fill in your card details.

4. Your money should arrive in the specified currency (usually BUSD if you've transferred USD).

Trading sections

From the **Trade** menu, you can use **Binance Convert** to quickly convert your deposited funds into another token. For example, you might need USDT, so you select **BUSD** in your first field, **USDT** in your second, and click on **Preview Conversion**, which will tell you how many tokens you'll receive before converting. Note that you can also use **Limit** orders here (to only convert at a certain price).

Binance Convert

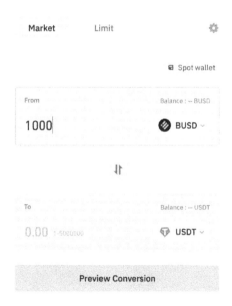

Figure 5.2 – Binance Convert

In the **Trade | Spot** menu, you'll find the interface for spot trading. Trading *on the spot* allows you to buy and sell tokens at the current market rate (which is known as the spot price). The trade usually happens immediately, as the order gets fulfilled.

Trade | Margin Trading allows you to borrow tokens so that you can sell tokens you don't have. Imagine you want to short the token (to bet that it will go down). What you actually do is borrow the token from the exchange and immediately sell it to get the funds at its market price. When the token goes down to your target price, you rebuy the token (but at a lower price now) and give the token back to the exchange, while retaining the funds that remained after buying it.

Derivates | USDⓈ-M Futures are **perpetual** or **quarterly contracts** settled in USDT or BUSD, or, in simpler terms, **futures trading**. This is what I'm usually trading and here's where we will trade (either directly or through intermediaries).

Long versus short

When we open a position that we expect to rise in value, we do it by opening a **long position**, going **long** or "longing."

When we open a position that we expect to fall in value, we open a **short position**, **go short**, or just **short** (a token).

Even though, theoretically, we can go in both directions at the same time (and some risk management strategies do this, for example, hedging), we usually go either long or short.

When we issue a long order, the CEX buys the token for our account. For example, we can send a market order to buy one BTC at market value and, after execution, we'll be **owning** (or rather our account on the CEX will be owning) one BTC.

When we open a short position at market value, what the CEX actually does is buy the token, and then instantly sell it at the price it bought it. When we close the short, the CEX rebuys the token at the new price, and we get the difference.

For example, we short 1 BTC at market value, let's say $42,000, and we close our short when BTC falls to $40,000. What happened was that there was 1 BTC bought at 42K and then sold instantly; then, when the price lowered to 40K, 1 BTC was bought again and the debt of 1 BTC was repaid.

Shorting is riskier because if the trade goes against us, we risk losing our collateral.

The following are a few activities I recommend you go through in order to better understand this topic. They will help you when you start trading on the exchange.

Activities

1. Watch the spot and margin tutorials on Binance. They are located here: `https://www.binance.com/en/support/faq/spot-margin-trading?c=3&navId=3`.

2. Understand the concepts of borrowing and repaying when using margin trading: `https://www.binance.com/en/support/faq/spot-margin-trading?c=3&navId=3#16-182`.

3. Go to **Trade | Spot** and watch the chart for BTC/BUSD on 4H. Note that you can change the chart type from **Original** (Binance's version) to **TradingView**, which is an embedded version of the chart on TradingView.

Even though there's a TradingView chart inside Binance, I definitely recommend you stick with `https://www.tradingview.com/` for your charting purposes. As a trader, you'll do some advanced charting and add custom indicators that you won't find there.

Types of orders

There are numerous types of orders on Binance (and other CEXs) but I'm going to limit myself to the most important ones that are also supported by Binance, such as the following:

- Market orders

- Limit orders

- Stop limit orders

- Stop market orders (futures only)

- One-Cancels-the-Other (OCO) orders (spot and margin only)

- Trailing stop orders

Let's dive in!

Market orders

With **market orders**, you are buying at the current price, no matter what it is. A market order guarantees that the order gets executed because it will accept the price the token has at that moment. The following diagram shows how it works:

Figure 5.3 – A market order

Limit orders

Limit orders are instructions positioned in the order book that are only executed when the market price meets or surpasses the established limit price. You can use limit orders to purchase at a reduced price or sell at a higher price, contingent on the price reaching the desired point. See how it works in the following figure:

Figure 5.4 – A limit order

When you set a limit order, you're fundamentally determining the maximum amount you're prepared to spend when buying a cryptocurrency, or conversely, the minimum amount you're willing to accept when selling it.

Stop limit orders

A **stop limit order** has a stop price and a limit price. It's basically a limit order that only gets triggered when the price reaches the stop price.

For example, the price has reached a support line and you only want to buy if it tries to rise from there, but you still want the price near the support. So, you put a stop limit order, with the stop above the support line (when you judge that there's a tendency for the price to rise) and the limit at the support line. If the price falls through the support line, the stop limit order doesn't get triggered, but if it tries to bounce from support to your chosen stop price, then a limit order will be put near the support, for when the price gets there.

Another example is to buy when a token shows momentum. If ETH is at $1,100 and you put a stop limit with the stop at $1,150 and the limit at $1,200, the limit order will be placed once the price reaches $1,150, basically allowing you to buy up until the $1,200 limit.

One other example would be to sell your token if the price drops too much. When prices fall too quickly, big sell limit orders might not get filled entirely because the price falls over your limit too quickly and limit orders only sell at your limit price or better. So, if you've bought at 42k, you put a stop at 40.5k and a limit at 40.4k. Essentially, your limit sell order set at 40.4k only activates when the price drops to 40.5k, enabling you to sell as the price continues to decrease, up until it hits the 40.4k mark. Here's what it looks like:

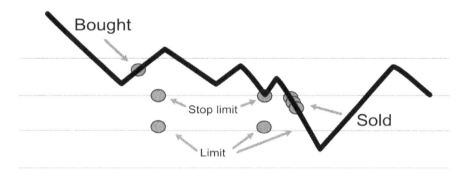

Figure 5.5 – A stop limit order

On some CEXs, you can place a time limit for your stop orders (both stop limit and stop market) or mark them as **good-till-canceled** (**GTC**), meaning that they will remain active until you cancel them manually.

Stop market orders (only available in the futures markets)

Stop market orders are just like stop limit orders but instead of a limit order being placed when the price reaches the stop price, a market order is being placed there. So, in the previous example, if the price is falling and there's a stop market order, you'll sell starting at the stop price at market price, up until you've sold your whole position. The following figure shows how it works:

Figure 5.6 – A stop market order

OCO orders (spot and margin markets only)

OCO orders combine a stop limit and a limit order in which if one is triggered (even if not filled), the other is canceled.

For example, if ETH is trading in a support range between $1,100 and $1,200, and you want to trade the range and the breakout, you can put an OCO buy order like this:

- The limit order is at $1,100 (basically you buy low in order to sell at the end of the range, at around $1,200)

- The stop limit order has its stop at $1,210, with the limit at $1,220 (buying when you consider the price breaks away from the trading range)

- Basically, you buy either if it's too low or if it's too high, but you don't want to buy both and your OCO will cancel the second buy order once the first is filled

Here's what it looks like:

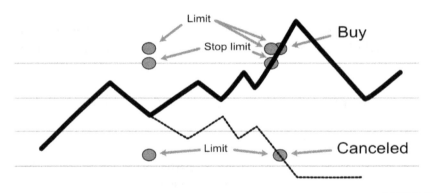

Figure 5.7 – An OCO order

Another example is when you want to limit your risks. Let's say you've bought ETH at $1,100, estimating it will increase in price up to $1,200. Still, in case you are wrong, it's better to protect your money by also selling if it arrives at $1,050. So here's the OCO order that you create on the exchange:

- The (sell) limit order is at $1,200.

- The (sell) stop limit order has its stop at $1,050 and the limit at $1,050 (selling when you reach that point).

- Note that the stop and the limit are identical. The limit order will sell at any price >= $1,050, so putting the stop order at $1,050 will trigger a sale at that price.

In both examples, the OCO orders will make sure that once you do one action, the other is canceled and you don't forget about an order that might lose you money.

Trailing stop orders

A **trailing stop order** shares similarities with a stop limit order, with one crucial distinction: the trailing stop order adjusts with the market, maintaining a set percentage distance from the current market price, thereby *trailing* the price in the direction you desire. This means it continually adjusts to stay the same distance away as the price moves favorably. However, when the market price moves against your desired direction, the trailing stop order remains static. It ceases to *trail* the price, thus creating an opportunity for your trade to be executed when the price hits the established stop level.

For example, when you want to follow a rising market, you can enter a trade with a trailing stop 2% from the price. When the price rises by 5%, the trailing stop will follow, keeping your exit 2% from the new (risen) price. It follows it until the price starts to fall when it catches the fall at 2% from the highest point it reached.

Check how the trailing order follows the price in the following figure:

Figure 5.8 – A trailing stop order

Other types of orders

There are more types of orders (depending on the exchange) but I don't use them and I'm only listing them here for your information:

- **Post-only orders** post the orders in the order book without trying to match them with an existing order first. This decreases the fees as you are a **market maker** (you put orders in the order book), not a **market taker** (you fill orders from the order book).

- **Reduce-only orders** are not found on Binance. They help you reduce your position without having to cancel it.

- **Iceberg orders** are used when you have a very large sum, and you don't want to affect the market. What it does is place a limit order of a smaller value and, every time the order is taken, places another limit order at the same value.

- **Hidden orders** are limit orders that are not placed in the order book.

- **Time in force orders**:

  - **GTC** – These orders don't expire

  - **Immediate-Or-Cancel** (**IOC**) – This order executes immediately and, even if only partly filled, is canceled if it cannot be instantly fulfilled

  - **Fill-Or-Kill** (**FOK**) – This order executes immediately in full and gets canceled if cannot be fully filled (so you don't get a partial fill)

- **Time-Weighted Average Price** (**TWAP**) orders are used when you want to spread the order in time to prevent a bad purchase (by averaging the entries) or when entering the market with a large sum (so you don't kill the liquidity).

There are more types of orders, but you won't necessarily need them, and I wanted to present to you the main ones found on the top crypto CEXs.

In the upcoming section, we will delve into a discussion about the spot market and the futures market, highlighting the differences between the two.

Spot versus futures

A **financial instrument** is a contract or a document that represents a legal agreement involving monetary value. It can include assets, such as stocks and bonds, or contractual rights to receive or deliver cash, such as bank deposits, loans, and derivatives.

A **spot market** is a market where the financial instrument being traded is immediately delivered.

A **futures market** is a market where the financial instrument is being delivered at a later date. You buy (and sell) derivative contracts that represent the value of the asset.

Futures trading is typically the choice for traders, thanks to its unique advantage of enabling profits from any market direction. On the other hand, spot trading is a popular choice among investors due to its simplicity. It enables them to easily buy and hold tokens.

Here is a table with the main differences between spot and futures trading:

Spot	Futures
You own the token (and can use it for staking and with other instruments)	You do not own the token
You are betting on rising prices	You can profit from either direction.
You pay the price of the asset	You can use leverage to pay less (or buy more)
You pay the normal fees	You pay fees and a (small) difference, which can also be negative

Table 5.1 – Differences between spot and futures trading

Let me explain some of the benefits of futures trading:

- It allows you to profit regardless of the market direction, as you can choose to go long or short. This versatility paves the way for sophisticated strategies such as hedging, where you counterbalance risk in one direction by taking a position in another, and arbitrage among others.

- Futures trading enables you to trade with leverage, allowing you to hold more tokens for a lower initial outlay. While this approach is capital-efficient, it also heightens the risk to your portfolio. In spot trading, $100 equates to $100; however, in futures trading on platforms such as Binance, leverage of up to 125x can be utilized, potentially commanding a position around $11,660, although this is slightly less due to associated fees.

- Futures trading also boasts higher liquidity, thanks to traders operating with leverage, which facilitates larger and more frequent transactions. This dynamic ensures traders can have their orders filled more swiftly compared to the spot market.

- The fee structures also vary between spot and futures trading. In spot trading, you pay for the token price, which is determined by supply and demand, along with taxes. In futures trading, you incur the carrying cost of the futures contract, which can sometimes be negative, implying that you get paid. In addition, an overnight fee may apply if you hold your futures contract over an extended period. However, Binance does not impose this fee for perpetual futures, which is our focus in this discussion.

There are disadvantages to futures trading, which can be summed up as a higher risk of losing money.

The main disadvantage is the risk associated with the exchange selling your position (because your trade went the other way while using high leverage with small collateral). Imagine opening a position of 11k with $100 in your futures account, leaving $1 as collateral. You will get liquidated when the price drops by 0.86% because your collateral cannot sustain your position.

Binance supports perpetual futures, which allows you to trade without a period of expiration on your contracts, which is the easiest route to understand and trade futures. I will not go into delivery trading in this book, we'll only use perpetual futures.

When you first enter your Binance Futures account, you'll get a video with step-by-step information on how to open the account, and a quiz that you need to complete accurately to get access to the trading interface. Do your homework, take the quiz, and voila! You now have access to futures trading and can begin transferring assets to your Futures account.

Before we go to the next section, *Leverage and liquidation*, I recommend a few activities for you to better understand futures trading.

Activities

1. In the **Futures** interface, in the upper tab, you also have **Information | Guide** (`https://www.binance.com/en/support/faq/crypto-derivatives?c=4&navId=4`), which describes each setting in detail. Go through it and learn more about the **Futures** interface on Binance.

2. Read all about (crypto) futures on Investopedia.

3. Binance provides a simple calculator for futures trading for **profit and loss (PNL)**, **target price**, **liquidation price**, **max open**, and **open price**. Get familiar with it. The calculator is at `https://www.binance.com/en/futures/BTCUSDT_PERPETUAL/calculator` and its instructions are here: `https://www.binance.com/en/support/faq/how-to-use-binance-futures-calculator-360036498511`.

Leverage and liquidation

When we talk about leverage (in crypto), we refer to trading using borrowed money to increase your potential for profits (and losses).

Leverage is shown in ratios such as 1:2 (2x), 1:5 (5x), 1:50 (50x), and up to 100x (on most CEXs).

This is indicative of how much your initial entry is multiplied by. This means that if you have $100, with 2x leverage, you can enter a position of $200. With 5x leverage, you're entering a $500 position.

You enter these bigger positions by borrowing money against your balance, by leveraging your balance against your position.

The money that you borrow from is called **collateral**, and before you can start trading using leverage, you need to have collateral in your futures account. This account is usually separated from your spot account so only the money transferred into it might get lost.

Margin trading is when you borrow money against your collateral and use that money to open a position. Margin refers to the collateral you have or the difference between the total value purchased and the loan amount. **Buying on margin** happens when you buy an asset (or open a position) using that collateral. Yes, I know it's a bit confusing, and several exchanges confuse it further by providing slightly different definitions, but you don't actually need to have the specific terminology here in order to understand how it is used. Let's work through examples.

Say we want to open a position of $1,000 worth of BTC at 10x leverage. You need $100 ($1,000/10) in your account as collateral for the funds you'll be borrowing. That's your margin, $100, and you have borrowed $900.

When using margin, you'll need what we call a **maintenance margin** for your trades (Binance also calls it a **margin threshold**). What happens is that if the market goes against your opened trades and the margin gets lower than your margin threshold, you'll have to add additional funds to your account.

Let's say that you've opened that position of $1,000 with $100 (10x leverage) and your position is up 10%. Congratulations, you've just made $100. If you wouldn't have used leverage, you'd have made $10.

If the position is down 10%, you've (virtually) lost $100 from your collateral, but if you don't have that $100 lost in your collateral, and you only have $90 in your trade as margin, you will get liquidated (your balance will go to 0). Before that happens though, you will get an email from the exchange (depending on the exchange, Binance does this) to fund your account so that it can sustain this loss.

Let's talk more about liquidation here. **Liquidation** in the crypto futures market represents a protection mechanism against incurring (further) losses. It happens when losses exceed the maintenance margin.

If you open a position of $1,000 worth of BTC at 5x leverage, you need at least $200 as collateral in your account ($1,000/5).

If you have $1,000 in your account (including the open position), then there's no liquidation because if your position drops by the maximum amount, $1,000, you'll lose the $1,000 you have in your account.

However, if you only have $200 and you use it to open the position, you'll get liquidated when the price drops to $803.21 (according to https://www.binance.com/en/futures/BTCUSDT_ PERPETUAL/calculator). This is because a ~$200 drop in the position actually "*eats*" the money in your balance (the initial $200 you've used to open this position). The $3.21 represents fees (including a liquidation fee).

Note that the process is a bit more complex, and it includes, on Binance, an insurance fund, a method to auto-deleverage liquidations, a **Unified Maintenance Margin Ratio**, and various other calculations, but you don't need all these details at this stage of the game.

I perceive leverage more as "*amplifying spikes*" rather than merely "*investing less capital.*" In fact, it can serve as an effective insurance method to avoid storing large amounts, such as 50k, on an exchange. Many associate leverage directly with multiplying their standard position size by 10x, which naturally leads to increased risks and higher fees. However, it's often overlooked that leverage can be used to achieve a desired position without committing as much capital upfront. Positions of $300 at 10x leverage and $3,000 at 1x leverage are essentially equivalent.

A word of caution here: misuse of leverage can result in the loss of your entire balance within a span of just 10 seconds. Therefore, my advice is to initiate leverage trading only with small multipliers, say between 2x and 4x. However, this step should be taken only after you've amassed substantial experience trading without leverage, and you're consistently making profitable trades. We'll talk more about this in *Chapter 6*.

Next, I propose two activities regarding liquidation, which is an important part of futures trading. Make sure you understand how liquidation works before you go to the next section.

Activities

1. Read about how liquidation works on the exchange you'll be using. For Binance, read `https://www.binance.com/en-ZA/support/faq/how-liquidation-works-in-futures-trading-7ba80e1b406f40a0a140a84b3a10c387`, `https://www.binance.com/en-ZA/support/faq/how-to-reduce-your-chances-of-getting-liquidated-25edcd7fe0e544839d0847b8cbb2e400`, `https://www.binance.com/en/support/faq/liquidation-protocols-360033525271`, and `https://www.binance.com/en/support/faq/how-does-liquidation-work-in-the-binance-portfolio-margin-account-ff4b1ab6c27b4ed6b3ebe8e4ed1572f8`.

2. Play with the **Liquidation Price** section (and the other sections) of the Binance calculator: `https://www.binance.com/en/futures/BTCUSDT_PERPETUAL/calculator`.

The order book, market depth, commissions, spreads, and slippage

In this section, we will delve into key elements of trading dynamics such as the order book, market depth, commissions, spreads, and slippage. The **order book** is a vital tool, showing a list of buy and sell orders for an asset. **Market depth** represents the volume of orders at different price levels, providing insights into supply and demand. **Commissions** are fees paid to brokers for their services, while **spreads** denote the difference between the buying and selling price. Lastly, we'll look at **slippage**, a phenomenon that occurs when a trade is executed at a different price than expected due to market volatility. Together, these components form the backbone of any successful trading strategy.

I've mentioned the term "*order book*" before but I haven't explained what it is yet. It's a very complex topic (entire books have been written about it) and knowing what it is and how it works will help you understand the subtleties of trading.

So, what is an order book?

In short, it's a list of orders that are sorted by the price they target.

When you post a limit order to buy BTC at $42,000, it gets posted in the order book.

Here's what it looks like:

Price(USDT)	Amount(BTC)	Total
27977.61	0.77912	21,797.91550
27977.52	0.20000	5,595.50400
27977.48	0.16160	4,521.16077
27977.45	0.00065	18.18534
27977.37	0.07400	2,070.32538
27977.22	0.20000	5,595.44400
27977.20	0.05362	1,500.13746
27977.11	0.00065	18.18512
27976.77	0.00065	18.18490
27976.63	1.20000	33,571.95600
27976.53	0.96260	26,930.20778
27976.15	0.00632	176.80927
27975.45	0.03016	843.73957
27975.37	0.01910	534.32957
27975.34	0.20000	5,595.06800
27975.12	0.28717	8,033.61521
27975.09	0.44670	12,496.47270
27974.81	0.00714	199.74014
27974.75	7.54439	211,052.42415
27,977.48 $27,977.48		More
27974.74	3.73197	104,400.89044
27974.73	0.00675	188.82943
27974.71	0.00651	182.11536
27974.69	0.00953	266.59880
27974.68	0.01296	362.55185
27974.61	0.33952	9,497.93959
27974.52	0.29956	8,380.04721
27974.48	0.35253	9,861.84343
27974.41	0.00036	10.07079
27974.39	0.00065	18.18335
27974.38	0.31897	8,922.98799
27974.30	0.36131	10,107.39433
27974.24	1.19361	33,390.33261

Figure 5.9 – The order book

As you can see in the figure, we have prices from low (at the bottom) to high (at the top). These are the closest orders to the current price. The order book is bigger (it basically extends to the complete list of orders), but this is what's relevant now.

Each item in the order book has a price, an amount, a total, and a quantity (shown by the amount of green or red background color). In the book, you will be able to see a light gray area over the prices, which represents the quantity, but on Binance, it's red in the upper part of the image and green in the lower part. Here's what the columns in *Figure 5.9* mean:

- **Price:** This is the price at which the limit orders were set.

- **Amount:** It represents the total quantity of tokens within those limit orders.

- **Total:** This is the combined value of all the tokens in that price range, indicating the price required to purchase all of them.

Additionally, when you hover over the table, it will display the total amount needed to raise the price to your desired level by summing the totals up to the point you're hovering over.

Also, see the background color in the limit order. That visually represents the total.

The price in the middle is the last traded price, sometimes followed by an arrow indicating in which direction it traded from the previous trade and then by the marked price (which is the global spot price index plus a decaying funding basis rate, but let's not go into that, unless you insist: `https://www.binance.com/en/blog/futures/what-is-the-difference-between-a-futures-contracts-last-price-and-mark-price-5704082076024731087`).

We, as traders, can exploit the order book in various ways.

For example, when we see a lot of limit selling happening (big red background), we can quickly identify a local resistance there and put our sell order right under it. That way, it will have a higher chance of getting filled.

There are other imbalances that we can look for, such as a limit order of a specific size that gets filled followed by another one at the same price point and of the exact same size, which might show an **Iceberg order** being present (indicative of a hidden support or resistance line at that point).

The market depth or depth of the market

The **depth of the market** (**DOM**) is the total volume of limit orders placed in the order book. It represents the ability of the market to absorb large market orders without (significantly) impacting the price of the token. It's also called the DOM.

If we click on the **Depth** button on the interface, we'll see the following figure:

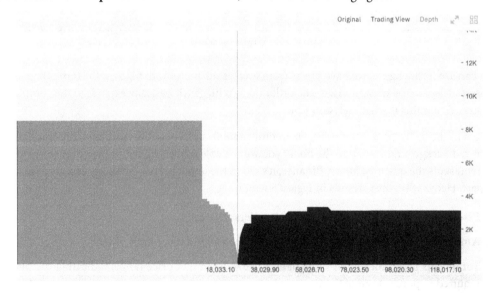

Figure 5.10 – DOM

It's a real-time boxing match between the bulls and the bears. You can interpret this as two waves; the one on the left (the green one on Binance) is the wave of buyers and the one on the right (the red one on this platform) is the wave of sellers. When there's a big wave on one side, it usually (and metaphorically) absorbs the smaller wave on the other side, moving the price in that direction.

In the figure, you can see how the bulls are winning the battle with big orders under a certain price, absorbing the sellers and driving the price up.

You can use this information to put a limit order before a big support (or resistance) block so that it will get executed quicker or to see the real-time dynamics and predict the short-term price direction based on the price volatility. Here are some other pictures of various DOMs:

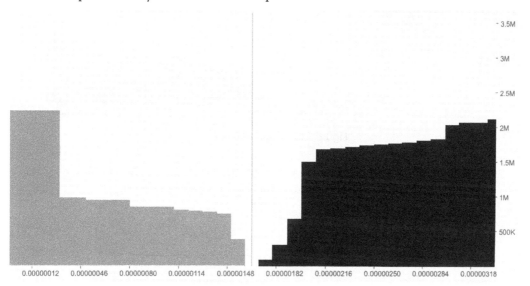

Figure 5.11 – Sellers winning

Here, the sellers have a bigger wave and are catching all the orders. It's hard for the price to move up past all of those limit sales and I wouldn't put a take profit order *"that high on the wave."*

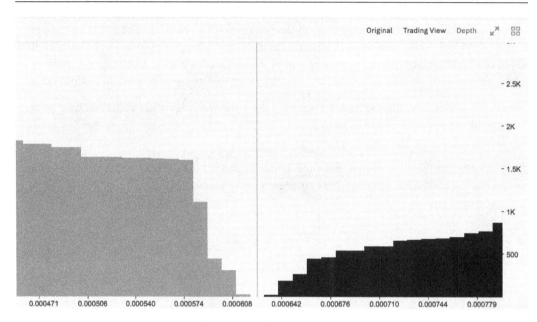

Figure 5.12 – Buyers winning

Here, we have the opposite scenario. Buyers have strong limit buy orders in the order book and it is harder for the price to be driven down (it needs extremely strong market orders).

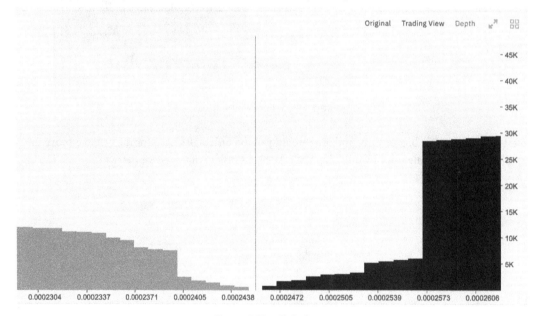

Figure 5.13 – Fight later

There is a fight, but it's not now. We know from this DOM that there is a point that will block the bulls from pushing the price up, but there's balance until that point. The fight will happen later.

Liquidity

When we talk about liquidity, we talk about how easy it is for an order to get filled (or how active the order book is). On smaller CEXs, for some tokens, we might see a static order book that has some buy orders at a low price, some sell orders at a higher price, and no transactions happening. That's a token without liquidity.

Think of the market as a vast ocean, with the price being a ship navigating its waters. The ship can move freely, but sometimes its path is obstructed by icebergs. These icebergs represent "*liquidity*" in the form of limit orders. In this vast ocean, some icebergs are gigantic and hard to bypass, while others are smaller and easier to navigate around.

To forge ahead, the ship needs to break through these icebergs. The force that allows the ship to break or melt away the ice is akin to a "*market order*." When a market order is placed, it chips away at the iceberg, thinning its mass. Once the iceberg is completely shattered or melted, the ship can continue its journey, only to encounter the next iceberg in its path.

The bid-ask spread

The difference between the highest bid price (the last green buy order) and the lowest ask price (the first red sell order) is called the **spread**.

Many brokers in traditional markets monetize the bid-ask spread (they are using market makers to provide liquidity on their platform). In crypto, the clients usually have direct access to the order book, directly placing orders there so exchanges don't (usually) monetize the spread and, instead, they use trading fees.

Slippage

When we talk about slippage, we talk about a market order being filled at a price point other than the one requested. This happens because there's not enough liquidity to fill at that specific price (not enough limit orders there to cover your order), because of the bid-ask spread, because the price has moved quickly from that point, or maybe because of a delay between the time you submitted it and the time the order was executed. Limit orders do not suffer from slippage, but they can be partially fulfilled for the same reasons as those mentioned previously. Slippage can also be positive, as the price you get might be better than the one you initially requested.

Market makers

When we talk about market makers, we talk about companies that provide slippage to CEXs via automated algorithms that submit limit orders in the order book. They, as market makers, provide liquidity so that market takers (traders who use market orders) can get their orders executed.

A lot of companies that I've worked with needed a market maker, especially during the listing phase where there's a lot of buying pressure from fans and selling pressure from investors. That pressure needs to be handled so that the token increases in price. The ones doing the handling are the market maker companies.

Note that there are market participants who want to trade a higher number of tokens than the usual traders who do so outside the classical order book. For example, I've worked with an NFT marketplace that wanted to sell its business and its tokens. The selling wouldn't happen as a dump on the market but as a wallet-to-wallet transaction, without impacting the order book. These situations are happening in dark pools, on private exchanges, or alternative trading systems where investors can transact without impacting the price of the token. Imagine the impact it would have if the NFT marketplace announced that it was going to sell. Instead, they announce that they have been acquired by a bigger company (thus minimizing impact or even turning it into bullish news) and that is it.

The following is an indispensable tool I employ daily for my trading pursuits – 3Commas. This platform presents a distinct approach to facilitating trading across a variety of CEXs. It cleverly bridges the gap between slight variances in terminology and trading nuances, effectively bringing them all under one comprehensive umbrella.

A metaphor for it all – 3Commas

3Commas (`https://3commas.io/`) is a crypto trading bot platform that is very affordable for people starting out. It features smart tools for trading, a TradingView subscription inside its platform, connections to multiple exchanges, crypto signals, portfolio management, cryptocurrency trading, a trading terminal, and various bots: DCA, SMART, Options, GRID, and HODL.

I mostly use it for its **Smart Trade** feature and its ability to connect to multiple exchanges (and to trade on them in parallel). This is its main site where you can create a free account:

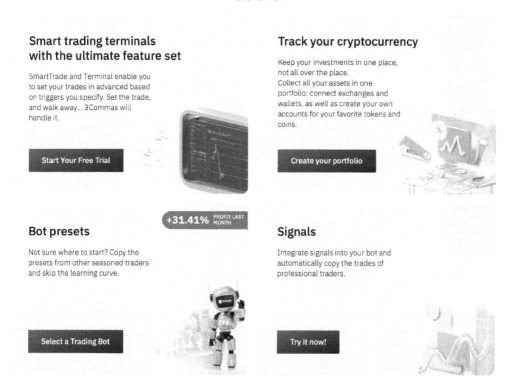

Figure 5.14 – 3Commas site

After signing in, you are presented with an onboarding process where you can connect to an exchange and learn about its interface. Alternatively, if you skip it, you are presented with this interface:

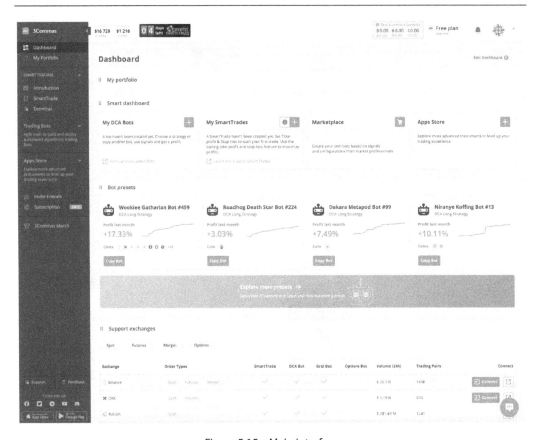

Figure 5.15 – Main interface

The first step you have to take is to connect to an exchange such as Binance. Note that you can connect to multiple exchanges at the same time and use 3Commas as a portfolio management system, checking, at a glance, all of your balances across all exchanges.

On the left, you have an **Introduction** section where you can learn more about its **Smart Trading** feature, and the **Terminal** section from which you can quickly trade on any connected exchange.

I won't get into the other sections but feel free to use their academy to learn more about the platform: `https://3commas.io/crypto-trading-academy`.

Connecting to an exchange

To connect to the exchange, you can go to **Dashboard | Supported exchanges** (or **My Portfolio | Exchanges**) and click the **Connect** button of your preferred exchange, situated to the right of the exchange name.

Figure 5.16 – Connecting to Binance

SmartTrade

The **SmartTrade** terminal is the main reason I use 3Commas:

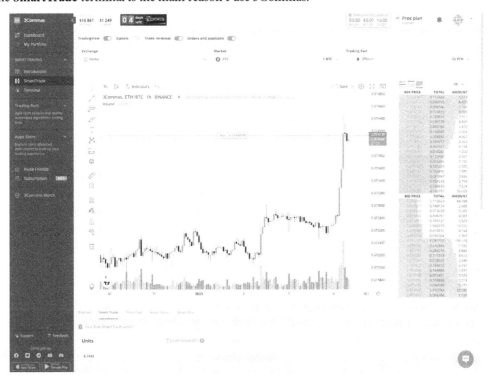

Figure 5.17 – SmartTrade section

It consists of four sections:

- **TradingView** is a direct connection to TradingView, allowing you to use the charting tools while in 3Commas without paying for a subscription there. On its right, you can also see its bid-ask spread.

- **Signals** are buy and sell signals 3Commas offers for various trading pairs. I don't use this at all. It basically lets somebody else (usually an algorithm) suggest trades, which 3Commas can take.

- **Trade terminal**, or the smart trading terminal, is a terminal for issuing advanced orders to your connected exchanges, orders they might not even have in their own terminals. Don't confuse this with the **Terminal** section on the left of the page.

- **Orders and positions** shows your open positions and what you can do with them (edit, close, add funds, etc.).

Here's a picture of the **Trade Terminal** (the tools at the bottom of the previous figure):

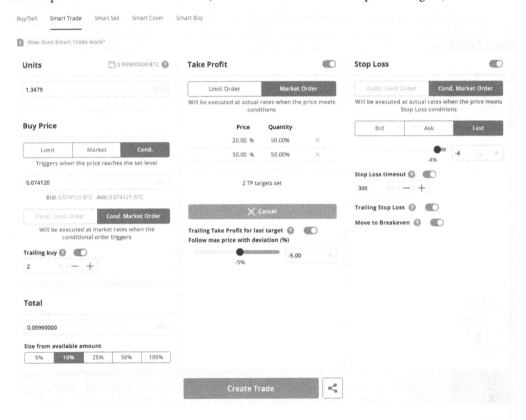

Figure 5.18 – SmartTrade view

The **Trade terminal** section has the following SmartTrade tools:

- **Buy/Sell**, which is used to quickly buy and sell at **Limit** or **Market**. The **Terminal** section on the left has the same tools.

- **Smart Trade** can be used to buy at **Limit, Market**, or **Cond.** (Stop Limit or Stop Market). You can also use the **Trailing buy** option there (which is the trailing stop mentioned at the beginning of the chapter, in *Types of orders*). It also has a **Take Profit** section with a limit order or market order that supports split targets (you take profit multiple times), including a trailing take profit (similar to the trailing stop). And, did I say that it also has a **Stop Loss** section, which uses a conditional limit or market order with **Stop Loss timeout** (in case there's a sudden spike or liquidity grab, which is quickly corrected), **Trailing Stop Loss**, and... wait for it... **Move to Breakeven** (which will move the stop loss to break even after you hit your first profit target) options? You can do all of this manually, but 3Commas (3C) will allow you to automate everything under one roof.

- **Smart Sell** is used to get rid of tokens you already own. It uses most of the tools that Smart Trade uses to do that. Note that there are links to more information under each section giving you details and ways to use each tool.

- **Smart Cover** is useful when you want to sell your tokens now and buy them again at a better price. It can be used as a classical short tool, where you want to make a profit from a downtrend, or it can be used to repurchase tokens after you got a successful long and you're waiting for a quick drop in price before bouncing up again.

- **Smart Buy** is the opposite of **Smart Sell** and it's generally used when you have open short positions in Futures. You basically use **Smart Buy** to take control of the open shorts (that you've created either outside of 3C or using bots inside 3C).

From here, we'll use Smart Trade for longing and Smart Cover for shorting.

You see that our terminology suddenly changed. *Stop Limit orders* became *Conditional Limit orders*, *Trailing Stop* became *Trailing buy*.... Well, this happens when you hop from exchange to exchange, each having its own slightly changed naming conventions and interface. Where 3C shines is in the way it unifies all the exchanges you're trading on under one roof that has the same set of (advanced) features.

Paper trading/demo account

After creating your 3C account, you'll see **Paper Trading balance** in the top section.

Figure 5.19 – Top view

Clicking on it will switch to an environment that you can use to test your trading skills. You'll be able to trade here safely, without using real money, so that you can hone your skills until you become profitable.

Your first (demo) trade

Let's say I see this situation: BTC/USDT at 26766.66 in a downtrend.

Figure 5.20 – TradingView on 3Commas

I want to short the market BTC/USDT so I go to **Smart Cover | Units** and use $2,482 to short, at the market price (currently 26759). I also enable **Take Profit** and **Stop Loss**:

Figure 5.21 – Smart Cover

Now I have three lines (or four if I've enabled an additional take profit) on my graph, which I can move manually or edit using the fields from the previous figure:

Figure 5.22 – Four new lines

I then create the trade:

Confirmation of a transaction ✕

Pair:	₿ BTC/USDT
Units:	0.09277 BTC
Sell Price:	26759.99 USDT Market
Stop Loss:	Last: 26858.00 USDT +0.36% Cond. market
Take Profit:	26537.04 USDT -0.83% Limit 50.00%
	26627.84 USDT -0.49% Limit 50.00%
Total:	2482.52427230 USDT

☑ test trade

Confirm

Figure 5.23 – Trade confirmation

Now I'm monitoring the trade. I love the **Status** section and the **Profit/Loss** section from which I can quickly find out how my trades behave:

Figure 5.24 – Monitoring the trade

If I want to add more funds, reduce funds, close at market price, share the trade with someone, or edit the trade (modifying the take profit and stop loss conditions), I can do that in the right menu:

Figure 5.25 – Active trades – right menu

Here's how it looks after a while:

Figure 5.26 – Monitoring the trade again

And this is the final figure, with the trade results:

Figure 5.27 – The trade ended

The following exercises are designed to deepen your understanding of trading on 3C. It's crucial that you engage with them prior to beginning your trading journey.

Activities

1. In 3Commas, connect to your preferred exchange. You can use this tutorial for the process: `https://help.3commas.io/en/articles/3109051-binance-how-to-create-api-keys-fast-connect-also-explained?_ga=2.68036947.330265515.1672729298-379498444.1672729298`.

2. Next, go to **Paper Trading | SmartTrade | Trade terminal** and click on the **How does X work** links for each of the smart trading tools (like in *Figure 5.28*).

3. Go to **Buy/Sell** and create a buy market order (always in **Paper Trading**). Figure out what type of order was sent by 3Commas to the exchange when it bought the token.

4. Now create a sell order.

5. Go through each section – **Buy/Sell**, **Smart Trade**, **Smart Sell**, **Smart Cover**, and **Smart Buy** – and create a trade on each one. Make sure that you don't enable any advanced options at first (such as trailings). Follow those trades until their completion and make sure you understand what happened there (what order was sent to the exchange when it opened the trade, when it sent the order, what order 3C sent when it closed the trade, and why it worked the way it worked).

6. Repeat until you are confident you understand how the **Smart Trade** section works. 3Commas provides you with enough examples to make everything clear but it takes a while and you need to dedicate time to this.

7. Use the Paper Trading account to play with the tools. Initiate a few trades and see how they behave when the market moves in one direction or the other. Edit trades, close trades, add funds to them, trade in different markets, and, all in all, learn how to use the 3Commas tools for trading.

The following figure shows the location of the link to the 3Commas knowledge base:

Figure 5.28 – How does X work?

> **Important**
>
> When creating the API in the exchange (e.g., Binance), don't enable withdrawals. Give only the minimum access that 3Commas needs to do its job.

Summary

This chapter went into depth regarding the various trading tools that you have at your disposal on the CEX.

My goal was for you to understand the types of orders you can issue on an exchange, how they behave there, and what actually happens when they get executed. Basically, you got to know the tools you'll be using in the later chapters.

I left you with a lot of activities to do, but (I hope) you haven't started trading just yet. That's because in the next chapter, we'll cover risk management, which is a must-read before any money is involved.

6

Money Management

In this chapter, we will delve into key aspects of effective trading strategy management. This includes understanding how to limit losses, the importance of position sizing, the benefits of keeping a trading journal, the necessity of a well-defined trading plan, and the decision between trading in dollars or Bitcoin.

The goal of this chapter is to equip you with vital risk management tools that are crucial to any successful trading journey.

Here are the specific topics we'll cover:

- Limiting losses
- Position sizing
- Keeping a trading journal
- Your trading plan
- Dollars or Bitcoin?

Limiting losses

Martingale is a gambling system in which the stakes are doubled after each loss.

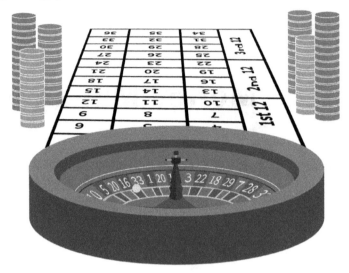

Figure 6.1 – Playing roulette

If you play roulette, bet $10 on red, and you get red, congrats, you've won $10. If you get black, you lose the initial $10, then you double down, betting $20 on red. Black is the outcome again; you lose $20, and you bet $40 on red. Red comes and you've won $40 minus the row of losses totaling $30, so you've actually won $10.

This might seem a smart system until you calculate the budget you need in order to win the $10 that you've bet on red after getting black 10 consecutive times. That's $20+$40+$80+$160+$320+$640+$1,280+$2,560+$5,120+$10,240 = $20,460.

So, would you risk $20,460 to win $10?

What if there are 11 consecutive blacks?

You do the math.

Even though most traders started trading to gain profits, one of the most important aspects of trading and investing is how to limit your losses.

In trading, even though you can theoretically gain a big amount of money in a short amount of time, you have a certain amount of capital that you're starting with and, if you're not careful with it, you might lose it before you start winning, as in the following example.

Let's say you have $10,000 starting capital and you're using a strategy backtested over a year and also over a bear market, a sideways market, and a bull market that has a total profit of 13% a year with a win/loss ratio of 53% and a **max drawdown (MDD)** of -50%.

This means that you could get 13% a year with this strategy; that's around $1,300 (assuming you're all-in with the strategy) but what happens if the drawdown starts when your strategy runs, bringing you to $5,000 total capital?

You've just started with a $5,000 loss. Getting 13% a year would net you around $650, taking you 5 and a half years to recover your initial capital.

This example shows why we can't look at a strategy from one angle only.

When a trader shows a strategy that they've been testing for the past month, that strategy might still have a big chance of failing if it wasn't properly (algorithmically) tested.

There are some key points I'd like to talk about here that will definitely prevent you from losing money but you also need to use common sense and manage your feelings. Trading is not a get-rich-quick scheme.

Limiting losses strategically

From a strategic perspective, the solution lies in **asset diversification**. Subsequently, I'll delve into three crucial strategies that foster asset diversification: mixing up your investment types, operating across varied markets, and mitigating overexposure in trades or on **centralized exchanges** (CEXs). However, if you spread yourself too thin, you could be taking on more risk for smaller payoffs. So, nailing the sweet spot is pretty important.

Mix your investment types.

Depending on your capital, you can invest in different asset classes such as real estate, stocks, bonds, and crypto or diversify across countries and industries. Make sure that the securities that you're diversifying with are not too correlated or you'll risk fishing in the same pool of water.

Limiting losses in the trading account

Trade across different markets.

Use `https://www.coingecko.com/` | **Categories** to check the various categories that exist. Categories such as exchange tokens (such as BNB for Binance), Blockchain tokens (such as AVAX for Avalanche), meme coins (such as DOGE), NFTs (maybe AXS and SAND), privacy coins, yield farming, **decentralized exchanges** (DEXs), and gaming.

Or split by market cap, that is, large caps (think top coins), mid caps, and small caps (think low interest/volume).

There were low-cap coins that handled the 2022 bear market pretty well, but they weren't traded on CEXs.

Still, the idea here is not to rush it by trading a lot of tokens over various categories. My suggestion for you is to start trading BTC because most of the market is married to BTC. Once you know how to trade it, you'll be able to trade other tokens. Then, follow with ETH and a few other blockchain tokens. They are high-volume, so you'll be able to trade them easily. After you do this, start exploring.

Don't be in trades or on CEXs with the majority of your portfolio.

In 1697, Willem de Vlamingh, together with his crew of Dutch explorers, arrived in Western Australia, becoming the first Europeans to see black swans with their own eyes. Before that time, all of Europe knew swans as only white and there was an expression regarding black swans that referred to a thing being impossible. Yet the impossible happened and Europe discovered black swans.

In trading, a black swan event refers to an event that is almost impossible to happen and yet happens. Imagine somebody hacking Binance and taking all your money from there. Imagine a CEX becoming illiquid and filing for bankruptcy.

If you think it's rare, well, on the 11th of November 2022, FTX's CEO stepped down from FTX and the company filed for bankruptcy. A lot of people lost money there, money they were holding on a reputable exchange (found in the top five in the world). And yes, I also lost part of my portfolio from that event, though luckily, most of it is on the chain, out of any CEX's reach.

This is what you (and I) can learn from this:

- Don't put all of your money on one particular exchange. Distribute money across different exchanges or, better yet, hold it in your on-chain wallet and only send it to the exchange when you are trading. What this means is that in the case of a black swan event like the FTX collapse of 2022, you'd only lose the money you have on FTX, not your whole trading account.

- I would recommend the "*heat*" on your total portfolio stays between 15% and 30%. That means that in the case of a sudden market crash, you're risking at most 30% of your account (in case everything goes bad and your trades don't find liquidity to exit with a stop-loss order).

Limiting losses in trading

Next, I'll discuss two strategies for limiting losses in trading: implementing position sizing when placing trades and controlling your emotions effectively.

Use position sizing when deploying trades.

In traditional trading, one rule of thumb is to risk at most 2% of equity in any particular trade and a maximum of 6% of your portfolio over a month.

For a 10K portfolio, that would be a $200 risk per trade with a total risk of $600/month. However, once your portfolio increases (even during the same month), you can risk more, proportionately to the increase.

This can be achieved through **Fixed Fractional Position Sizing**, which we'll discuss in the *Position sizing* section.

Handle your emotions.

This is one of the most important aspects of trading. If you can't handle your emotions, in time, you will lose more than you win.

A lot of people are posting high returns in leverage plays (a 50x leverage with $100 is $5,000). What they don't do is show you all the other money they've lost until that win and, maybe even more importantly, what they'll do with their winnings (lose them in 50x leverage $5,000 trades). Of course, statistically, there are always outliers who will win despite gambling, but chances are you won't find yourself there if you gamble.

Before we go any further, let me introduce to you the concept of **R**.

"R" is a standard unit for evaluating the potential reward and risk of trading strategies and individual trades.

R represents your optimal risk amount. We define this as your "*standard position*" size in our trading plan.

R-Multiple is our profit or loss on a trade, divided by the amount we planned to risk. For instance, if we risk $500 and earn $2,000 (2000/500), this is a 4R trade. If we forgo a stop loss and lose $750 when we intended to only risk $500, that results in a -1.5R trade (750/500).

Calculating a risk/reward ratio for a trade is directly related to your emotions. Traders suggest an R of 1.5 to 2, meaning a risk/reward ratio of 1.5x to 2x. This means that if you risk losing $200, you also have a chance of winning $300-$400. This looks good and it feels good, but it actually has no impact on your profits. That's because you can be profitable with an R of 0.2 as well, meaning for every $200 you risk losing, the gain can be $40. If your strategy has a very high win rate, this is perfectly acceptable. But if you're trading it manually, you can go on a losing streak, lose a few hundred bucks, and hate the strategy. What the 1.5x - 2x risk helps with is your emotions. Even if your trades have a win rate of less than 50%, you still have a chance of making a profit.

The following are four activities to help you better understand and improve your ability to diversify and limit losses.

Activities

1. Read about diversification: `https://www.investopedia.com/terms/d/diversification.asp`.

2. Go to `https://www.coingecko.com/` and find what the top 10 coins are by market cap. Go to TradingView and compare their charts on 1D. How similar are they? Bonus task: find out where and why they diverged.

3. Go to `https://coinmarketcap.com/` (an alternative to Coingecko) and repeat the process. On both platforms, you can create a portfolio that can mirror your investment strategy and keep a balance of your holdings. I wouldn't use it for trading, but it's great for investing.

4. **Value at Risk (VaR)** calculates the potential loss (based on a specified probability) that a group of investments might experience during normal market conditions over a defined time frame, such as a day. Read more about it here: `https://www.investopedia.com/terms/v/var.asp, https://www.investopedia.com/terms/v/var.asp`.

5. Learn more about the R concept and dive into the fractional R trades and terminology such as R-Theoretical and R-Actual at `https://tradethatswing.com/what-r-means-in-trading-in-terms-of-risk-and-profit/`.

Position sizing

In trading, we always want to increase returns and reduce risk, so we need to understand how much money to put in our trades in order to have a good risk/reward balance.

Figure 6.2 – Position sizing

There are various position sizing methods such as YOLO (no method); (addictive) gambling, also called emotion-driven trading; fixed-size (0.05 BTC for each trade); fixed-value ($1,000 for each trade); a fixed amount of equity; a percent of equity; percent volatility; the Kelly formula; the max drawdown method; fixed risk/fixed fractional; the profit-risk method; margin target; leverage target; optimal f; and more.

I'm going to present to you two of those methods. I've used both at various times.

Method 1 – percent of equity (variation)

With the **percent of equity method**, you make sure that the value of your position is equal to your chosen percent of account equity. I've fine-tuned this method to crypto because of the various black swan events that happen here, so you'll see modifications from the standard method.

I use the max heat system as I find it applies better to crypto. In traditional trading, your broker is usually insured, and the companies are a bit more stable, whereas in crypto, the risks are bigger, from the CEX disappearing overnight or getting hacked to hackers getting access to your account and siphoning money to the dark web.

So, I prefer to know via the max heat method how much I always have in stake, between 15% and 30% of my equity. That means that if my trades disappear (no liquidity, CEX hacks, or other issues), I would lose a maximum of 15 to 30% of what I have. I'm using this technique because I'm also trading via decentralized platforms, sometimes through **distributed exchanges** (**DEXs**) that have anonymous teams behind them. If you are trading traditionally, on a CEX, or just starting out, feel free to use my second method, presented next.

Besides max heat, I also use 3 fixed risks: a conservative 2.5% of my equity, a moderate 5%, and an aggressive 10% risk, which I rarely use.

For a 10k portfolio with a max heat of 15%, that would be $1,500 in-game at any given time. A 2.5% conservative risk of 10k equals $250, which would allow me 6 max positions ($1,500/$250). If I open 6 conservative trades of $250, I'm risking 15% of my portfolio, which is the max I want to risk.

Note that using this method, the risk affects the initial sum, not the difference to the stop loss plus fees.

Here's an example:

```
Initial deposit: $10,000  Current balance: $10,000

Max heat (%): 15%

Max heat ($): $1,500    Remaining heat ($): $1,500

Fixed risk (%): 2.5%    Fixed risk ($): $250

Max positions: 6    Remaining positions: 6
```

The current balance excludes open trade.

Max heat ($) is calculated as the initial deposit * the max hit (%).

Fixed risk ($) is the current balance / the fixed risk (%).

The remaining positions are calculated as the remaining heat / the fixed risk ($).

I'm entering a trade with $250:

```
Current balance: $9,750

Remaining heat: $1,250

Fixed risk: $195

Remaining positions: 6
```

I'm entering another trade with $195:

```
Current balance: $9,555
```

```
Remaining heat: $1,055
```

```
Fixed risk: $191.1
```

```
Remaining positions: 5
```

Then, I close the first trade, bringing back $695:

```
Current portfolio: $10,250
```

```
Remaining heat: $1,537.5
```

```
Fixed risk: $205
```

```
Remaining positions: 7
```

This is the first method. You can refer to the GitHub link for the spreadsheet.

Method 2 – fixed fractional position sizing (also known as fixed risk position sizing)

What I love about **fixed fractional position sizing** is that it directly takes the risk of the trade into account, making it ideal for futures trading. Note that the first method considers the risk of the whole environment of trading while this method focuses on the trade risk (and can be used outside of crypto).

In fixed fractional position sizing, you take into account only how much you'd lose if the trade would stop in a loss (you would sell with a stop loss).

For a 10k portfolio and a 2% (traditional) risk, that would be $200 at risk for the first trade. I recommend you start with a 1% (conservative) risk and only increase it once you're confident in your trading skills.

In addition to this, we're also limiting the risk per month to around 6% of the portfolio, thus recommending you to be in a maximum of 3 trades of $200 risk at any one time.

A short example: I want to go long on token CAS. It is currently trading at $10 and I'm setting my stop price at $9. That means I can lose $1 per token bought. My portfolio is $50,000 and my fixed risk is at 1.5% ($750). That means I can buy 750 CAS tokens (risking $1/CAS with a total of $750). My max loss is $750 or 1.5% of my portfolio value.

Let's see the algorithm in action now:

```
Initial deposit: $10,000  Current balance: $10,000
```

```
Max heat (%): 6%
```

```
Max heat ($): $600    Remaining heat ($): $600
```

```
Fixed risk (%): 1.5%    Fixed risk ($): $150
```

```
Max positions: 4    Remaining positions: 4
```

The max heat here is calculated using the current balance (not the initial deposit, as in the previous method).

The remaining heat is the max heat minus the risk that we are in trade with (the risk from all open trades).

The fixed risk is a percentage of the current balance.

The max position is calculated by dividing the fixed risk from the remaining heat.

Let's say token DAB is trading at $230 and I'm shorting it with a stop loss at $240. I'm risking $10/token with a fixed risk of $150 so I can buy 15 tokens. I'm entering a trade with $3,450 (ignoring taxes):

```
Current balance: $6,550
```

```
Max heat ($): $393
```

```
Remaining heat: $243
```

```
Fixed risk: $98.25
```

```
Remaining positions: 2
```

I'll be rounding up to two decimals; it won't impact the statistics (that much).

There's a token CAF that is trading at $15 and I'm longing it with a stop at $13. I'm risking $2 and with a fixed risk of $98.25 I can buy 49.13 pieces. That's $736.95:

```
Current balance: $5,813.05
```

```
Max heat ($): $348.78
```

```
Remaining heat: $100.53 (348.78-150-98.25)
```

```
Fixed risk: $87.20
```

```
Remaining positions: 1
```

My first position closes with a profit of $600.95, totaling $4,050.95:

```
Current balance: $9,864
```

```
Max heat ($): $591.84
```

```
Remaining heat: $493.59 (591.84-98.25)
```

```
Fixed risk: $147.96
```

```
Remaining positions: 3
```

I'm currently using this method because I find it statistically relevant to my performance as a trader. Its only issue is that you can find yourself with a lot of money in trade and on CEXs and you need to take this into consideration. This method too can be found in the GitHub repository.

The following activities will help you better understand position sizing. I understand that there's a bit of mathematics involved, but this is the kind of mathematics that saves you money. It's just like doing your taxes, hard at first, but once you do it you see the value it brings.

Activities

1. Go to `http://www.adaptrade.com/MSA/MSA3UsersGuide.pdf` | **Page 42** to read more about the different position sizing methods listed. Check the **Profit Risk Method** as an alternative to fixed fractional position sizing (it's the same as the initial method when it starts but it risks more when you've gained more).

2. Play with this calculator, which finds out the position size you can take based on your account value, percentage available to risk, entry price, and initial protective stop: `https://chartyourtrade.com/position-size-calculator/`. Make sure you understand the process.

Keeping a trading journal

Robert Collier said, "*Success is the sum of small efforts, repeated day in and day out.*" Lao Tzu said, "*The journey of a thousand miles begins with one step.*" Charles Atlas said, "*Step by step, and the thing is done.*"

Figure 6.3 – Trading journal

They all talk about success in steps, but the thing is, success is also a feeling – when you look back and see what you've built. And once you've identified that feeling, it becomes easier and easier to build toward it.

Now, how can you look back if you're trading without logging all of your trades, studying what you did well and what you did wrong, and learning from it?

I would argue that a trading journal is a must for any person who calls themselves a trader. You need to have a historical perspective on each trading method you've used, to know how good it is, how it behaved in past markets, and also your overall performance.

Adjusting to the market

When you look at your past trades, you might notice that one technique that works in bear markets might not work in bull markets, and note it down. I have specific strategies for bull markets, bear markets, and side markets. For example, it's easier in a side market to trade a parallel channel, taking longs at the bottom and shorts at the top.

Some strategies "*expire*" after the market adapts to them. You might notice how their performance degrades over time, modify to account for the market, or mark them as obsolete as something new works better.

Different timeframes offer different opportunities, volatility impacts stop-loss orders, and the trade duration might indicate you should get out before it's too late.

Handling emotions

Having a trading journal helps you handle your emotions. You might notice how you're continuously ignoring the starting point of your strategy, entering either too soon or too late, or maybe with a bigger amount than specified. By having a clear account of what you did, you'll be able to better organize your thoughts and handle your emotions while riding the wave of the market. Profitability will begin to feel earned, not a random section of events, and losses will have a reason attached, being considered in the bigger picture. You'll also be able to feel better about what you do and be able to prove your success to yourself.

Planning your trades

The best traders out there have a clear plan on how they trade. They know when to enter, when to exit, and in what situations to change that. Most of them don't follow their trades second by second and have either alarms, multiple take profit orders, or stop losses to make sure everything is taken care of.

Before they enter the trade, they document everything about the situation they are trading in, including a picture of the chart, so that when the trade ends, they can compare what they saw in the beginning to what happened in the end. This, in time, will provide an intuitive feeling of how the market behaves. In my coaching sessions, I sometimes have a bias toward the direction of the market even on lower timeframes. It's an intuitive feeling that, even if it lacks clear proof, it is more right than wrong.

Logging your trades in the trade journal also allows you to paper-trade. You can test a trading strategy without using any money for a month or two, just by entering the trade in your journal and watching it on the chart as if it were a real trade.

I've provided you with a *Trading Journal* in the GitHub link.

Next, we'll explore your trading plan, discussing how to outline conditions for entering and exiting trades, determining risk, and planning for profit.

Your trading plan

A trading plan means setting conditions for getting into and out of trades, establishing how much money to risk, and preparing a path with an expectation of profit.

Figure 6.4 – What is a trading plan?

You can base your trading plan on multiple factors and conditions; let's see a few of them:

- **Timeframe** (position trading, swing trading, day trading)
- **Market type** (bull market, bear market, sideways market)
- **Entry strategy** (trade a breakout or a parallel channel without leverage)
- **Exit condition** (exit after two red candles or at channel top)
- **Position size** (2% risk)
- **Expectations** (weekly profitability > x% for day trading)
- **Analysis** (going over all trades one week after they closed and checking whether there's something to improve)

A trading plan can be a lot of things.

It can be a sentence such as *"a swing trade in a bull market, entering with a 2% risk every time BTC drops by 10% and exiting at a 10% profit"* or *"depositing $1,000 into a mutual fund every month and taking a percentage out when it grows by X%."*

My personal trading plans are always tied to profit. If my profitability is over my expected percentage, I'm not checking anything too close. If it is under the percentage (even if still profitable), I dedicate time to identify what didn't work or whether the conditions changed (the market changed, maybe specific news had an emotional influence on the market, etc...).

In the upcoming section, we'll discuss the choice between trading in dollars or Bitcoin, examining the effects of market conditions on profitability perceptions, and considering the personal beliefs and goals that guide this decision.

Dollars or Bitcoin?

An interesting thing that happens during the bull market is that you'll see a lot of videos of people making money in trading. They will show you their accounts and you will literally see how the money grows. This phenomenon rarely happens during the bear market.

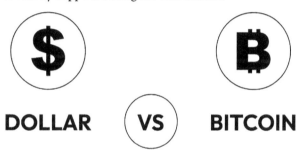

Figure 6.5 – Dollar or Bitcoin?

That is because in the bull market, if you keep your winnings in BTC and if BTC grows by 13%, let's say monthly, and your trading system's monthly profit is -2%, your total account growth in dollars is 11%. You can show your account balance, and everybody will see how good you are as a trader.

Still, if you check your balance in BTC, you're actually losing 2% each month. Hmm...

In the bear market, if you keep your money in BTC and BTC decreases by 5% and your trading system is 1% profitable, your total account growth in dollars is -4%, and in BTC, it's 1%. Hmm again.

So, you can see how people can show different perspectives of their account and it will look as if it's profitable even if it's not (though that's a bit harder when BTC drops).

One thing that you'll need to decide when starting trading is how you'll measure your account growth. You can usually do it in dollars or in Bitcoin. I'm not recommending you trade in euros or other currencies, as the charts will look a bit different and you won't understand why round numbers are ignored by Price Action.

I would recommend you measure your account in dollars. Measuring in BTC is for people who dream of BTC going to the moon and being able to afford to buy little islands where they can retire. Measuring in dollars is for people who will see their account grow monthly and be able to afford a new car, even a new house, while still in their youth.

It all depends on your beliefs here and even though a lot of crypto enthusiasts will swear by daddy bitcoin during the bull run, you won't hear them so enthusiastic in the bear market.

Summary

In conclusion, effective money management in trading hinges on limiting losses, correct position sizing, diligent record-keeping in a trading journal, and the formulation of a solid trading plan. Implementing these strategies can substantially increase your chances of achieving trading success.

My goal for this chapter was to provide you with strategies to limit losses and also with the capacity to properly formulate a trading plan, track its progress, and ensure proper risk management before and during the trade.

In the following chapter, we'll delve into the essentials of a trading system, emphasizing the importance of understanding your strategy intimately, testing it thoroughly, and being prepared for any market conditions.

7

Finding Your Edge

As we embark on this chapter, we will take a comprehensive journey through the various stages of developing and implementing a successful trading strategy. We will kick off with a solid foundation by understanding the essentials of a trading system, followed by identifying potential trading patterns that can shape your strategy. An essential aspect of our discussion will revolve around defining entry and exit points, a vital component for mitigating risks and securing profits.

Next, we'll plunge into the rigors of backtesting and forward testing, which enable us to evaluate the potential viability and profitability of our strategy. Once we are confident with our strategy's theoretical success, we will move on to paper trading, or "*a dry run*," providing us with a risk-free environment to evaluate the strategy in real-time market conditions. With sufficient confidence and preparation, we'll transition into live action, bringing our tested strategy to real-world application. Finally, a well-rounded testing checklist will assist us in ensuring we have thoroughly covered every aspect of strategy development and implementation.

My goal for this chapter is for you to go through a detailed and enlightening exploration of the process of creating and perfecting your trading strategy.

These are the topics we're going to talk about to get there:

- Trading system essentials
- Identifying a trading pattern
- Defining entry and exit points
- Backtesting
- Forward testing
- Paper trading (the dry-run)
- Live action
- Testing checklist

Trading system essentials

In the previous chapter, we discussed holding your assets in dollars versus holding them in Bitcoin and I explained how even if a strategy loses a total of 1% per month, if BTC is rising by 4% in 1 month, you'll have made a 3% profit in dollars for that month.

You need to be very careful when checking for strategy performance, as anyone showing you a strategy can show it against Bitcoin or against the dollar (based on which looks more profitable). They may also demonstrate a tiny, statistically insignificant sample (such as a live trade of 15 minutes) or showcase a strategy that was effective in a bear market during recording but may not work in the current bull market, among other situations.

Thus, in order to protect your money and invest successfully, I'd recommend you find *your own* edge in trading. This doesn't mean you need to develop a strategy from scratch, but it does mean that you need to intimately know each strategy that you'll be developing. You need to make sure it is clearly defined, to backtest it, forward-test it, paper-trade it, and see how it behaves when you trade it live and you scale the money. You should be able to recite its setup at 3 a.m. if you wake up from a nightmare (where a black swan event suddenly happened).

In order to help you better define a trading strategy, I've developed a template, which you can find in the GitHub repository.

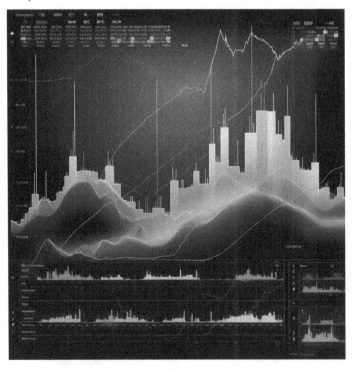

Figure 7.1 – Complexities of a trading system

Here are its elements and how you're going to use them.

Filters

In order to trade using a strategy, we must first define what we don't want to trade. Filters prevent us from trading in a situation where our strategy wouldn't actually work.

A **filter** is a precondition to us looking for a setup for our entry.

For example, we might have a strategy that we've only tested on Bitcoin (so we can exclude any other tokens until we've tested it somewhere else). That's called a filter by **market**.

We might also filter by **market capitalization**. For example, we can filter for large caps (tokens with large capitalization) to make sure we have trading volume.

Another filter might be a **timeframe**. We might use an indicator such as **Pivot Points** that works better on lower timeframes (5 to 30 minutes) or our swing strategy might only work within a 4-hour timeframe.

It can also be a **trend** such as an ascending trend (which usually happens in a bull market), a descending trend (sometimes at the beginning or during a bear market), a sideways trend, or a trending "*trend*" (when it is ascending or descending but not sideways).

A **chart setup** filter would be able to filter for a triangle breakout or a specific support line being touched.

A **volume** filter would look for a rising volume on a rising price (for example, if we have a rise in price without a rise in volume, we wouldn't trade if we had that filter).

Then, we can also have a **price** filter, maybe a specific candlestick that we're looking for (for example, we only trade after three dojis).

These filters help us quickly look for our specific trading conditions by scanning various charts. What I usually do is have a list of tokens that I prefer to trade (around 10-20), which I quickly skim through on various timeframes for my top 3 strategies. If my filters exclude everything in that list, I don't trade. It's akin to looking up the weather before planning a picnic. If the weather is poor, you won't even bother searching for the perfect picnic spot.

Don't run for the trade, let the trade come to you!

The setup

After filtering out what doesn't work, we're left with what could work.

Our setup is our preparation for the trade. It's the moment we're really watching the chart, waiting for the price to do our bidding.

Here, we set the specific conditions that we need before we search for entry points.

To go **long**, we might need a bullish trend on a higher timeframe (if we're trading 5-minute, we might go to 1-hour to make sure it's a bullish trend). For **shorts**, we reverse the conditions (we look for a bearish trend on 1H).

Other setups might be as follows. If we're looking for a triangle to trade, the setup might wait for the price to be close to its apex. If we're trading a parallel channel, a filter will find the channel while a setup will wait for the price to be close to one of the parallel lines of support or resistance.

The entry trigger

Here we have the **initial entry conditions**, for example, when there's a crossover with the **Relative Strength Index (RSI)** indicator and the price is above the **Volume Weighted Average Price (VWAP)**.

Then we have the **confirmation**, which brings an additional argument to our trade. We can, for example, increase our entry size if the RSI is not overbought or if the price is at a pivot point support line.

Then there's the **re-entry** condition. In some trades, the stop loss gets triggered, and we are out of the trade even if the entry conditions are still there. We can specify a situation where we enter the trade again.

These conditions need to be specified both for **longs** and **shorts** (in case we're going in both directions).

The stop loss

The **initial stop** can be based on an **Average True Range (ATR)**, a support/resistance line, a Fibonacci level, a whole number, an order book condition, or some other specific triggers. For example, we can set the stop loss to be at 2.5 ATR from the entry point. I find ATRs and **Support and Resistance (S&R)** lines to be the best for common stop losses.

Then we have the **confirmation**, which we already know how it works.

We can also set a **risk-free** condition. For this, we can move our stop loss to our entry point when certain conditions are met (for example, the price rises above local support, or the first take profit is triggered, or we just move it after a specific price percentage increase).

Then, we might have an **early exit** condition or trade **invalidation**. This can happen when you go long and you see a double top or a strong resistance line... or maybe you're in the trade too long without the price going either way.

The take profit

The **take profit type** can be based on R (2:1 from the stop loss), on a resistance line, a Fibonacci sequence, or on other **conditions**.

You can also have **split** profit **targets**. In a trade on 4H, you might take the first profit on a local, 4H resistance line, then the next profit before a weekly resistance line, and the last one before a very strong monthly resistance line.

Optional

Optional to our strategy, you can have an additional indicator or a size split (if 3 triggers are met, enter with $X, if 2 more triggers are found, add 0.5 * X and so on).

We can also have more leeway or have a discretionary strategy (though these strategies can't be automated). A good example here is a parallel channel, which is never perfect. You can define the support and resistance lines that encompass the current channel, but they need to be fine-tuned continuously.

Then, we can mark the strategy as being still in backtesting, forward testing, paper trading, or execution mode.

The review

No strategy works without reviewing it properly.

Here we have the **emotional/psychological** section where we note down various situations that we've encountered where we made a mistake, or we felt that we wanted to do something that was against the strategy.

One example that I often find when coaching is that people wake up in the morning, get to their chart, and see a trade that they've just missed. They enter it because it's just a bit different and then they wonder why the strategy didn't work. I usually make them mark these trades as using the "*emotional strategy*" and we check the results at the end. Just a hint regarding why this doesn't work: when your strategy will let you enter between $10 and $16 (that's the price range where all the conditions are met) and you enter at $17, just a little above that price range... it's actually not $1 above the entry conditions; it's $4 above the average entry point of $13.

In the spreadsheet, we also have a `Technical/extra conditions or screening` section. Here, while trading based on RSI and with additional confirmation of Pivot Points, you might also check whether the strategy works better with an **Exponential Moving Averages** (**EMAs**) intersection. You don't want to trade based on this, but you want to keep it in mind or just look at EMAs when trading to see whether you notice any potential correlation before testing it out. These ideas might come while testing the strategy or, if your strategy is a modified version of a public one, maybe you took some of the ideas people had from the discussions around that strategy.

Then we have the **ideas/improvements** section where you dump various ideas on how to improve the strategy (maybe adding another filter, ignoring the shorts in a bull market, an additional take-profit target, etc.).

Finally, the **backtesting** section shows (or links to) the results of your tests and the details of the test conditions.

The following section is about the journey of identifying profitable trading patterns and understanding when they work and when they don't.

Identifying a trading pattern

Finding a pattern to trade is not hard but knowing that what you are trading is actually profitable over the long run is. Besides finding the pattern, it needs to be tested over various markets, then it needs to be tested live, and finally, you can start trading (initially with a small amount, which increases as you become confident in the technique).

Figure 7.2 – Identifying a trading pattern

YouTube/Twitter/Telegram/Discord/TradingView and other social channels

You can get a pattern by watching YouTubers that do exactly this, develop and test patterns over numerous trades. Please make sure you test these patterns carefully as influencers are pressured by their business model to come up with new content. When one shows you new strategies every week, you can be sure they didn't test them properly.

Twitter is another good source for strategies as it's focused a bit more on content than on influencers. Even if there are a lot of comments from people who "*made money*" using the strategies, they can be outliers, exceptions to the rule that enthusiastically write about their experiences while the majority of people (for which the technique doesn't work) think that there's something wrong with the way they have implemented it.

TradingView also has a section dedicated to **Trade Ideas**, and though I wouldn't call it a social channel, the section allows comments and most of the commenters are traders. Some of the people there know their business but most of the comments are from people that have no idea how to trade and that want to skip steps and get to the money.

TradingView's indicators and strategies

When I first started out, I thought that I could run a strategy and see whether it was profitable. If it wasn't, I could revert it and then I'd be profitable for sure. Little did I know that these strategies don't show the correct profitability of the method and, even if they do, they can't guarantee further profitability.

My recommendation here is to learn about some basic indicators and trade a bit with them. Only when you're comfortable trading with MA, RSI, ATR, and **On-Balance Volume** (**OBV**) should you add a new indicator, outside of the ones suggested. There are some gems out there, such as *VuManChu*'s Cipher indicator (`https://www.tradingview.com/u/vumanchu/#published-scripts`) and you can also follow some of the good coders such as *LonesomeTheBlue* (`https://www.tradingview.com/u/LonesomeTheBlue/#published-scripts`) and *prosum_solutions* (`https://www.tradingview.com/u/prosum_solutions/#published-scripts`). Their coding skills are amazing, and their indicators are doing what they should.

In time, you'll develop a taste for what works and what doesn't.

All of these indicators can be used as additional data points when building your strategy but don't forget that you need your data to come from different indicator categories. Just a reminder, these categories are trend analysis, trend indicators, momentum indicators, volatility, and volume. Don't use three trend indicators in the same strategy as they will probably use the same data to tell you the same thing.

Learning PineScript or Python and get hired as a coder

When I started out with trading, I wanted to develop my own tools for the job. That's why I've learned PineScript, which I used religiously in my early trading years (before switching to Python and to algorithmic trading).

When I saw a strategy from someone on Twitter that sounded practical, I coded it and also sent the strategy to them. This is how I became friends with *EmperorBTC* (`https://twitter.com/EmperorBTC`) who is a great teacher for newcomers to crypto. He has the ability to explain simply and clearly some pretty advanced stuff and gets all my respect for the work he does. He also helped me out a lot when I started out and introduced me to my first advanced trading group with people that I'm still friends with.

After publishing some strategies on TradingView, I've received messages from people wanting to get their own strategy developed. Most of them didn't work, but the smart people out there knew that to find out a strategy doesn't work is almost as precious as finding out it works. And some of them did work. I kept in touch with the traders who successfully used those strategies and helped with some further development, thus bettering them and also getting permission to use them for my own portfolio. I'm still using two of these strategies even now, years later.

If you are a coder or if you have the mind for coding, learning PineScript could be a step in the right direction.

Developing your own

Ah! The beauty of creating something on your own!

In my free time, I sometimes paint, and I love how I sometimes create something wonderful out of nothing. It makes me feel creative, joyful, and fulfilled.

Developing your own strategy is not impossible. It actually becomes easier and easier as you go through the process again and again.

One quick method of doing so is by choosing three indicators from three different categories from our indicators template located on GitHub in *Chapter 4* and seeing whether they complement themselves well and whether you can derive some specific conditions in which trading by them could work.

For example, you could choose S&R, RSI, and Keltner Channels.

Next, set the S&R monthly and weekly lines on the BTC chart and see how the price behaves around those lines.

Would adding the RSI and trading only when it gives a specific signal work, such as being oversold, being overbought, or by identifying a divergence?

When adding the KC to the graph, is the picture clearer? Do they fit with the other indicators in pinpointing a specific place to long or to short?

Maybe the chart is too complex, and you think you're missing trades. Should you take out RSI and leave only KC and the S&R lines? Should you add another indicator to pinpoint the exact entry or maybe filter out a specific market type?

You play around, find something that seems to work, and then test it for 20 trades. After 20 trades, you get the hang of how everything fits together and can decide whether you want to test it properly (starting from 100 trades for each trend direction: ascending, descending, or sideways) or tweak it some more.

After understanding the basic approach to identifying trading patterns and strategies, it's now important to discuss how to pinpoint your entry and exit points in a trade. This involves a blend of technique and mindset to minimize losses and enhance gains. Let's delve into the nuances of making entries, crafting exits, and adopting the SHIELD mentality in trading.

Defining entry and exit points

A lot of questions I get from people starting out is how to pinpoint the perfect trade entry (and the perfect trade exit). In my experience, you can't do that. You can't time the market because most of the cost you'd incur waiting for the perfect moment would exceed any profit you'd make from the trade.

What you can do, though, is use a few entry and exit techniques as well as a specific mentality that helps prevent loss.

Figure 7.3 – Finding a good trade

Entries

Regarding entries, my rule is that if your entry conditions are triggered, it's an entry (and the size of the entry is based on your risk management and strategy conditions).

Let's say that you've just arrived in front of the computer and, even though the entry conditions are there, you note that the price already went 10% in your trade direction. Do you still enter? Wait for a pullback before entering? Ignore this trade?

I'd still enter, again, *as long as the entry conditions are triggered*. I'd also mark/tag this in my journal as not being the perfect timing for later, when I want to automate the strategy.

Even though the entry is valid, a bot would take the perfect entry when the conditions were met; it wouldn't wait this long so it wouldn't actually be in this situation. You need to take this into account when calculating the profitability of the strategy.

Other situations that might occur should be added to your trading strategy template. Don't give yourself too much leeway as leeway cannot be automated (nor can its success be calculated).

It's all right if you want to be a discretionary trader and add intuition and feelings to your trade... after at least a year of technical trading. You're not born with that intuition; you develop it with sweat and money.

Another thing to look at, after the trade has ended (and your emotions cool down), is whether, with all the knowledge you had then, you should have used another entry point instead of the one you took. Of course, every trade is random, but when you see a pattern develop, you might add another precondition to your strategy and improve your profitability.

Exits

Just like entries, there are no perfect exits, and my recommendation here as well is to exit per your strategy conditions.

But in crypto, there's one thing happening that doesn't just happen in traditional stock trading. Sometimes, crypto tokens go up exponentially. And you'll notice, after trading for a while, that you exit the trade, but the token continues to grow, grow, and grow.

In order to take advantage of this, I almost always leave 10% of my initial entry to go to a higher resistance line, or I just keep it in tokens. It's like I get taxed for 10% of my profits but I'm keeping the taxes.

This helps me accumulate some of the tokens I like over a period of time without thinking about it.

Does it impact my profits?

Of course it does. Just like taxes do.

Should you use this method?

Maybe not at first but keep it in mind for when you become profitable (and start missing these exponential growths).

The SHIELD mentality

Losing money is hard. Especially when you could have invested it instead of trading it away. But in order to do this, you need a larger bank.

First, trade only in markets where you'd also like to invest (around this time).

Then, don't put a stop loss on your trade; just mark it on TradingView.

If your stop loss gets hit (on the chart), don't manually sell your position. Switch your hat from the trader's role to the investor's role and consider the money invested in the token.

Basically, you're accumulating the coin with the help of unprofitable trades.

And if this puts too much pressure on your capital, you can also set a take profit at 0% profit, just to get your initial amount out (but without investing, in this case).

Note that you also need to mark this as a loss in your trading journal. Don't cheat on your strategy performance!

But this method has its drawbacks. Firstly, it doesn't teach you to be a better trader (maybe quite the opposite); secondly, you'll have a large portion of your capital stuck in investments, capital that can be used in trading; and thirdly, if your timing is bad, you might be at the beginning of a bear market and have all of your investments in coins that will quickly get devalued and may take years to come back to their original price.

When I wrote this section, I kept asking myself whether I should offer this suggestion or not. It feels like cheating, and it doesn't necessarily prepare you to be a better trader. But I think that everyone should judge for themselves how they want to play this game.

This is just a technique that you can add to your repertoire and use only when and if needed.

Moving forward from defining trade entries and exits, we need to validate the efficacy of our trading strategy. This is achieved through a process known as backtesting. In the following section, we'll explore an effective approach to backtesting a trading technique.

Backtesting

In this section, I'm going to present to you an efficient way to **backtest** a trading technique. It's not meant to be perfect, you aren't doing it automatically via an algorithm using multiple conditions, but it does its job, and it separates strategies that might not work from the strategies that might work.

You've identified a potential trading pattern and defined it as a strategy. You know its filters, the setup, the entry trigger, the stop loss point, and the take-profit point(s), and you have some ideas on how to improve it.

Now it's time to see how well it worked in the past.

In order to do this, you need to have a period where the market was in an uptrend, a period when it was in a downtrend, and a period when it was in a sideways trend. These periods should be of the same range and in the same timeframe as your strategy.

For example, you could look at the BTC/USDT pair during 2020-10-04 – 2021-01-09 (around 3 months) on the daily timeframe and consider that an uptrend.

The following figure shows other markets with a somewhat clear direction:

Market examples				
MARKET	COIN	TIMEFRAME	START	END
UPTREND	BTCUSDT	DAILY	4.10.20	9.01.21
SIDEWAYS	BTCUSDT	DAILY	10.02.21	13.05.21
DOWNTREND	BTCUSDT	DAILY	24.02.20	17.03.20
UPTREND	ETHBTC	DAILY	1.01.18	1.02.18
SIDEWAYS	ETHBTC	DAILY	23.04.18	23.05.18
DOWNTREND	ETHBTC	DAILY	5.02.18	5.03.18
UPTREND	XRPUSDT	DAILY	5.11.20	24.11.20
SIDEWAYS	XRPUSDT	DAILY	6.09.20	5.11.20
DOWNTREND	XRPUSDT	DAILY	25.11.20	30.12.20

Figure 7.4 – Uptrend, downtrend, and sideways markets

In order to test your strategy, go to TradingView and add two vertical lines at the start of the uptrend and at its end. It looks like this:

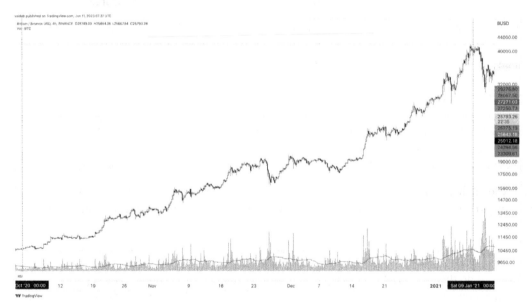

Figure 7.5 – Testing range

Then, activate **Bar Replay** mode, a feature of TradingView that simulates historical data bar by bar, as if you're experiencing real-time market conditions. Set your preferred timeframe, and methodically apply your strategy candle by candle within your testing range.

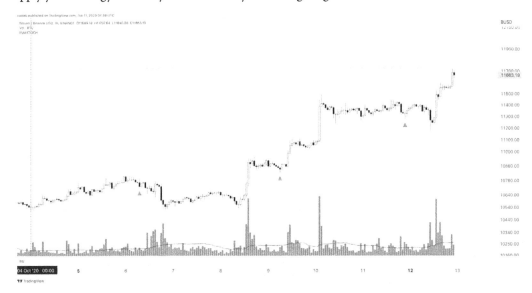

Figure 7.6 – Testing the strategy in Bar Replay

Here are some things to note:

- Some strategies work only during specific moments or in specific markets and within specific timeframes. If it doesn't work in one place, it's up to you to decide whether you want to test it in the others. I have specific strategies for bear markets (where there aren't many uptrends) and others for bull markets and sideways markets.

- While **Bar Replay** is a useful tool, it's not flawless. It doesn't facilitate intrabar testing, meaning that a strategy might not be triggered during a candle formation, even if it would have been triggered in real time. There may also be discrepancies in how TradingView presents strategy outcomes. Nonetheless, these limitations are typically seen as part of the learning journey in technical analysis.

Test your strategy for 20 trades. This is not statistically relevant, but I find it is enough to make small changes to the strategy based on your intuition. The longer you trade, the better this intuition will be and the quicker you'll figure out what modifications you need to make.

Test it again with 20 trades and repeat this process for any other modifications you might make.

When you are happy with your strategy, continue testing for at least 100 trades and in all 3 market directions. Maybe add different timeframes and different markets. Does it work as well? Or better?

Here's what my process looks like:

Figure 7.7 – I have spreadsheets and spreadsheets of these calculations

Next, calculate your results. I have a template for you in the GitHub link.

Make sure to calculate your successful trades, your failed trades, your strategy's R, and your success ratio.

Just a reminder, and also building a bit on the R term: R is the amount you are risking. For a risk-reward ratio of 2:1, you are risking 1R for a potential 2R profit (for example, risking $50 for a potential profit of $100). If you've risked 1R for a 4R profit and you've made the profit, then you've risked 1R and, if you've lost it, your strategy nets a total of 3R (4-1). Knowing your strategy's R allows you to understand how well it works in practice.

Save the chart with your tests for reference and smile. You've finished backtesting your strategy.

Prior to delving into forward testing, I would recommend undertaking a few activities to enhance your comprehension of backtesting. The learning journey doesn't stop with backtesting; rather than immediately deploying our newly minted strategy with real finances, the next crucial step we need to take is known as forward testing. This technique enables us to deal with a host of scenarios that might not have come to light during the backtesting phase.

Activities

1. Find out three strategies that you're going to test using the suggestions in the previous section, *Identifying a trading pattern*.

2. Using the strategy tester template from GitHub, backtest these strategies in the three different market scenarios. Ask yourself why they work in one market and not in the other. Would you use them in practice? When? When not? How do you know when would be the proper time for that?

3. Read more about what "R" means in trading here: `https://tradethatswing.com/what-r-means-in-trading-in-terms-of-risk-and-profit/` (in case you haven't read it in the previous chapter).

4. Add a TradingView strategy from the **Indicators** button and check how it works, the entries and exits it has, and its results. Understand it well as you might make something similar in the future. (You can, for example, search for *RSI strategy*, *Supertrend strategy*, or *Parabolic SAR strategy*.)

Forward testing

After you backtest your strategy, don't jump right into using money for your newborn strategy. You still need to do forward testing.

Forward testing allows you to address a few more situations that you don't actually encounter during backtesting and you need to address them while you're still not trading with real money.

In order to do this, open TradingView for the marketplaces you've backtested your strategy with and follow the tokens.

You might put alarms so that you get (phone) notifications when the setup is ready and you need to monitor the token, for example, and notice that you're getting notified too late. Then, you prepare your setup (or your alarm) so that you have time to get to the computer and check the situation at hand.

Another situation would be that you've just arrived in front of TradingView and you see a trade that still checks your entry trigger, yet the token has already gone up a bit. Questions might go through your head now; are you going to start a trade at this point? If so, will the stop loss be put as your strategy specified? If it's specified under a support line and your support line is now farther away, will you still put it there? Then, a take profit would probably be a bit above what you'd normally set it. Is this all right? And, after these modifications, are you still applying your strategy or a derivation? Maybe you should tag it differently, so you don't add its results to the original strategy.

Should you enter a long when you can clearly see the token price is falling even if your strategy checks? Or enter just a bit and add as it goes down? Should you modify the strategy?

What about the situations when you have 5, 10, or 20 consecutive failing trades? Is this part of your strategy's profitability, a random losing streak, or has the market changed? Does your strategy still work? When would you consider the strategy to not be working anymore? (Note that even strategies that get obsolete have the potential of being rejuvenated after a market cycle.)

You'll have other questions, and they will only appear once you do forward testing.

I recommend you forward-test for at least 100 trades just so that you can better understand how the strategy is impacted in a live market.

Paper trading (the dry-run)

And now, after forward testing, the next step I recommend is **paper trading**. *3Commas* allows you to trade with paper money, thus protecting your capital until you see it rise due to your own abilities.

Always paper-trade new strategies until you are profitable for at least one month (though other traders would say one to three months).

You might ask yourself why do a forward test and then a paper trade; shouldn't you just paper trade after the backtest?

My answer to you is that forward testing is not used to calculate the R, the profitability of the strategy, but to tune it some more against a real-life scenario.

After that, paper trading is where you actually put your strategy into practice, and this is the place where you'll get as close to the real R as possible.

Live action

After you get confident in your strategy, this is the time for live action. Now you're putting real money at stake.

Figure 7.8 – You, after a year of successful trades

Besides the lessons already learned about risk management, there is another safety tip I can give you. You can start by putting a smaller amount, let's say $15, when you enter the trade and continuously increase that sum up until your fixed risk percentage (1.5%-2% of your capital).

Live action will bring up emotions that you didn't have during testing. Emotions of thrill and euphoria, panic, and addiction. You need to manage them while also staying on course and following your trading plan.

First, I recommend you go through all of these steps as I've shown them to you. Always backtest for at least 100 trades in each market, always forward-test for 100 trades, and then paper-trade for at least a month. After you develop three strategies that work and you're confident in your ability to work through the method presented here, you can skip a few steps. For example, you can paper-trade and forward-test at the same time (since you've already processed your emotions and you've also worked through most of the forward trading challenges before). But I strongly recommend you don't do this for your first three strategies. Go through the process as you need to build that mental fortitude and winning history that will help you succeed in the trading world.

Testing checklist

When testing strategies, run through this checklist to make sure you haven't forgotten anything. Also, note that you might not be able to manually test everything, and that's all right. It's okay to not be perfect and to have some unknowns when you trade a strategy. But ideally, know the unknowns:

- How many trades did you have? Testing over 3 months with 3 trades is different from testing over 1 week with 100 trades and they tell you different things.

- Did you test it through ascending, descending, and sideways trends? But did you also test it in the previous X days/weeks/months (depending on the timeframe)? Did you test through a period where the market changed direction (situation: your filter identified a bull market, you trade it, but it takes a while for the filter to identify that the market became bear while your strategy is still running)? Was the dataset detrended?

- Are proper filters in place? Is it biased toward a certain condition/market direction/timeframe/ market? When testing in different markets, did you take into consideration that tokens might get unlisted or dumped? Does your filter take this into account (by trading large caps, for example)?

- Does it take into account lower timeframes, intraday candles, repainting, slippage, fees, drawdown, and maybe even black swan events?

- Do you take into account delays such as receiving the market data late, API delays if you're using external tools, overfitting, and underfitting?

- Did you account for the various situations that occur during live trading (as opposed to backtesting)?

- Can it be tested automatically (for example, in a TradingView script)?

- Can you give this strategy to a friend who is trading, and can they reproduce your results using your conditions?

- Does it work in other markets (forex, stocks, etc.)?

A note on advanced testing

There is more to testing a strategy than meets the eye, but I feel that what I've given you here is enough to develop your first productive strategy. Still, I'd like to mention all the things that make testing an arduous process. Some keywords are alpha and beta (`https://www.investopedia.com/ask/answers/102714/whats-difference-between-alpha-and-beta.asp`), Sortino/Calmar/Sharpe ratios (`https://towardsdatascience.com/sharpe-ratio-sorino-ratio-and-calmar-ratio-252b0cddc328`), expectancy, total days in trade, drawdown, overfitting, and more.

Here are some scenarios.

The strategy performs better than BTC (and the "*buy & hold*" enthusiasts), yet BTC is in a downtrend. Is it a good strategy?

Backtesting shows a profitable strategy with a huge drawdown. It might be that you live-trade exactly when the strategy has a string of losses and you lose a very big percentage of your portfolio. (Then you'll need 100% profit to recover from a 50% loss, or 400% profit to recover from an 80% loss.)

How do you compare your strategies? Do you use a ratio such as Sharpe, VaR, total profit in percentage, or accumulated profit? What happens if you have a strategy that's better in one test and another that outperforms the first one in another test? (Tip: that's when you start learning statistics.)

If your strategy stays too many days in trade, it might catch market spikes/news/volatility grabs/ SL hunting and act too random. This might look good in backtesting, while the randomness might just as well prove to be bad during live runs.

I test my strategies with 60% training data, 20% validation data, and 20% test data. During the training, I use all my knowledge to develop the strategy and make it beat the market as much as possible. Then, I test it on the next 20% of data (20% of a time range) and do some modifications or maybe hyperopt it better. The last 20% is tested only once, after I commit my strategy to my private repository. Making modifications then would overfit my strategy to the final testing set. But what would happen if the 60% training data was during a downtrend and the last 40% (validation and test data) was on an uptrend? A long-biased strategy might look better than it is. That's why you can use advanced models such as **GroupTimeSeriesSplit** to better distribute your data: `https://www.kaggle.com/code/jorijnsmit/found-the-holy-grail-grouptimeseriessplit/notebook`.

Summary

In this chapter, I helped you navigate through the complex landscape of developing and implementing a robust trading strategy, right from understanding the system's essentials to conducting backtests, forward tests, and even paper trading before plunging into the live market scenario.

My goal for this chapter was to ensure you gain a comprehensive understanding of trading strategy development, with a particular focus on identifying trading patterns, defining critical entry and exit points, evaluating strategies via backtesting and forward testing, simulating real-time trading through paper trading, and finally, applying the tested strategy in live action.

In the next chapter, we're going deep, right into the art of coding and automating your strategy. Prepare for the geeky part of the trading process.

8
Automated Trading

In this chapter, we are going to delve into the technical side of trading strategies by focusing on the process of coding. Our journey will begin with creating a custom indicator in **TradingView**, a platform renowned for its robust charting capabilities and custom scripting language, **Pine Script**. Crafting your own indicator can empower you with the ability to analyze markets in ways that align with your unique trading philosophy.

Following that, we will move on to the task of coding a strategy in **Freqtrade**, an open source algorithmic trading bot that supports cryptocurrency trading. With Freqtrade, we can take our custom strategies and convert them into algorithmic trading bots capable of executing trades 24/7 with precision and speed. This section is not merely about writing code but also about combining your trading ideas with technical execution to create powerful, automated trading systems.

Whether you are a seasoned coder or a novice in the field, my goal for this chapter is not to teach you how to code or about the inner workings of Pine Script but to show you its potential and how you can take advantage of it later, after you have your own working strategy that you trade manually. I'm not expecting you to understand all the coding that's happening here; this is not a book about coding, but as long as you know the tools presented here exist, you'll be able to come back to them when the time is right. Having a tool to test your strategies automatically and to deploy them 24/7 is a unique angle to trading and you should take advantage of it!

Here are the topics we'll be covering:

- Coding trading strategies – from Pine Script to Python and beyond
- Coding an indicator in TradingView
- Coding a strategy in Freqtrade
- Trading ideas

Technical requirements

As Freqtrade uses Python, a basic understanding of Python is a prerequisite. This book does not cover Python programming; however, I've provided a link to an Udemy course titled *Cryptocurrency algorithmic trading with Python and Binance* that will expedite your Python learning journey, covering Python, Pandas, algorithmic trading, and statistics.

Let's start!

Coding trading strategies – from Pine Script to Python and beyond

In the intermediate phase of my trading journey, I found myself crafting Pine Script indicators and strategies for clients. Pine Script is the coding language used to create custom indicators on the TradingView platform. Initially, I began this journey by developing tools for my friends in our private trading circle. As my proficiency grew, my clientele expanded through their endorsements.

Interestingly, many of the strategies proposed by my clients were not profitable. While these strategies had shown promising results over one or two months during the manual development and backtesting stages, they often failed to generate profits when deployed live. At times, any profits realized were more attributable to Bitcoin's general bullish trend rather than the efficacy of the strategy. However, amidst this sea of underperforming strategies, some stellar performers sustained profitability over the years. The majority of the strategies found their niche in specific market conditions, exhibiting profitability either during bull or bear markets, generating moderate returns monthly, or showing high profitability with an inherent risk of significant initial **drawdown** (a drawdown is a decrease in the capital, which, when it occurs right at the beginning of testing, reduces your starting balance, thus making recovery of losses more challenging.).

The game-changer in my journey was the transition from Pine Script to Python. Python unlocked a universe of advanced tools and techniques, including statistical analysis, correlation studies, and advanced mathematical models. This level of sophistication facilitated the creation of highly accurate strategies and allowed for precise replication of their results. However, Pine Script remains a highly accessible language for beginners and is widely adopted among traders. Moreover, it offers a treasure trove of pre-built strategies ripe for tweaking and customization, making it an excellent starting point for this journey.

We will commence with price-derived indicators and strategies, a common approach among trading coders. However, I would like to challenge you to venture beyond the conventional. Once you gain confidence with price-based indicators, consider exploring information not directly derived from price. We have an array of data streams at our disposal, such as news, market sentiment, social media influence, economic calendars, announcements from the Federal Reserve, and more. However, traders often limit themselves to **Open, High, Low, Close** (OHLC) data, neglecting valuable insights from these additional sources.

Unlocking these alternative perspectives is akin to reaching a level-3 quest in algorithmic trading. However, let me reassure you that this journey doesn't demand deep coding expertise. Even creating a basic indicator that distinguishes bullish, bearish, or sideways trends could be invaluable for your strategy. The consistency of applying the same code across different strategies will lend a sense of stability in the unpredictable world of trading.

Many traders still follow traditional indicators, some dating back to the 1950s and even earlier. For instance, Ralph Elliot's *Elliot Waves theory* is still prevalent, despite its creator passing away in 1948 and the method's statistical shortcomings. Similarly, indicators such as the **stochastic oscillator**, the **Relative Strength Index** (**RSI**), the **Moving Average Convergence Divergence** (**MACD**), and the **On-Balance Volume** (**OBV**), all developed between the 1950s and 1970s, continue to be widely used.

In today's world, the creation of new indicators is commonplace. However, like the underappreciation of contemporary art in favor of classical masterpieces, the vast array of modern indicators often remains unexplored. The challenge lies in sifting through the sea of indicators to find the one that truly adds value to your trading strategy.

Coding an indicator in TradingView

Pine Script, the scripting language native to TradingView, allows users to construct their unique indicators and strategies. It operates on TradingView's servers, meaning it doesn't burden your machine's resources beyond displaying data, and the scripts are stored on TradingView. Furthermore, TradingView offers access to over 100,000 community scripts.

As of the time of writing this book, Pine Script is in its fifth version, which will be the focus of our discussion. Importantly, with each new version, backward compatibility is maintained, enabling the running of older scripts. While I have updated some strategies from V3 to V4 and subsequently to V5, others remain in their V4 form.

However, it's essential to clarify that this book will not delve deeply into Pine Script. My aim is to introduce you to Pine Script, show you how to modify existing scripts to create your own, and provide resources for further learning. The primary focus of this book isn't on coding in Pine Script.

Editing existing indicators

Let's go to TradingView and open an advanced chart for a market, let's say BTCBUSD on 4H, and click on the **Pine Editor** tab in the lower bar of the screen. On the right side, go to **Open | Indicator**, and you will get this output:

Figure 8.1 – Pine Editor | indicator template

This is the empty template of code found there:

```
// This source code is subject to the terms of the Mozilla Public
License 2.0 at https://mozilla.org/MPL/2.0/
// © vaidab

//@version=5
indicator("My script")
plot(close)
```

The code tells us that you'll be using V5 of the scripting language and that the name of the indicator is My script and it will plot the close of the candle.

Now click the **Add to chart** button on the left and voilá, you now have your script results displayed under your main chart. You can close it with the **X** that appears when you hover over the chart or the other **X** that appears when you hover over the script's name. Let's close it for now:

Figure 8.2 – My script, added to the chart

Now, let's say that you have an indicator such as **Hull Moving Average** (**HMA**) that you are using in your trading. HMA is a type of moving average that was developed by Alan Hull. It is a highly effective tool in identifying the current market trend more quickly than other moving averages, yet without sacrificing smoothness.

Add it with the **Indicators** button in the upper-right menu (or press the shortcut /). Then, go to its name in the upper-left part of the chart and click the {} button. This will open its code.

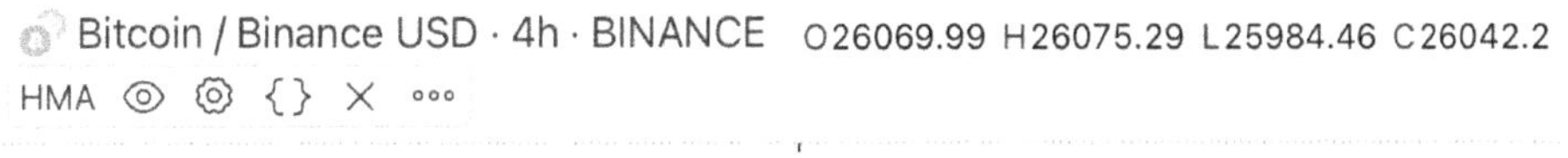

Bitcoin / Binance USD · 4h · BINANCE   O26069.99 H26075.29 L25984.46 C26042.2

HMA ◎ ◎ {} ✕ °°°

Figure 8.3 – HMA source code and X buttons

This is what its source code looks like:

```
//@version=5
indicator(title="Hull Moving Average", shorttitle="HMA", overlay=true,
timeframe="", timeframe_gaps=true)
length = input.int(9, minval=1)
src = input(close, title="Source")
hullma = ta.wma(2*ta.wma(src, length/2)-ta.wma(src, length), math.
floor(math.sqrt(length)))
plot(hullma)
```

The title is Hull Moving Average and overlay=true means that it will be displayed on the main chart.

The indicator takes two inputs, a length value (integer), representing the historical candles taken into account, and a Source value (which can be OHLC, open-only, close-only, or other combinations), which is used to take the values from.

Then the value of each candle is calculated by a weighted moving average formula and the results are plotted.

> **Note**
> For a more in-depth understanding of each function, I encourage you to refer to the *Pine Script Reference Manual* (and *User Manual*). You'll find the links later in the chapter. For the time being, my aim is to provide a glimpse of the potential that Pine Script holds.

You can use ChatGPT to walk you through an explanation of what the code does, like in this figure:

 Walk me through this code:

```
//@version=5
indicator(title="Hull Moving Average", shorttitle="HMA", overlay=true, timeframe="",
timeframe_gaps=true)
length = input.int(9, minval=1)
src = input(close, title="Source")
hullma = ta.wma(2*ta.wma(src, length/2)-ta.wma(src, length), math.floor(math.sqrt(length)))
plot(hullma)
```

 This Pine Script code is calculating the Hull Moving Average (HMA) for a given length and then plotting it on the chart. Let's break down the code to understand it better.

1. `//@version=5`

   This line defines the version of Pine Script that is being used. In this case, it's version 5.

2. `indicator(title="Hull Moving Average", shorttitle="HMA", overlay=true, timeframe="", timeframe_gaps=true)`

   This function creates a new indicator with the full title "Hull Moving Average" and short

Figure 8.4 – Using ChatGPT to understand code

Next, remove the HMA indicator from the upper-left part of the chart but keep the code and make a copy by clicking on its name, under the **Pine Editor** button. Rename it to `Private HMA v1`.

Change the line starting with `length` to the following:

```
length = input.int(12, minval=1)
```

Click **Save** and **Add to chart**.

This is how it will look:

Figure 8.5 – HMA with modified defaults

Now you have your own HMA indicator which defaults to a length of 12 (it takes a larger period into consideration when making the calculations).

You can use Pine Script to see how an indicator works *"under the hood"* and to go through the formula manually, change default script settings, add alarms to indicators that you're using, connect two or more indicators to one indicator that's fit for your trading style, and create strategies (indicators that have trading logic that allows them to be backward-tested and forward-tested).

> **Note**
>
> I'm using the term strategy interchangeably to refer to a (1) trading strategy and (2) TradingView strategy. The first one represents the strategy you're developing for trading (the specific filters and entry and exit criteria), while the second one represents a way of writing scripts that can show the results if you have entered and exited trades when the script told you so (all automated by TradingView). You'll understand from the context to which I'm referring.

Making your own indicator

Add the following code to a new script. You get a new script by deleting everything, clicking to the three dots on the right of the Pine Script window, and clicking **Save script as....** to give it a new name:

```
//@version=5
indicator("Private MA Cross Indicator")
shortLen = 9
longLen = 21
shortMA = ta.sma(close, shortLen)
longMA = ta.sma(close, longLen)
plot(shortMA, color = #9e2f24)
plot(longMA, color = #228227)
isCross = ta.cross(shortMA, longMA)
plot(isCross ? shortMA : na, color=#144ce7, style = plot.style_cross,
linewidth = 6)
```

This indicator will not be overlayed and, in its chart, it will put crosses on the intersection of MA 9 with MA 21.

Add this line at the end to be able to create a custom alert at the EMA intersection:

```
alertcondition(isCross, title="Enter trade")
```

That is it. Save it and you'll be able to add the **Enter trade** custom alert when adding an alert on the chart. Note that the final code can also be found in the `PrivateMACrossIndicatorWithAlert.psl` file on GitHub.

The next figure shows what everything looks like, in the end:

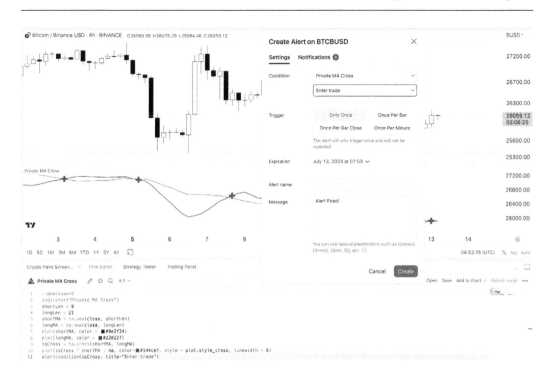

Figure 8.6 – Private MA cross indicator with alert

Of course, from here, things can get complicated, but if you code your indicators step by step, in no time, you'll be able to create the tools that can complement your trading.

Converting an indicator into a strategy

The beauty of TradingView is that we can quickly add trade logic to our indicator and transform it into a (TradingView) strategy, which we can test.

In order to do that, we add a few lines of code to our previous indicator. Let's say that we go long when the short moving average crosses over the long moving average and we go short when it crosses under the long moving average.

In order to do this, we change from the `indicator()` function to the `strategy()` function and add the trading logic.

Here it is:

```
//@version=5
strategy("Private MA Cross Strategy")
shortLen = 9
longLen = 21
startDate = timestamp("01 Jan 2022 00:00")
endDate = timestamp("31 Dec 2022 23:59")

shortMA = ta.sma(close, shortLen)
longMA = ta.sma(close, longLen)
plot(shortMA, color = #9e2f24)
plot(longMA, color = #228227)

inDateRange = (time >= startDate) and (time < endDate)

if (ta.crossover(shortMA, longMA) and inDateRange)
    strategy.entry("long", strategy.long)
if (ta.crossunder(shortMA, longMA) and inDateRange)
    strategy.entry("short", strategy.short)

isCross = ta.cross(shortMA, longMA)
plot(isCross ? shortMA : na, color=#144ce7, style = plot.style_cross,
linewidth = 6)
```

I added a time range for our strategy (so it can test a specific period) and the conditions for going long and going short. When the short MA crosses over the long MA, it goes long, and when it crosses under, it switches to short. Since we're always either in a long or a short, we don't need logic for closing trades; we're just switching directions.

If we run this strategy on BTCBUSD 4H and go to the **Strategy Tester** tab, we'd get a -1% net profit. If we switch to the 1H tab, we'd get a 0.02%-0.03% net profit:

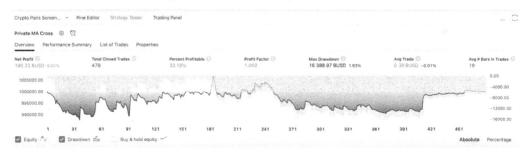

Figure 8.7 – Strategy Tester results

So it's not profitable, right?

Well… let me change that for you. Update the timestamps to the following:

```
startDate = timestamp("27 Mar 2020 00:00")
endDate = timestamp("27 Mar 2021 23:59")
```

Now, go to BTCBUSD 1D and you get a 2.61% net profit.

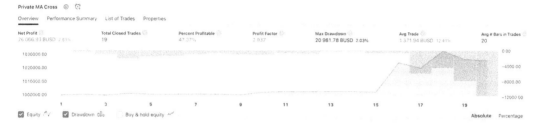

Figure 8.8 – Strategy showing profit

Next, comment out the lines where our strategy goes short and add an exit condition instead:

```
// if (ta.crossunder(shortMA, longMA) and inDateRange)
//     strategy.entry("short", strategy.short)
if (strategy.position_size > 0 and ta.crossunder(shortMA, longMA))
    strategy.exit(id="exit long", stop=close)
```

And voilá! A 3.74% profit in 1 year on BTCBUSD 4H. Take a look at the following graph for the output.

Note that percentages might differ lightly:

Figure 8.9 – Strategy showing even more profit

That's not much, but I can tweak the strategy to show you 20% or even 100% profitability.

… and I'd be lying.

Because what I'd do is just overfit the strategy to the specific market I'd be testing it in.

Change the first line in your strategy to this one:

```
strategy("Private MA Cross Strategy", default_qty_value=100000)
```

Now, it looks like this:

```
//@version=5
strategy("Private MA Cross Strategy", default_qty_value=100000)
shortLen = 9
longLen = 21
startDate = timestamp("27 Mar 2020 00:00")
endDate = timestamp("27 Mar 2021 23:59")

shortMA = ta.sma(close, shortLen)
longMA = ta.sma(close, longLen)
plot(shortMA, color = #9e2f24)
plot(longMA, color = #228227)

inDateRange = (time >= startDate) and (time < endDate)

if (ta.crossover(shortMA, longMA) and inDateRange)
    strategy.entry("long", strategy.long)
// if (ta.crossunder(shortMA, longMA) and inDateRange)
    // strategy.entry("short", strategy.short)
if (strategy.position_size > 0 and ta.crossunder(shortMA, longMA))
    strategy.exit(id="exit long", stop=close)

isCross = ta.cross(shortMA, longMA)
plot(isCross ? shortMA : na, color=#144ce7, style = plot.style_cross,
linewidth = 6)
```

Compile it and... oh my god! It brings you a 374,353.5% net profit!!!!!! You must sell your apartment and bet everything on these lines of code!

Here's what it looks like visually:

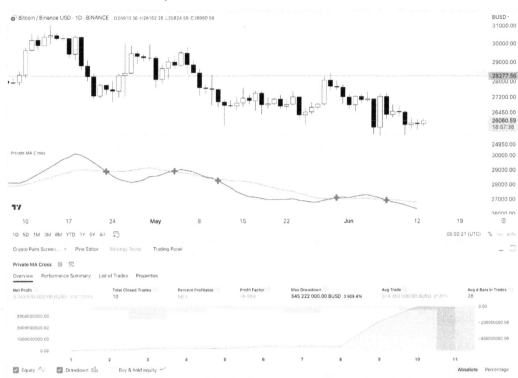

Figure 8.10 – Are you really betting your house on this?

(And, of course, we ignore **Max Drawdown**, which shows how amateur our thinking is. We want followers, after all.)

I'll leave you to understand for yourself what happened here and why this result was displayed. It's your time to shine now.

Note that you can also find the code in the `PrivateMACrossStrategy.psl` file at the GitHub link.

What I'm trying to say in this example is never trust results that somebody else shows you. Understand what they are trying to do and try to recreate their strategies. Notice how they "*forget*" to test in specific market conditions or how they "*overlook*" situations where the strategy drawdown would create enough loss for you to have to recover for years before you got profitable. Remember the example in which I just added one option to a function and disguised a strategy as being profitable?

You'll need to do the work here, and this is what the work looks like:

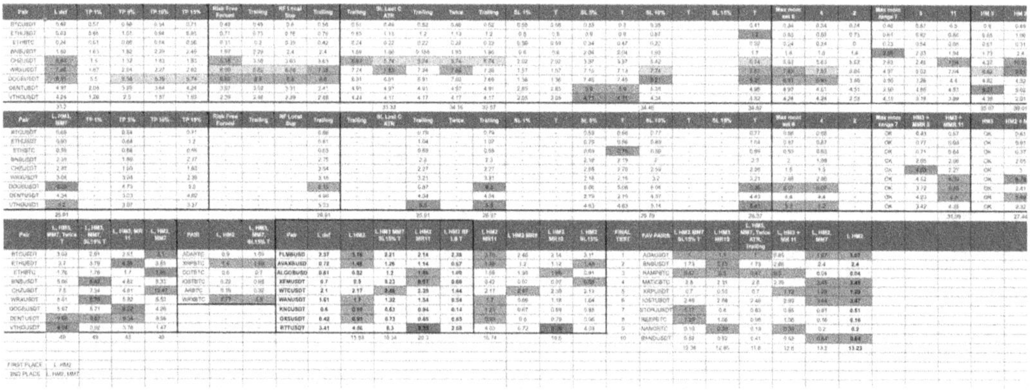

Figure 8.11 – "The work"

Caveats when coding Pine Script strategies

Here's a list of issues and things to take into account when you use the Pine Script/**Strategy Tester** combination:

- Conditions are calculated at bar close (so you will have situations when entries and exits would be triggered in real life but they wouldn't be in the script). This can be circumvented by forward-testing with `calc_on_every_tick`.

- The lack of intrabar calculations (did the price go from Open to High or to Low first?).

- The preceding situations lead to repainting (situations where the indicator showed a specific entry point and, after a while, it displayed another entry point instead). It *"looked into the future."*

- Testing with other types of candles.

- Peeking into the future: `https://www.tradingview.com/support/solutions/43000614705-strategy-produces-unrealistically-good-results-by-peeking-into-the-future/`.

Linking the strategy to a 3Commas bot

A nice feature that 3Commas offers us is the ability to connect to your TradingView indicator.

Here's an article that provides step-by-step instructions on how to connect the Hash Ribbons indicator to 3Commas – `https://3commas.io/blog/using-the-hash-ribbon-to-start-bot-deals` – and its knowledge base article that explains the process in detail: `https://help.3commas.io/en/articles/3108938-how-to-use-tradingview-custom-signals`.

What this means is that once we figure out a profitable indicator, we can code it using Pine Script, add alerts to it that trigger 3Commas signals, and we've just created an automated trading bot.

Some of my clients had strategies that they had been trading manually for years before I gave them this idea. You know the kind, the old-school traders that had an edge figured out and then they stuck with it. Well... automating that edge has now become simple to do, so why not have a bot trade for you while you sleep?

Now, let's venture into the next phase of our journey – coding your strategy in Freqtrade, a toolkit that provides you with an arsenal to fully backtest, automate, and deploy your trading strategy.

Coding a strategy in Freqtrade

Having written numerous strategies for TradingView, I noticed a degree of dissatisfaction among some of my clients. Their meticulously crafted strategies, once thought to be effective, fell short of expectations. While these strategies did generate the anticipated entry and exit points, they invariably led to financial losses when tested over more substantial periods and sample sizes.

They were losing due to statistics.

For instance, a strategy might show promising profitability, but if it's accompanied by substantial drawdowns, its practical implementation becomes exceedingly risky. Consider a scenario in which the strategy suffers a 25% loss in the first month, reducing the capital from $10,000 to $7,500. In such a situation, it would need a 34% return just to break even.

There are other issues such as days in drawdown or weeks with no trades, which can affect your psyche if you're live-trading.

Of course, every problem has a solution. For instance, if you're using a trend trading algorithm, you can complement it with a mean reversion strategy that exhibits a negative correlation to your initial trend trading approach. Alternatively, you could sacrifice returns in order to reduce risk, or slowly close positions during drawdown. However, you might also be **overfitting**. Overfitting means creating a trading strategy that performs very well on past data but fails to predict future market performance due to its specificity to the historical dataset. Basically, you are tuning your strategy so that your past results are good.

I personally keep the drawdown less than 20% during backtesting, which gives me a less than 30% drawdown during live trades, but that is not a rule. There are other high-risk, high-reward strategies that have a bigger drawdown.

In order to understand all of this, I recommend you delve deeper into the world of statistics and finance fundamentals. I have put some links in the *Further reading* section, that you might find helpful.

I could delve deeply into statistics, but I want this book to be concise and straightforward. Therefore, I'll focus on Freqtrade, an outstanding tool I'm highlighting here. Freqtrade not only allows you to develop and test trading strategies but also facilitates in-depth analysis of the results. Moreover, it can automatically execute your strategies, making it a complete environment for algorithmic trading.

Freqtrade intro

Freqtrade is a robust, open source trading bot specifically designed for cryptocurrency trading. It's built using Python and comes bundled with everything you need to craft a strategy from pandas and Jupyter Notebook to the libraries required for backtesting, plotting entries, and interfacing with multiple crypto exchanges. Additionally, it offers advanced features such as AI automation, parameter optimization, and various other modules.

Take note, Freqtrade is not a subscription-based service selling a *"profitable"* trading bot. I've extensively tested such bots and, in my experience, their profitability is overhyped or context-dependent. In contrast, Freqtrade is a toolkit that empowers traders with all the tools necessary to vet and deploy automated strategies for successfully trading crypto.

Its official website, `https://www.freqtrade.io`, is rich with detailed information, as shown in the following screenshot. I strongly recommend perusing it once before delving into this section. You may not grasp everything at first glance, but revisiting relevant sections while reading this book will help you connect the dots.

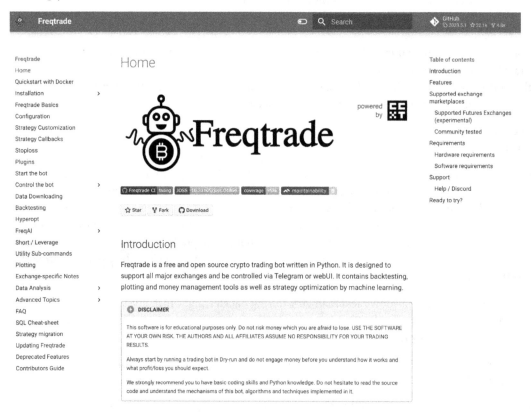

Figure 8.12 – The Freqtrade website

If you find coding uncomfortable, feel free to skim through this chapter and revisit it when you're ready to bring your profitable strategies to life.

Directions for installation and configuration

Since the software is frequently updated, relying on its up-to-date online resources ensures you're following the most current installation process. Visit its GitHub page (`https://github.com/freqtrade/freqtrade`) for the latest release and installation instructions and also use its Discord server (`https://www.freqtrade.io/en/stable/#help-discord`) if you need assistance or have specific queries.

I strongly suggest setting up Freqtrade with Docker (`https://www.docker.com/`) on a remote virtual machine, which is capable of running the bots continuously, 24/7. Many of my coaching clients have successfully utilized servers from Amazon AWS (`https://aws.amazon.com/`), Oracle (`https://www.oracle.com/`), and Contabo (`http://contabo.com`).

The 10 basic steps to get a Freqtrade instance running are as follows:

1. Get a remote server or virtual machine (optional).
2. Install Docker.
3. Download the latest stable Freqtrade version.
4. Configure Freqtrade.
5. Run it inside Docker.
6. Connect to the user interface.
7. Download data for the pairs and timeframes that you'll be trading.
8. Create a strategy.
9. Backtest, plot results, update strategy, backtest, plot, optimize, backtest, and so on.
10. Run a live instance connected to Telegram to get notifications.

Here is an article detailing a quick-start installation via Docker: `https://www.freqtrade.io/en/stable/docker_quickstart/`.

A few quirks that need your attention (and that might be resolved by the time you're reading this book) are these:

- Read the docs on downloading data and download data for trading pairs in advance so that you can backtest your strategies quickly.

- Hyperopt takes a lot of processing power; once you're profitable, you might want to have a virtual machine with multiple cores that will continuously run Hyperopt on your strategies and that you don't use for anything else.

- Always search GitHub and Discord for issues you encounter; most of them already have an answer there.

- The indicators used are not always 100% correlated with TradingView's indicators. Small differences in the algorithm might produce totally different results, so I recommend you plot via Freqtrade if you trade via it.

- Mastering this tool requires time and patience, so take it slow and do not rush through the process.

Creating your own strategy

You can find the strategies inside the Freqtrade directory, in `user_data/strategies`, with `SampleStrategy` (`sample_strategy.py`) provided as an example.

```python
# pragma pylint: disable=missing-docstring, invalid-name, pointless-string-statement
# flake8: noqa: F401
# isort: skip_file
# --- Do not remove these libs ---
import numpy as np  # noqa
import pandas as pd  # noqa
from pandas import DataFrame

from freqtrade.strategy import (BooleanParameter, CategoricalParameter, DecimalParameter,
                                IStrategy, IntParameter)


# --------------------------------
# Add your lib to import here
import talib.abstract as ta
import freqtrade.vendor.qtpylib.indicators as qtpylib


# This class is a sample. Feel free to customize it.
class SampleStrategy(IStrategy):
    """
    This is a sample strategy to inspire you.
    More information in https://www.freqtrade.io/en/latest/strategy-customization/

    You can:
        :return: a Dataframe with all mandatory indicators for the strategies
        - Rename the class name (Do not forget to update class_name)
        - Add any methods you want to build your strategy
        - Add any lib you need to build your strategy

    You must keep:
    - the lib in the section "Do not remove these libs"
    - the methods: populate_indicators, populate_entry_trend, populate_exit_trend
    You should keep:
    - timeframe, minimal_roi, stoploss, trailing_*
    """
    # Strategy interface version - allow new iterations of the strategy interface.
    # Check the documentation or the Sample strategy to get the latest version.
    INTERFACE_VERSION = 3

    # Can this strategy go short?
    can_short: bool = False

    # Minimal ROI designed for the strategy.
    # This attribute will be overridden if the config file contains "minimal_roi".
    minimal_roi = {
        "60": 0.01,
        "30": 0.02,
        "0": 0.04
    }

    # Optimal stoploss designed for the strategy.
    # This attribute will be overridden if the config file contains "stoploss".
    stoploss = -0.10

    # Trailing stoploss
    trailing_stop = False
    # trailing_only_offset_is_reached = False
    # trailing_stop_positive = 0.01
    # trailing_stop_positive_offset = 0.0  # Disabled / not configured

    # Optimal timeframe for the strategy.
    timeframe = '5m'
```

Figure 8.13 – SampleStrategy

Here is also a list of strategies already coded for Freqtrade that you can take a look at and modify at your convenience: `https://github.com/freqtrade/freqtrade-strategies/tree/main/user_data/strategies`. Remember the code that gave us 374,353.5% net profit in Trading View? It functioned by purchasing at a moving average crossover and selling when a crossover occurred in the reverse direction. It looked like this:

```
//@version=5
strategy("Private MA Cross", default_qty_value=100000)
shortLen = 9
longLen = 21
startDate = timestamp("27 Mar 2020 00:00")
endDate = timestamp("27 Mar 2021 23:59")

shortMA = ta.sma(close, shortLen)
longMA = ta.sma(close, longLen)
plot(shortMA, color = #9e2f24)
plot(longMA, color = #228227)

inDateRange = (time >= startDate) and (time < endDate)

if (ta.crossover(shortMA, longMA) and inDateRange)
    strategy.entry("long", strategy.long)
// if (ta.crossunder(shortMA, longMA) and inDateRange)
    // strategy.entry("short", strategy.short)
if (strategy.position_size > 0 and ta.crossunder(shortMA, longMA))
    strategy.exit(id="exit long", stop=close)

isCross = ta.cross(shortMA, longMA)
plot(isCross ? shortMA : na, color=#144ce7, style = plot.style_cross,
linewidth = 6)
```

I'm going to transition this into Freqtrade. Bear in mind that there will be some variances, but my intention is to show how it looks in Python and how the backtesting results appear. At this point in the chapter, I don't expect you to grasp every single detail (unlike in the earlier chapters). Rather, my aim here is for you to follow along, gaining an understanding of the general concept and the direction we're heading in.

The following is the Python code for Freqtrade. It's pretty big, so I broke it down into sections:

```
# --- Do not remove these libs ---
import numpy as np  # noqa
import pandas as pd  # noqa
from pandas import DataFrame

from freqtrade.strategy import (BooleanParameter,
```

```
                    CategoricalParameter, DecimalParameter,
                                            IStrategy, IntParameter)

                    # -------------------------------
                    # Add your lib to import here
                    import talib.abstract as ta
                    import freqtrade.vendor.qtpylib.indicators as qtpylib
                    from functools import reduce
```

We can leave the initial imports as they are:

```
                    class PrivateMACross(IStrategy):
                        INTERFACE_VERSION = 3
```

We're using the latest version of the Freqtrade interface, v3. We will use the class name, `PrivateMACross`, to call the strategy from the command line:

```
                        timeframe = '1d'
                        ma_short = 9
                        ma_long = 21

                        startup_candle_count: int = ma_long
                        can_short: bool = False
```

We are running this strategy at a daily timeframe by default and using moving averages 9 and 21 for it. The last two lines tell us that we need at least 21 candles loaded before we take any action and that this strategy can't short:

```
                        minimal_roi = {
                            "0": 10.5
                        }

                        stoploss = -1.0
                        trailing_stop = False

                        process_only_new_candles = False

                        use_exit_signal = True
                        exit_profit_only = False
                        ignore_roi_if_entry_signal = False
```

We don't use `minimal_roi`, `stoploss`, `trailing_stop`, and so on. If you're wondering how they work, all of these parameters can be found on the Freqtrade website with detailed explanations and examples (`http://freqtrade.io`):

```python
order_types = {
    'entry': 'market',
    'exit': 'market',
    'stoploss': 'market',
    'stoploss_on_exchange': False
}

order_time_in_force = {
    'entry': 'gtc',
    'exit': 'gtc'
}

plot_config = {
    'main_plot': {
        f'sma_short_9': {'color': 'red'},
        f'sma_long_21': {'color': 'yellow'}
    }
}

def informative_pairs(self):
    return []
```

We left the defaults for the orders and added the moving averages to `plot_config` so that we can plot the entries if we want to.

Next, we fill a dataframe with the values of the moving averages:

```python
def populate_indicators(self, dataframe: DataFrame, metadata:
dict) -> DataFrame:
    dataframe['sma_short_9'] = ta.SMA(dataframe, timeperiod=self.
ma_short)
    dataframe['sma_long_21'] = ta.SMA(dataframe, timeperiod=self.
ma_long)
    return dataframe

def populate_entry_trend(self, dataframe: DataFrame, metadata:
dict) -> DataFrame:
    conditions_long = []
    conditions_long.append(qtpylib.crossed_above(
        dataframe[f'sma_short_9'].shift(1),
        dataframe[f'sma_long_21'].shift(1)
```

```
            ))

        if conditions_long:
            dataframe.loc[
                    reduce(lambda x, y: x & y, conditions_long),
                    'enter_long'] = 1

        return dataframe
```

`populate_entry_trend()` is the function that sets the buying conditions. Here, it will trigger a long every time MA 9 crosses MA 21:

```
    def populate_exit_trend(self, dataframe: DataFrame, metadata:
dict) -> DataFrame:
        conditions_exit_long = []
        conditions_exit_long.append(qtpylib.crossed_above(
            dataframe[f'sma_long_21'],
            dataframe[f'sma_short_9']
            ))

        if conditions_exit_long:
            dataframe.loc[
                    reduce(lambda x, y: x & y, conditions_exit_long),
                    'exit_long'] = 1

        return dataframe
```

And finally, we exit when MA 9 crosses below MA 21.

You can find the code in the `PrivateMACross.py` file in the `Chapter_08` folder on GitHub.

Basically, just as in our TradingView strategy, we buy every time SMA 9 crosses over SMA 21 in the time range 27 March 2020, 00:00 to 27 March 2021, 23:59 on BTCBUSD 1D and we sell when SMA 21 crosses over SMA 9.

Next, we backtest it:

```
docker-compose run --rm freqtrade backtesting --config user_data/
config/config-backtesting-book.json --strategy PrivateMACross
--timerange 20200327-20210328 --timeframe 1d -p BTC/BUSD
```

And here's the output:

```
Result for strategy PrivateMACross
================================================================== BACKTESTING REPORT =======================================================================
|    Pair    | Entries | Avg Profit % | Cum Profit % | Tot Profit BUSD | Tot Profit % |   Avg Duration    | Win Draw Loss Win% |
|------------|---------|--------------|--------------|-----------------|--------------|-------------------|--------------------|
| BTC/BUSD   |    8    |    31.67     |    253.36    |   253602.486    |    25.36     | 29 days, 15:00:00 |  5    0    3  62.5  |
|   TOTAL    |    8    |    31.67     |    253.35    |   253602.486    |    25.36     | 29 days, 15:00:00 |  5    0    3  62.5  |
=================================================================== LEFT OPEN TRADES REPORT ===================================================================
|   Pair   | Entries | Avg Profit % | Cum Profit % | Tot Profit BUSD | Tot Profit % |   Avg Duration    | Win Draw Loss Win% |
|----------|---------|--------------|--------------|-----------------|--------------|-------------------|--------------------|
|  TOTAL   |    0    |     0.00     |     0.00     |      0.000      |     0.00     |      0:00         |  0    0    0   0   |
==================================================================== ENTER TAG STATS =========================================================================
|  TAG   | Entries | Avg Profit % | Cum Profit % | Tot Profit BUSD | Tot Profit % |   Avg Duration    | Win Draw Loss Win% |
|--------|---------|--------------|--------------|-----------------|--------------|-------------------|--------------------|
| TOTAL  |    8    |    31.67     |    253.35    |   253602.486    |    25.36     | 29 days, 15:00:00 |  5    0    3  62.5  |
===================================================================== EXIT REASON STATS =======================================================================
|  Exit Reason  | Exits | Win Draws Loss Win% | Avg Profit % | Cum Profit % | Tot Profit BUSD | Tot Profit % |
|---------------|-------|---------------------|--------------|--------------|-----------------|--------------|
|  exit_signal  |   8   |  5    0    3  62.5  |    31.67     |    253.35    |     253602      |    253.35    |
==================================== SUMMARY METRICS ==================================
| Metric                      | Value                  |
|-----------------------------|------------------------|
| Backtesting from            | 2020-03-27 00:00:00    |
| Backtesting to              | 2021-03-28 00:00:00    |
| Max open trades             | 1                      |
|                             |                        |
| Total/Daily Avg Trades      | 8 / 0.02               |
| Starting balance            | 1000000 BUSD           |
| Final balance               | 1253602.486 BUSD       |
| Absolute profit             | 253602.486 BUSD        |
| Total profit %              | 25.36%                 |
| CAGR %                      | 27.01%                 |
| Sortino                     | 8.12                   |
| Sharpe                      | 0.23                   |
| Calmar                      | 357.67                 |
| Profit factor               | 34.47                  |
| Expectancy                  | 12.55                  |
| Trades per day              | 0.02                   |
| Avg. daily profit %         | 0.07%                  |
| Avg. stake amount           | 99999.989 BUSD         |
| Total trade volume          | 799999.269 BUSD        |
|                             |                        |
| Best Pair                   | BTC/BUSD 253.35%       |
| Worst Pair                  | BTC/BUSD 253.35%       |
| Best trade                  | BTC/BUSD 191.31%       |
| Worst trade                 | BTC/BUSD -4.94%        |
| Best day                    | 191498.977 BUSD        |
| Worst day                   | -4941.581 BUSD         |
| Days win/draw/lose          | 5 / 297 / 3            |
| Avg. Duration Winners       | 40 days, 9:36:00       |
| Avg. Duration Loser         | 11 days, 16:00:00      |
| Rejected Entry signals      | 0                      |
| Entry/Exit Timeouts         | 0 / 0                  |
|                             |                        |
| Min balance                 | 1014845.847 BUSD       |
| Max balance                 | 1258544.067 BUSD       |
| Max % of account underwater | 0.39%                  |
| Absolute Drawdown (Account) | 0.39%                  |
| Absolute Drawdown           | 4941.581 BUSD          |
| Drawdown high               | 258544.067 BUSD        |
| Drawdown low                | 253602.486 BUSD        |
| Drawdown Start              | 2021-03-02 00:00:00    |
| Drawdown End                | 2021-03-27 00:00:00    |
| Market change               | 775.84%                |
=====================================================================

Backtested 2020-03-27 00:00:00 -> 2021-03-28 00:00:00 | Max open trades : 1
================================================================ STRATEGY SUMMARY ============================================================================
|   Strategy     | Entries | Avg Profit % | Cum Profit % | Tot Profit BUSD | Tot Profit % |   Avg Duration    | Win Draw Loss Win% |    Drawdown     |
|----------------|---------|--------------|--------------|-----------------|--------------|-------------------|--------------------|-----------------|
| PrivateMACross |    8    |    31.67     |    253.35    |   253602.486    |    25.36     | 29 days, 15:00:00 |  5    0    3  62.5 | 4941.581 BUSD 0.39% |
=====================================================================
```

Figure 8.14 – Backtesting PrivateMACross in a bull market

We have 8 entries with a 62.5% win rate, a total profit of 25.36%, a cumulative profit of 253.35%, and a drawdown of 0.39%. That's because we caught the entire bull run in our time range. Congratulations :)

Looks like a good strategy, right?

But what would a bear market look like?

```
docker-compose run --rm freqtrade backtesting --config user_data/
config/config-backtesting-book.json --strategy PrivateMACross
--timerange 20210811-20220812 --timeframe 1d -p BTC/BUSD
```

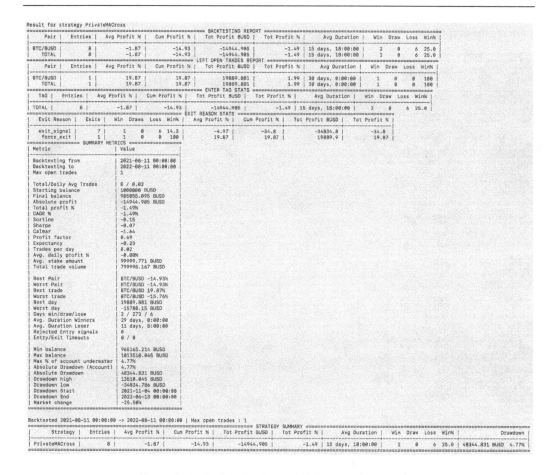

Figure 8.15 – Backtesting PrivateMACross in a bear market

Here, we've still got 8 entries but with a total 25% win rate, a profit of -1.49%, and a cumulative profit of -14.93%.

(Note that if you want to go down the rabbit hole, just add `--timeframe-detail 30m` to the backtesting process. Suddenly, the results vary. I'll let you figure out why.)

So… in a bull market, this strategy provides a clear win, and in a bear market, a clear loss. Guess you'll need to figure out when they happen, right?

The core objective when developing your own strategy is to pinpoint a set of straightforward rules that yields solid results without precipitating massive drawdowns. The trick is to analyze the trades that fail and devise additional rules to filter those out while avoiding overfitting. Begin with a simple, profitable system and then backtest it and observe its performance in a paper-trading environment.

Next, establish rules that the system must invariably follow or avoid. This not only preserves the profitable strategy but also enhances its **return on investment** (**ROI**). Any objective input added should be rigorously tested to confirm its positive impact before it's permanently incorporated, as these are the elements that can lead to overfitting during backtesting.

Crafting a strategy in Freqtrade entails considerable effort, including a command of Python, a deep understanding of backtesting, and a touch of statistics. However, the more you immerse yourself in the process, the more straightforward it becomes, to the point where you can swiftly evaluate strategies proposed by well-known Youtubers and find amusement in their outcomes. The task of discovering your own effective strategy is an entirely different story. It requires a fair share of sweat equity, but rest assured, it's a form of toil that pays dividends.

In the subsequent section, I'll share a few trading ideas and angles that you may consider researching and maybe transforming into trading strategies.

Trading ideas

The following is a collection of trading concepts, presented without a particular sequence. Feel free to explore and utilize any that appeal to you. However, bear in mind that you might come across some that are initially difficult to comprehend and that might require further research:

- Start easy. Learn about some good indicators for beginners such as the ones I mentioned in the indicators template provided in *Chapter 4* (and also found in the `Chapter_04` directory on GitHub).

- Most of the strategies that work in bull markets don't work in bear markets and vice versa. Instead of creating a new strategy, why not dedicate your time to defining a correct trend (bullish or bearish), maybe coding a TradingView indicator, and setting an alarm for when the trend changes? Then, you can trade (automatically) using the proper strategies for the current market. (Technically, look into **ADX**, **MA crosses and gaps**, **Hidden Markov Models**, and the **Hurst exponent**.)

- If a strategy gives very bad results, try to inverse its conditions. It's not that simple (there are other inconveniences such as fees), but see what happens.

- Many individuals, including novices and experienced traders alike, actively trade RSI divergences. Look further, maybe into indicators that work with volume, as this is an area most traders ignore. Keywords are **market profile**, **time-price-opportunity charts**, and **volume profile**. One of my ideas is that tokens with a normal trading volume move in the general market's direction and are dominated by high-frequency algorithms and institutional traders, so why not ignore them and check for a big change in volume before trading? Tokens with high volume relative to their history might move independently of the market.

- Study token launches. See how the token reacts in bull markets versus bear markets. Most tokens have a liquidity deposit at the listing, after which their price drops (because the public round investors are selling the tokens), and then the price drops some more, regularly (when public, private, and seed round investors are selling). After the coffers are dry, the token shows its potential by rising (or staying down). One of my best (manual) strategies is figuring out when the token is drained enough and starting to rise.

- Volatility trading is a good angle. Think something along the lines of if a system is X% volatile, exit after Y number of candles if at least Z% profit is gained. Instead of identifying an exit condition, find the best entry and then exit when you are profitable enough due to volatility.

- Think of BTC's volatility and its general uptrend. Why not have a pseudo-grid bot that performs a martingale-style DCA during BTC's volatility? It would suffer from heavy drops (by running out of stake) but it would work in any uptrend or sideways market and even on slow downtrend markets. Always take profit on the rise. Move it to other good coins for increased profits. (Technically, for BTC, you could use $500 buys in steps from 18k to 25k and when you successfully run this strategy, add other big tokens with good fundamentals).

- I'm a technical trader and love the calculations involved there, but there are good fundamental traders and news-based traders out there. Figure out a news source that powerfully impacts the market (such as the FED announcements or a very famous YouTuber) and backtest trades such as "*buy instantly on positive FED comment, sell after x%*" or "*wait for a YouTuber to release a video on a low cap coin and buy instantly, sell after x%.*" Make sure it works before you put it into practice. I did this from another angle: I've linked a bot to various launchpads' Telegram announcement channels and bought the instant those launchpads announced they were providing a crypto project for investment to their token holders. Here, the more creative you are, the better the returns are.

- Create a graveyard for your strategies. I have over 100 strategies in my graveyard, sorted by indicator category (and trend). When I'm bored, I venture there, feeling like Frankenstein, attempting to revive one of his creations. It sometimes works, and when it does, you have a strategy that you are familiar with.

- Modify the indicators that are already (kind of) working. Change their parameters. For example, most indicators are fit for trading the stock market, which is closed during the weekends, so they are typically trading for 22 days. Crypto trades for 30-31 days so maybe by adding more historical candles to the indicator, we can fit it into a particular cycle. That's just an idea but play with it; who knows where it could lead you.

- After a market crash, I trade a short-term mean reversion strategy around the lines of when the token falls by x% buy, sell after it gets back to x%. This strategy works when the fundamentals of the token are sound, but it has limited upside and unlimited downside. You might find yourself with a bag and you might run out of capital doing it if the market drops further. It also fails when the direction is more down than up. Think of adding a martingale strategy to it and it could work. The strategy only works because of the volatility (which is pretty big in crypto).

- Think of trading on **decentralized exchanges** (**DEXes**). There, you don't always have **Market Makers** on the listed tokens (who play with the price, affecting how the market looks) so trading is a bit more straightforward. Also, tokens that have not been listed on CEXes and that have a low market cap have the potential of doubling and even tripling in price (or they can also go to 0). Higher risk, higher reward.

- Test these scenarios: momentum strategies and the bull flag on small tokens (small caps or low volume ones), support and resistance strategies on medium tokens, and moving averages and price reversal strategies on large tokens. I'm currently running an ATR-based strategy that's focused on volatility spikes on small caps and it's pretty successful.

- Check for power plays: use **Crypto Pairs Screener** to filter for **Relative Volume** of at least **1.5**, high ATR, big volume, and a high % change. Something big is happening there; figure out what and trade it.

I want to learn more about algorithmic trading

I've mentioned that this book is not dedicated to algorithmic trading, I'm just scratching the surface, but Packt did release a relevant book: *Learn Algorithmic Trading – Build and deploy algorithmic trading systems and strategies using Python and advanced data analysis* by Sebastien Donadio and Sourav Gosh (`https://amzn.eu/d/aUOx0Kv`). It has over 350 pages talking about **algorithmic trading fundamentals**, **trading signals generation and strategies**, **algorithmic trading strategies**, **building a trading system**, and **challenges in algorithmic trading**, and I highly recommend it.

Summary

In this chapter, we explored the intersection of trading strategy and technology by touching on the learning aspect of how to code a custom indicator on TradingView and an algorithmic trading strategy on Freqtrade. This process allows us to convert our unique trading philosophies into precise, automated systems capable of continuously monitoring and executing trades in the cryptocurrency market.

My goal here was to illustrate the potential of Pine Script and Freqtrade. This chapter was designed to ensure you're aware of these tools, to be revisited when you have your own manual strategy. Embracing the ability to automatically test and deploy strategies 24/7 is a key advantage in trading.

The following is our final chapter in which we conclude our journey together and I will give you some further resources for the road ahead.

Further reading

- *Pine Script V5 User Manual*: https://www.tradingview.com/pine-script-docs/en/v5/Introduction.html

- *Pine Script V5 Reference Manual*: https://www.tradingview.com/pine-script-reference/v5/

- Pine Script primer: https://www.tradingview.com/pine-script-docs/en/v5/primer/index.html

- Community Scripts: https://www.tradingview.com/scripts/

- (Free) Pine Script Basics Course: https://courses.theartoftrading.com/courses/pine-script-basics-course

- *Pine Script (TradingView) - A Step-by-step Guide*: https://algotrading101.com/learn/pine-script-tradingview-guide/

- Some public indicators and strategies I've posted on TradingView: https://www.tradingview.com/u/vaidab/#published-scripts

- Python – a programming language that's very easy to use: https://www.python.org/

- pandas – data analysis and manipulation built on top of Python: https://pandas.pydata.org/

- pandas-ta – a Python library with over 130 indicators: https://github.com/twopirllc/pandas-ta

- Freqtrade's website: https://www.freqtrade.io

- Hummingbot, an alternative to Freqtrade: https://github.com/hummingbot/hummingbot/tree/development

- NautilusTrader, another alternative to Freqtrade: https://github.com/nautechsystems/nautilus_trader

- *Cryptocurrency algorithmic trading with Python and Binance*: https://www.udemy.com/course/cryptocurrency-algorithmic-trading-with-python-and-binance

- A list of Freqtrade strategies: https://github.com/freqtrade/freqtrade-strategies/tree/main/user_data/strategies

- Backtesting traps when using Freqtrade: https://brookmiles.github.io/freqtrade-stuff/2021/04/12/backtesting-traps/

9
What's Next?

Congratulations – you've reached the final chapter. Even though the book ends here, your journey is just starting out.

If you've followed me closely, you've learned sufficient theory (which I hope you've put into practice) and you've been able to develop a strategy that you trade manually or automatically.

What's next?

I recommend following this short roadmap:

- **Trading technically**: Learn about the tools used in Exocharts (http://exocharts.com) to become even more knowledgeable. Think volume profiles, Bid-Ask, Delta, imbalances, CVD, tick charts, range charts, and footprint charts.

- **Trading strategically**: Diversifying into stocks, bonds, or other investment vehicles, moving to different **centralized exchanges** (**CEXs**) based on fee offers (yes, when you trade 1,000+ times a day, the fees add up), and trading on **decentralized exchanges** (**DEXs**) (I recommend, I've also contributed to, and I've successfully traded with LimitSwap: https://github.com/tsarbuig/LimitSwap).

- **Trading the news**: Learn how to trade by news. There are bigger gains if you can estimate how the price reacts to the **Federal Reserve System** (**Fed**) announcements (you can even hedge on volatility, creating two trades in both directions that will close once the price decides where to go). And other announcements can happen. I've successfully traded a "*new coin listing on Binance*" strategy where I bought when the price came out of the initial dump hole and sold at 20%+. Other situations can't be defined algorithmically. There, you can put your creativity to use.

- **Learn more about statistics**: Learn how to properly test a strategy taking into account the alpha, the beta, the drawdown, the Sharpe ratio, transaction costs, volatility, annualized returns, and a lot more. Welcome to math :)

- **Get a coach**: If you want to accelerate your process, understand the steps, get answers to your questions, surpass the emotional difficulties, and build your own strategy with someone, or if you just need someone to double-check your work, contact me. You can email me at `contact@vaidabogdan.com`. Make sure your subject is *"trading coach"* so that I can quickly find your email, and expect a delay of around 48 hours until you get an answer (`mailto:contact@vaidabogdan.com?subject=trading%20coach`).

- **Take a vacation and take (real) breaks from trading**: Even though it starts as a passion, seeing all the money coming in and following trades at indecent hours adds up. You need to be able to separate this from your time dedicated to other things.

That's it!

I wish you the best on your journey!

BONUS – One Month of Trading

In the process of writing this book, I realized that while I fully believed in the materials I provided, there was a need for something more to instill confidence in you. I pondered various approaches, ultimately concluding that nothing motivates more than the prospect of success.

So, I've asked myself, what if I document a month of trading for you?

There will always be people that object to success, and they'll have their own opinions, like so:

- If I document 20+ trades, I choose the ones I won

- If I document multiple trades of $1,000+, I already made a big amount of money; now, it's easy

- If I document myself starting out, I'm not a beginner; I already know how to trade

- If I document a client's progress, I've helped them (or chosen the client that made more money from multiple clients)

- If I document myself during the bull market, of course, I'm making money – it's the bull market

With all of these objections, what can I do to provide you with proof that the methods in this book work?

Nothing really – there are always people who will say it works, people who will say it doesn't, echo chambers, and whatnot.

At the time of writing, we're in a bear market in crypto, and I love it. It's the period when I can dedicate time to writing and other leisurely activities, something I wouldn't really be able to do in the bull market. This is the time when projects build, investors protect their money, and traders lose some of theirs.

Yep, the bear market also has its downs – mainly, high spikes in volatility where trading goes against your well-defined strategies, and it's way harder to make money now than it is in the bull market.

So, even though we're in the worst period for showing off, in this chapter, I'm going to document one month of trading with a $10,000 account. I will show you what I'm doing, what my thought processes are, and how I adapt to this ever-changing game.

As a disclaimer, don't expect sensationalism. I'm 100% against that.

No, I won't double this account in a month. Actually, if I doubled it, I would rather remove the chapter than publish it because you wouldn't believe me. And it wouldn't be a normal month of trading.

I expect a conservative return of around 1–3%.

In the 3% scenario, that's $300 in the first month, and ~$4,257 after 12 months ($10,000 * (1.03)^12 = $14,257).

In the 1% scenario, that's $100 after one month and $1,268 after 12 months.

You can use this calculator to play with other figures: `https://www.thecalculatorsite.com/finance/calculators/compoundinterestcalculator.php`.

If that doesn't seem much, that's because I won't trade with leverage, bots, or other hacks. I just want you to see the process and the thinking behind it. You can always 10x this return with more trading (I only took 24 trades this month), proper leverage (that comes with higher risk), and the compounding process will take care of the rest.

Note that black swan events can happen, tokens might get unlisted, and APIs might not work, and I will also document those situations in which I might get a negative return. This can happen, and I did have one or two months a year when this happened, usually when doing algorithmic trading.

Also, my trading day is actually boring. When I'm trading live, I'm searching for specific situations that I've worked hard to define, situations that take into account a lot of things (including the S&P, the volume profile, the global trend, BTC correlation, and more). I'm not studying all of them in every trade, but I have the background information when I enter the trades, which adds to my chances. So, for example, even though I've suggested you should always check using three indicators from different categories when trading, I usually have three results in my mind (and I'm always biased regarding the direction of the trade). Also, I'm not a chart trader by default. I love trading on the chart, but I don't have the time to take into account all the info all the time. I love my life, I love traveling, and that's why I actually focus on algorithmic trading. Every few days, I run an idea through Freqtrade, and if it has merits, I go down the rabbit hole, developing a theoretical trading system, backtesting it, modifying it, backtesting it again, backtesting it in-sample and out-of-sample, and dry-running the result. I'm the type of guy who likes to have control over his own time, so this suits me better than strategies that force me to devour the screen every day.

This is a bonus chapter, and I will trade using all my knowledge, not only what I've taught you in the previous chapters. If you encounter a new terminology, a new indicator, or a different way of doing things, feel free to use Google, YouTube, or ChatGPT to better understand how it works. I will try to teach you one thing at a time through each trade I make, but make sure you understand every trade before you continue reading. I'm not asking you to do 100 trades using an indicator I didn't explain; instead, I'm asking you to read a bit about the indicator and what it does so that you understand the idea behind the trade. Also, if you notice days I didn't trade, I was either relaxing or busy with other work. I try not to force myself and to keep it fun.

Preparing the tools

June 7, 2023

Tasks for today:

- Create a Binance account (in my case, I just created a subaccount for this project in my main account; this feature is available for you after your account grows a certain size and you reach the VIP level on the platform)
- Create a 3Commas (3C) account
- Create a TradingView account
- Configure all the accounts
- Link Binance's API with 3C's API
- Set up the trading journal
- Allocate $10,000 for the account
- No trading for today

June 8, 2023

Tasks for today:

- Analyze BTC
- Set up a trade on TradingView
- Make a first trade on BTC
- Note it in the journal

> **Note:**
> We also provide a PDF file that has color images of the screenshots and diagrams used in this book. You can download it here: `https://packt.link/pXrot`.

Trading

June 8 – BTC analysis

The following is my monthly analysis of BTC, containing **support and resistance (SR)** lines, **round numbers**, the Fibonacci **Golden Channel (GC)**, and the **Volume Point of Control (VPOC)**.

Figure B.1 – BTC analysis on the monthly chart

Here are some notes on the preceding chart:

- I'm not including all possible SR lines but, rather, focusing on the main ones that are identified before and after significant price swings.

- I also focus on the two lines before and after the current price; I don't need to analyze a price range where BTC will not arrive for the next year.

- I'm not adding all the SR lines possible, only the main ones (found before and after big swings).

- I'm not adding the line on the precise price. I'm just looking for the area where the price will react. And since I'll be trading on the 4H and lower timeframes, I will adjust the lines when I get there.

- The only adjustment I made is a support line that I initially put at $19,960 and I've now moved to $20,000. I do this by double-clicking it, going to the coordinates, and changing the price manually. The reason for this is that I prefer for the round number to stand out when I go on the lower timeframe.

Here's a close-up:

Figure B.2 – The zoomed-in image

If you want to learn more about the Fibonacci GC, you can check out `https://www.investopedia.com/articles/technical/04/033104.asp`, and for the VPOC, check out this one: `https://phemex.com/academy/point-of-control-how-to-use-poc-in-crypto-trading`.

Now, we will move on to my weekly analysis.

The first thing I will do is open the **Object tree**, located in the lower-right section of TradingView, and move all of my charted objects into a folder, hiding monthly information until I chart the weekly info. It looks like this:

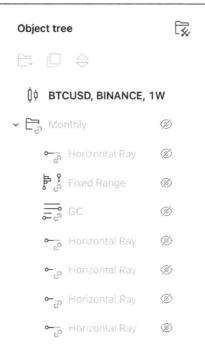

Figure B.3 – The object tree

After we've hidden the monthly objects, we will proceed with the weekly analysis.

Here's what it looks like:

Figure B.4 – BTC analysis on the weekly chart

Here are some notes:

- I've only added the two closest support lines and the two closest resistance lines. I'm not interested in weekly price movements but in 4H ones, so these are just for reference when we get to the 4H timeframe.

- I placed the second line from the top on the last swing in May this year, but then I noticed there was resistance in that area during May last year, so I moved it to the left to take that into account. I also adjusted it closer to the price, as mentioned before.

- I experimented with the **Volume Profile** and observed significant trading activity during BTC's fall from April to June 2022. However, I don't find its VPOC to be particularly relevant because it was a unique, singular situation. Charting the Volume Profile after the drop would position the VPOC under the last two SR lines, making it irrelevant to our trading. As a result, I won't include it in the weekly timeframe.

Now, I will move all the objects into a `Weekly` folder in the Object tree and then reveal the monthly objects. It looks like this:

Figure B.5 – Clutter

Next, I will adjust the following:

- Hide the lines that are well over and under the price. I do this by right-clicking on them and clicking **Hide**.

- I will delete the weekly resistance line at 29,998 because I have a stronger monthly line at 29,419. Remember, there are no exact prices in trading, only areas where the price reacts, and here the area is somewhere around 29,400–31,100.

- I will hide or delete the last three lines (19,960–21,471). If I hide them, when I redo the analysis, I will just unhide them and adjust the position. If I delete them, I will just add them again. It's your choice of how you prefer to work; I usually hide the monthly lines and delete the weekly and lower ones. And to answer your unspoken question, I usually analyze BTC on a weekly basis when I'm actively trading.

There are situations where the close of a candle in a monthly chart is lower than the close of the candles it consists of in a weekly chart, in which case I will have the monthly SR line closer to the price than the weekly SR line. I will always prefer to keep the stronger and closer line on the chart because I want to identify the earliest moment when the price reacts to that SR area. Remember, it's never a specific price; it's an area.

Here's the uncluttered version:

Figure B.6 – A weekly uncluttered version

Now, I'll quickly do the daily timeframe. I don't like the daily that much; I've only used it effectively when trading a modified **TD Sequential strategy** (originally created by Tom DeMark).

A note on why I don't trade the daily timeframe

The fact that I don't trade it doesn't mean that you shouldn't trade it. Still, take into consideration that trades on higher timeframes take a longer time to end, freezing your capital and leaving you at the mercy of the market. Sometimes, sudden market events generate abnormal behavior while you are still in trades, and even with a good strategy, you get stopped out.

On the daily timeframe, I add three lines that are actually close to the current price, and I'll hide the GC lines. The GC area typically serves as a potential bounce area when a price experiences a rapid decline. However, our price has remained in that area for an extended period, making it less relevant for our current analysis.

Here's our daily chart:

Figure B.7 – The daily chart

I find the 4H chart, followed by the weekly and monthly charts, to be the best ones to look at. The M and W charts provide strong SR areas, and the 4H chart is a great place to trade. The 1H -> 15m charts work too, usually on Altcoins, as BTC is quite volatile, and it might just catch your stop loss before it goes toward your desired direction. However, if your strategy is sound...

On the 4H chart, we can see some parallel channels:

Figure B.8 – The 4H chart

The second channel is a continuation of the first.

And we actually have another channel, which is a bit harder to determine and not that fluid:

Figure B.9 – The "hidden" parallel channel

I love trading parallel channels; I already have some ideas in mind...

I will add the **Volume** indicator, find out the VPOC, and also keep on the chart the closest channels (they overlap a bit, but I need to pay attention to them).

And with that, here's the final version, the one I will use for trading this week:

Figure B.10 – BTC/USD analysis

Note that I might readjust the SR lines if needed. The charting is not frozen in place, but the last figure provides me with the information I need to propose some trades.

Also, if I don't find anything to trade here, I will check lower timeframes or other tokens, but I won't go into charting again.

What are the conclusions here?

- In the short term, I see BTC in a downward channel
- There's a lot of fighting (and volatility) in the 27,000 area
- There's strong support in the 23K area and good support in the 24K area
- There's strong resistance in the 29K area and not much trading between 28K and 29K (we can see this by the lack of volume on the Volume Profile)
- If BTC continues its downtrend, we can trade the parallel channel (with a higher emphasis on short trades)

- If BTC takes off and gets out of the channel, we can expect a strong momentum until around 29K (a good long trade).

> **Note**
>
> Chart analysis can be self-fulfilling. Imagine all the traders putting support and resistance lines at theory-based levels, buying the double and triple bottoms, buying the breakouts, and basically, forcing the price to react by doing exactly what the pattern says it would do.

June, 10 – Trade 1 BTC/BUSD

Since we know BTC trades in a channel, and because the price dropped to the lower channel support, an opportunity for a long appeared. Here's my setup:

Figure B.11 – The trade setup for BTC/BUSD on 1D

I want to **long** BTC at 25,643 with a **stop loss (SL)** at 25,012 and a **take profit (TP)** at 27,271. I'm also adding a partial TP at 26,277, just in case the price rejects the middle of the channel (in some cases, the middle line acts as resistance and the price returns to the lower channel line). Note that these numbers (directly taken from TradingView) might change slightly in my 3C screenshots because of slippage when entering at market price, the price difference when switching tabs, fees, and so on.

Here's the 3C version of TradingView:

Figure B.12 – 3C's Trade Terminal

The following is a screenshot showing my trade setup. Note that I've checked the **Move to Breakeven** option, which will move my SL to my entry price after 3C arrives at the first TP.

Figure B.13 – 3C's Trade Terminal

Now, we confirm the transaction:

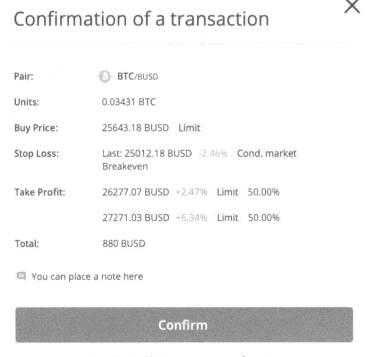

Figure B.14 – The transaction confirmation

Since BTC is currently trading at 25,656 and my buy limit price is at 25,643, I'll have to wait until it arrives at my trade. Never run for the trade; doing market orders to catch a price usually means that you have a **fear of missing out** (**FOMO**). Do limit orders and just accept it if they don't get triggered; there's always another trade to make. If you see me doing market orders, I'm usually doing that because of a running trend that I do want to catch, but I don't recommend you trade in the spur of the moment. I invite you to do the calculations and figure out how much I've lost (or won) by using market orders instead of limit orders. Alternatively, you can just use limit orders.

All right, let's look at the trade:

Figure B.15 – Trade #1

We'll usually start on minus because of the transaction fees.

Here's how it went:

Figure B.16 – Trade #1 – ended

The trade ended in a SL but with a profit. How is this possible?

Well, it is, because we've set two *TPs* and a *move to breakeven*. Basically, it took TP1 and then it returned to the entry price. On TradingView, it looks like this:

Figure B.17 – TradingView's view

And on 3C it looks like this:

Enter price (buy): 25643.18	Price with exchange fees. 25668.82	Close price: 25902.7	Stop Loss Price Condition: 25668.82	

Current Position: 0.0 BTC   0.0 BUSD

TP Condition

Price Condition	Quantity	Status
26250.79	0.01716000 BTC (50.0%) / 450.46360667 BUSD	Finished
27271.03	0.01715000 BTC (50.0%)	Cancelled

Buy steps:

Price	Volume	Status
25668.82	0.03431000 BTC / 880.69732330 BUSD	Finished

Figure B.18 – Trade #1 – the TP1 hit and then SL

It would've worked better if I'd added an **SL timeout** to prevent that short drop under the channel, which was actually pretty visible in the past. I've noted that down as a learning point.

> **A short note about risk management and the trading journal**
>
> Risk management and the trading journal were presented in *Chapter 6*. I think I included enough examples there, so we can skip them in this section. Journaling entries now would increase the size of the chapter quite a lot and would distract you from following the trades and the thinking behind them. Because of this, I will use $880 to enter each trade, with a few exceptions (where I'll show you the when, why, and how to add funds to a trade that goes against you). The fixed sum will allow you to compare the trades and their results over different timeframes.

Adding other coins to watch

Since I already have TradingView open, I will add a few other coins from `https://www.sandwich.finance/` | **BUSD perpetual futures**. That link gets me a `.txt` file, which I import from **Trading View | Watchlist and details**. Then, I click on the arrow down next to the current list name and then click on **Import list** and rename it `Binance Futures BUSD` (I'll leave the location of the rename button to you).

Note that even when I'm trading spontaneously, I like to trade tokens that hold some value, and those are usually the tokens that have made it to the perpetual futures market.

June, 10 – Trade 2 ETH/BUSD

After BTC, I usually look at ETH. It was trading in a parallel channel, but I found increasing volume in a break from that channel, so I wanted to trade that. It was also a hedge against the trend, as I was already long on BTC.

This is what I wanted to catch:

Figure B.19 – Trade setup for ETH/BUSD on 1H

And here's my setup in 3C

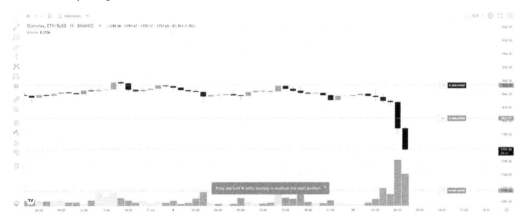

Figure B.20 – 3C's TradingView view

And here's my order:

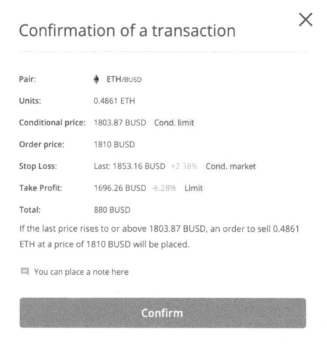

Figure B.21 – The 3C order

But the gods of trading wanted to humble me and I had to cancel my trade... because I didn't catch the train:

Figure B.22 – The trade ran from me

Using ATR bands

Let's introduce a new indicator to our trading. It's called **ATR Bands by TheTrdFloor**, and what it does is draw two bands, one above and one below the price based on the **Average True Range (ATR)**.

A trick when searching for an indicator or a strategy is to look at the number to the right of its creator:

| ☆ ATR Bands | TheTrdFloor | 3467 |

Figure B.23 – ATR Bands by TheTrdFloor

In this case, it's **3467**. This represents the number of people who have added the indicator, and the bigger it is, the better the indicator is (usually). With a low number, you can find some gems out there, but you'll mostly find indicators with mistakes in them.

These are the settings that I've changed:

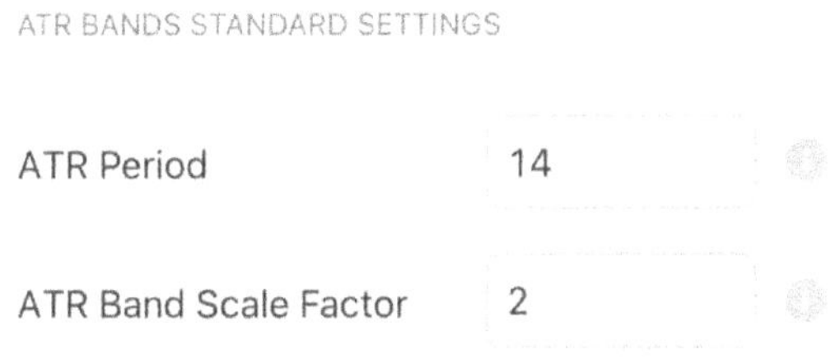

ATR BANDS STANDARD SETTINGS

ATR Period   14

ATR Band Scale Factor   2

Figure B.24 – The ATR Bands settings

Basically, it's calculating the ATR over 14 candles, and that result is multiplied by 2 and plotted on both sides of the close. There are additional settings, such as displaying a TP band based on the ATR, which is intriguing, but for now, this is sufficient.

June, 10 – Trade 3 DATA/BUSD

Now, I'm scrolling through my watchlist, which contains all the BUSD pairs listed on Binance. I usually work with a smaller watchlist, featuring the top coins I trade daily, but I wanted to identify where the ATR Bands indicator could best fit. I do this by searching for RSI divergences or oversold signals. This serves more like a filter to determine which coins I should consider for entries. Here's what I've found:

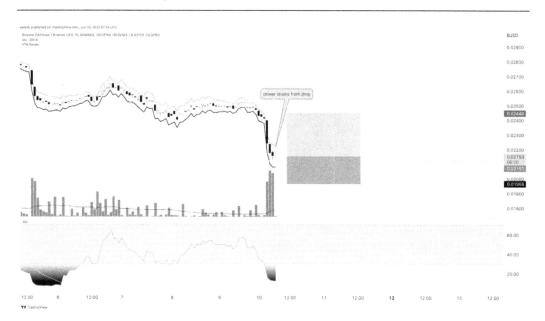

Figure B.25 – The DATA/BUSD entry

This is an interesting trade. RSI shows oversold. There's also an RSI divergence from the latest oversold section, but the volume is rising on a price decline.

In this game, you can always find valid reasons to contradict the arguments to enter a trade. What is important is to balance those reasons until you find one set is sufficiently bigger than the other to act upon. And if it isn't, it's always safer to protect your capital by staying out of that trade.

Normally, what other more cautious traders do is wait for the price to recover instead of trying to catch a falling sword. I agree with this, but there's also a potential pullback that I can take advantage of, even if the price continues to fall.

One thing to note is that the volume increases on smaller and smaller candles with lower wicks that get rejected. With BTC on the lower side of the channel, I expect a reversal here.

The arguments pro trade are as follows:

- Oversold RSI
- BTC on a support line (of the parallel channel) with a good probability of rising
- RSI divergence (though far apart and indicating a longer-term potential for reversal)
- Trend weakening due to smaller candles on higher volume with rejection wicks

The arguments against the trade are as follows:

- Rising volume on a price decline

- A falling sword (no confirmation of reversal)

It's a risky trade, but I like it.

The ATR bands help me when placing the SL. I am going for a risk/reward ratio of 1.6 (the distance from TP to **entry price** (**EP**), divided by the distance from EP to SL), making sure my SL is at least double the ATR volatility band.

Confirmation of a transaction   X

Pair:	**DATA**/BUSD
Units:	20455.6 DATA
Buy Price:	0.02151 BUSD Limit
Stop Loss:	Last: 0.01966 BUSD -8.6% Cond. market
Take Profit:	0.02448 BUSD +13.80% Limit
Total:	440 BUSD

🗨 You can place a note here

Confirm

Figure B.26 – The trade confirmation

Note that I'm trading with half the sum I would usually commit ($440). This is due to the higher risk. If BTC creates a lower wick mirrored by DATA's price movement and my confidence increases due to the nature of the price action, I might contribute the remaining amount later.

Six days later, still in trade:

Figure B.27 – DATA/BUSD 6 days later

I advise against holding onto any trade for an extended period (unless you're employing a trend-following system). The key reason is the risk of price fluctuations due to unforeseen events such as wars, US presidential elections, and pandemics. These could significantly impact your trade if it's held for too long. On a more immediate scale, consider an FTC hearing occurring on day three of your trade. The resulting volatility might trigger your SL (or TP). Even with a 50–50 outcome, such an event can influence your returns.

A note about price shocks

Price shocks are very hard to identify even when backtesting. Imagine that you overfit your strategy on a particular timeframe with two price shocks, catching both. You would think it's a very good strategy, but you actually catch the profit of a volatile situation that is unrelated to your indicators. What this means is that you might just as well catch the other end when trading with real capital.

Trade ended 10 days later. We can also see how the RSI gave an overbought signal.

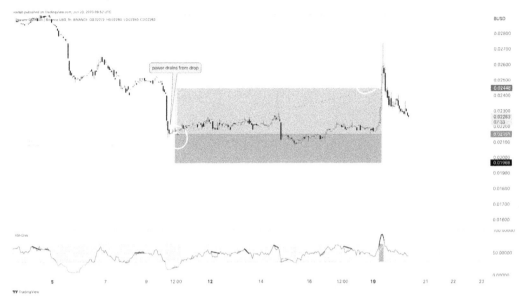

Figure B.28 – DATA/BUSD 10 days later

And here's our profit:

✔ Finished: 13.58%
Creation date 6/10/2023 10:55:58 AM

+59.81237896
+59.83$
+13.58%

Figure B.29 – The end result

June, 10 – Trade 4 GRT/BUSD

GRT/BUSD is a similar trade to DATA/BUSD, and taking the trade usually means that you are doubling the money on the same event, not that you've found another opportunity.

Here's my entry for GRT/BUSD:

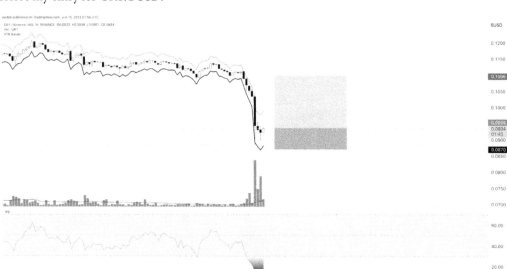

Figure B.30 – The GRT/BUSD entry

Note that there's a white (green) candle forming, so the price is trying to pull back.

The same conditions as DATA/BUSD and the same arguments for trading versus not trading apply. As I've mentioned, this is just doubling down on a (risky) trade:

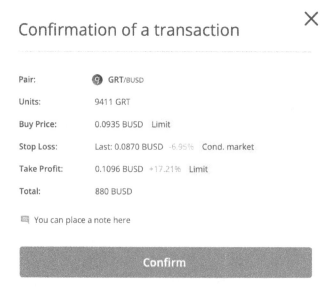

Figure B.31 – Trade confirmation

This is the result:

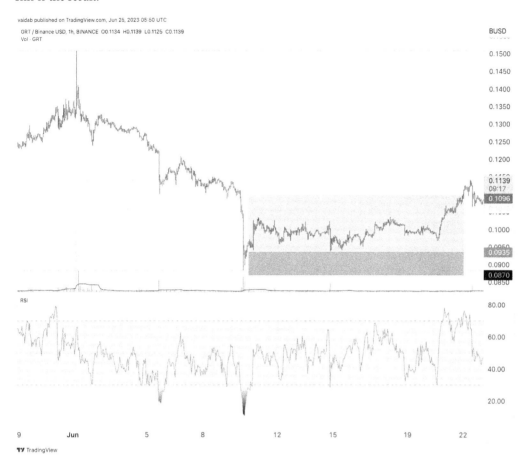

Figure B.32 – GRT/BUSD

And here's the profit:

✔ Finished: 16.99%
Creation date 6/10/2023 10:59:41 AM

+149.60572591
+149.62$
+16.99%

Figure B.33 – The end result

I did this second, almost identical, trade to illustrate a case. When you trade identical patterns that mirror BTC's move, on the same timeframes, around the same time, you just double down your money on your strategy. If you haven't tested it properly, this can lead to loss of capital. So, why not invest more time in thoroughly researching a potential trade and leverage your risk management strategy to determine the right amount to stake?

A note on the correlation of markets

An important thing to understand, when trading, is that most tokens on CEXes follow BTC. There are many reasons for this, such as market makers, arbitrage, correlation trading, and high-frequency algorithms.

When you trade, it's important to hone your skills on BTC and then go for the altcoins. Altcoins provide you with bigger rewards, but they are more volatile and have increased risk. For example, if BTC drops, they drop further; if BTC recovers, they recover better, and sometimes they don't correlate with BTC as you'd expect.

June, 12 – Trade 5 POLS/BUSD

Where are my mistakes?

Where are the losing trades?

I had four wins, right?

Wrong!

I actually had a partial TP for trade 1, BTC/BUSD, and then I couldn't catch the second trade, so that's a neutral outcome. Then, there are two trades that mirror each other, which could've been two losses.

So, it's two risky wins and one partial win.

I would've preferred to lose a bit at first, as this doesn't sound that realistic, but it actually is. It happens because I've analyzed the trend on BTC and I've followed the price action. And it also happens because of luck, as well as statistics and game theory (I'm in the lucky part of the month!).

Let's see how the story continues.

POLS is one of the tokens I usually watch. It is a launchpad that was very successful during the last bull market; taking a long there is also fundamentally safe (as there are a lot of buyers who intend to buy at lower prices).

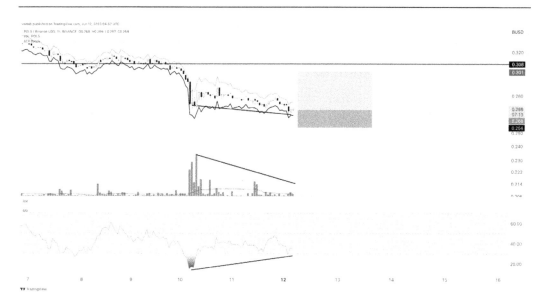

Figure B.34 – The POLS/BUSD entry

This looks nice. We have a bullish divergence there, a resistance line, and a downtrend on a lower volume.

A trick I use to speed up my trading is to take the values from TradingView's long (or short) position inputs, after I put them on the chart, and paste the TP and SL directly into 3C

By clicking on the long or short position drawing in TradingView, you get this screenshot:

Long Position		
Inputs Style Visibility		
Account size	10000	BUSD
Lot size	0.000068	
Risk	2.00	%
Entry price	0.268	
PROFIT LEVEL		
Ticks	33	
Price	0.301	
STOP LEVEL		
Ticks	14	
Price	0.254	
Template	Cancel	Ok

Figure B.35 – Taking values from TradingView

We confirm the trade:

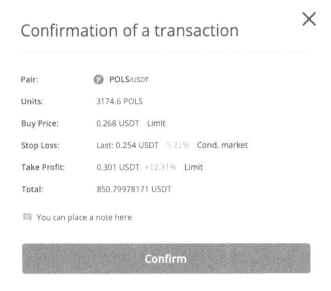

Figure B.36 – The trade confirmation

And it's a win.

Ignore the **/USDT** pairing; the pair was starred in my 3C account, and I traded it by mistake in my main account. I also entered the trade with $850 instead of $880. What can I say? It was a busy day, and I was multitasking.

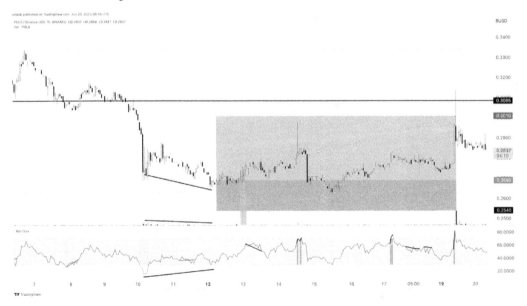

Figure B.37 – POLS/BUSD

Here's the end result:

✔ Finished: 11.67%
Creation date 6/12/2023 7:54:19 AM

+99.77767800
+99.78$
+11.67%

Figure B.38 – The end result

June, 14 – Trade 6 XVS/BUSD

I think you've got the gist of it. Now, let's move faster:

Figure B.39 – The XVS/BUSD trade

Here are the reasons for a long:

- Quadruple top
- A price pattern similar to a bear flag
- A price losing momentum
- A class B bearish divergence on the RSI

Here are the reasons against a long:

- No volume
- No indication the situation can't continue

We also have the **Keltner Channel indicator**, but we're not using it at the moment. It will help us with our next trade.

Here's the trade confirmation:

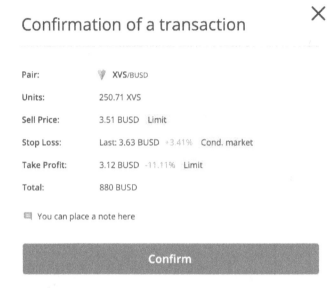

Figure B.40 – The trade confirmation

We lost:

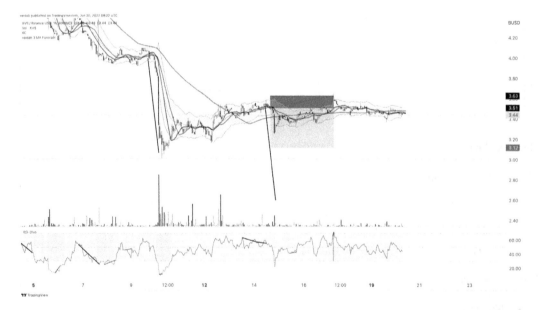

Figure B.41 – XVS/BUSD

Why did we lose here?

We can say statistics, the randomness of the market, and so on. We can also point out that our SL was caught by a wick. Maybe it was volatility; maybe it was SL hunting (a concept that will be explained further in this chapter). The end result is as follows:

✔ Stop Loss finished: -3.91%
Creation date 6/14/2023 5:21:03 PM

-34.38487649
-34.41$
-3.91%

Figure B.42 – The end result

June, 14 – Trade 7 VIDT/BUSD

The next trade is VIDT/BUSD:

Figure B.43 – The VIDT/BUSD entry

Here are the reasons for the entry:

- Upper wicks are rejected while the volume is high
- An overbought RSI
- A small divergence

Price fights very hard to stay at that level. This can be especially seen on the Keltner Channel indicator (modified with Multiplier = 2.25). The price is in the upper band and just wants to come down.

We enter the trade:

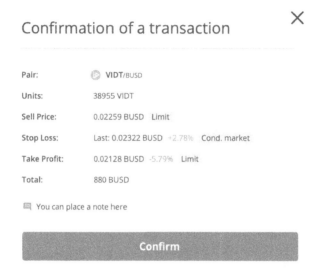

Confirmation of a transaction   ✕

Pair:	VIDT/BUSD
Units:	38955 VIDT
Sell Price:	0.02259 BUSD Limit
Stop Loss:	Last: 0.02322 BUSD +2.78% Cond. market
Take Profit:	0.02128 BUSD -5.79% Limit
Total:	880 BUSD

📋 You can place a note here

Confirm

Figure B.44 – The trade confirmation

And everything went as expected:

Figure B.45 – VIDT/BUSD

This is the end result:

✔ Finished: 5.61%
Creation date 6/14/2023 5:31:22 PM

+49.32209415
+49.32$
+5.61%

Figure B.46 – The end result

> **Important note**
>
> Almost all of the trades discussed in this chapter are purely discretionary and cannot be backtested. However, they offer valuable insights into various approaches to analyze price movements and present alternative perspectives on trading. While I have previously explained my recommendations to trade successfully, such as seeking confluence and backtesting strategies, it is important to note that when doing discretionary trading, I will ignore these rules in order to provide a more comprehensive understanding of the trading process. By breaking some of my own trading rules, taking riskier entries, and showcasing different perspectives when analyzing charts, I aim to enhance your learning experience and broaden your understanding of trading. Also, you don't want me to trade the exact same patterns in the same market conditions over and over (which is something that better resembles my normal trading day).

June, 14 and 16 – Trade 8 and 9 TOMO/BUSD

I'm entering the trade because of a pattern in the way TOMO/BUSD behaves. It's been on an uptrend in a channel sort of way since the beginning of the month, and looking at its history, it follows the RSI oversold/overbought signals very well. I'm going to short the upper part of the channel and long the lower part:

Figure B.47 – The TOMO/BUSD entry

Here's our trade:

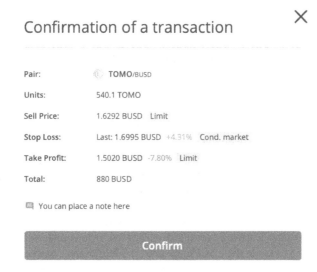

Figure B.48 – The trade confirmation

And surprisingly, it's a win:

Figure B.49 – TOMO/BUSD

I say surprisingly because I should've been stopped. I didn't set any SL timeout, so I should've been stopped with the spike that hit my SL.

I now move to the one-minute timeframe:

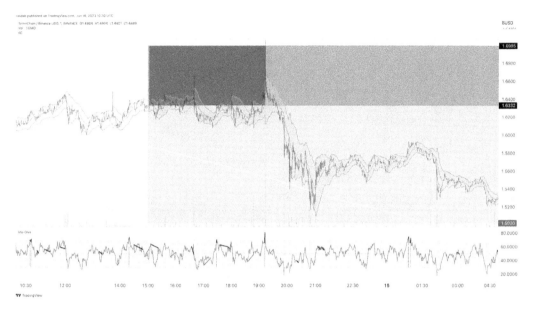

Figure B.50 – TOMO/BUSD LTF

And it seems that the spike took less than a minute. It probably was a huge buy order that caught a lot of limit sell orders, but it didn't catch mine. I don't really know why it didn't; sometimes, on very huge buy orders, the spread is so big that this happens. It's rare, but it does happen.

✔ Finished: 7.62%
Creation date 6/14/2023 5:36:11 PM

+67.00955888
+67.07$
+7.62%

Figure B.51 – The end result

So, this is a win...

Next, I have the long that I've promised:

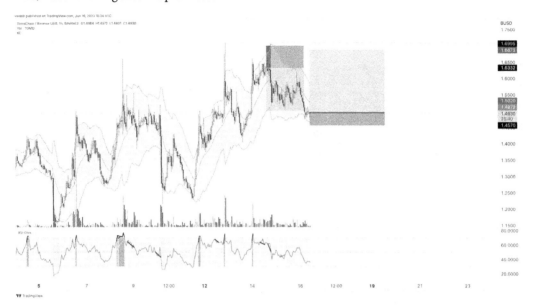

Figure B.52 – The TOMO/BUSD entry

It seems pretty straightforward. The only thing that worries me is that I didn't actually catch any oversold signal, and the price might get a bit lower. Basically, I'm running after the trade.

Figure B.53 – The trade confirmation and losing the trade

Why did I lose?

Well, there are numerous reasons, the randomness of the markets being my preferred one. The price follows the trend until the trend ceases to exist. Then, it might go sideways or follow another trend. In this case, it decided to go the other way:

✔ Stop Loss finished: -2.89%
Creation date 6/16/2023 1:33:33 PM

-4.44578132
-4.44$
-2.89%

Figure B.54 – The end result

June, 16 – Trade 10 CELR/BUSD

I was buying a pullback here. RSI oversold, and the price was exactly at a historical support and fighting on the lower band of the Keltner Channel:

Figure B.55 – The CELR/BUSD entry

Here's my entry:

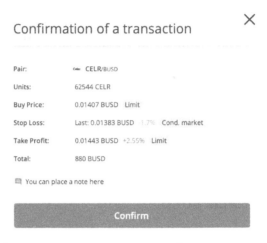

Figure B.56 – The trade confirmation

Aaand I got hunted. This is called **SL hunting**, and it's a sport supposedly played by some market participants that want to eliminate other players' positions by forcing the price to go to locations where they might place their SL orders.

Of course, markets are random. But this story helps us identify such places and protect ourselves against the wolves. Well, I got bitten:

Figure B.57 – CELR/BUSD

And my SL got triggered.

✔ Stop Loss finished: -1.97%
Creation date 6/16/2023 5:34:55 PM

-17.38035216
-17.40$
-1.97%

Figure B.58 – The end result

Finally, two losses in a row! I was beginning to think I shouldn't add this chapter to the book. Hey Siri, play *Not Afraid Anymore* by Halsey!

June, 16 – Trade 11 ANT/BUSD

Here, I looked at the RSI divergence on the upper band of the KC and the overbought RSI signal. I also looked at the last candle, which rejected the price increase (the long upper wick). This happened 13 minutes before the 1H candle closed, so I bet on this and shorted.

The reason for not making this trade was the volume. It increased during the rise, and it was pretty big during the black (red) candles that tried to bring the price down. There, the bears were fighting and not winning. There was also a structure forming there, which you can see later, in *Figure B.61* (I've highlighted it as a triangle), which I didn't notice:

Figure B.59 – The ANT/BUSD entry

Note that I'm taking two profits. That's because there was a resistance line near my first TP, which I'll illustrate in *Figure B.61*. But first, let's confirm this transaction:

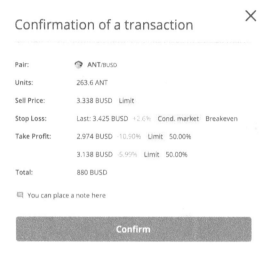

Figure B.60 – The trade confirmation

In the following diagram, I show the resistance line that turned into support (the reason for my first TP) and the structure that formed in the 3.27 price area (the rectangle):

Figure B.61 – ANT/BUSD

Still, the trade ended in a loss as the price maintained its upward trend.

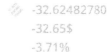

✔ Stop Loss finished: -3.71%
Creation date 6/16/2023 5:46:51 PM

-32.62482780
-32.65$
-3.71%

Figure B.62 – The end result

I now genuinely prefer the winning streaks after three losses in a row.

> **Note**
>
> The comments and explanations I add happen after the trade, so by default, they are biased. However, the reasons for entering the trade were noted when I entered, and those have not been updated. That's why I say things like, *"I didn't notice that..."*

Using vFMSS

It's time to bring out the big guns.

I've been trading the markets for quite a long time, and during that time, I've developed numerous strategies and indicators. One of the most successful ones was suggested to me by @EmperorBTC (http://twitter.com/EmperorBTC). He recommended I study Tom DeMark and the theory around his *Sequential indicator* (https://demark.com/sequential-indicator/) and provided insights into changing values to tune the indicator to the faster-moving crypto market.

We've traded the modified version for months, adapting it, bit by bit, to the crypto market. When the theory was sound, I created a private TradingView script for it, which everybody in our private group started using:

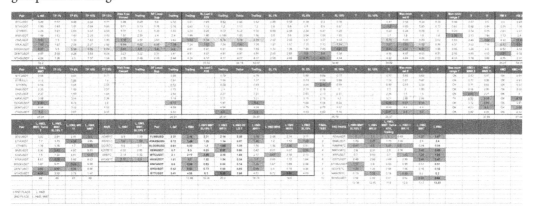

Figure B.63 – Some of the tests for the vaidab Faster Momentum Scalping Strategy (vFMSS)

Don't try to read the text in the preceding figure; it contains variations of the strategy's parameters. Just look at the big picture and all the (manual) testing that took place. Even in the world of automatic backtesting, manual testing has its place. It helps you better understand your strategy and how it behaves under various market conditions.

I've put a lot of work into this code, testing each variation on different markets and adapting it to market changes. I've also added protections and filters. It now literally filters the market through a unique perspective. And when I started using Freqtrade, I migrated the code to Python.

The code for the indicator is private, but I want to show you what you can achieve when you develop your own system and know it by heart. I'm not selling it, and I'm not providing signals. I was actually quite hesitant to put it here, but I wanted to show you the power of using a system.

June, 16 – Trade 12 BAKE/BUSD (vFMSS)

This was my first trade with vFMSS. I'm not following any other rules except what my indicator says, so you can ignore the RSI, the volume, and all the other information.

Basically, it's candle counting and setting specific candle conditions for strong pullbacks (or even a trend reversal).

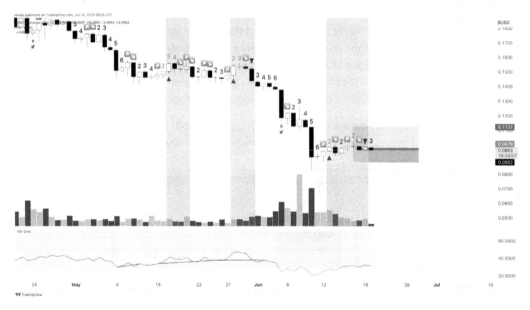

Figure B.64 – The BAKE/BUSD entry

I forgot to take the trade confirmation screenshot, but I took this one with all the data. My buy order is a buy limit one, so it took a few seconds to get caught:

Figure B.65 – The trade

And here's the win:

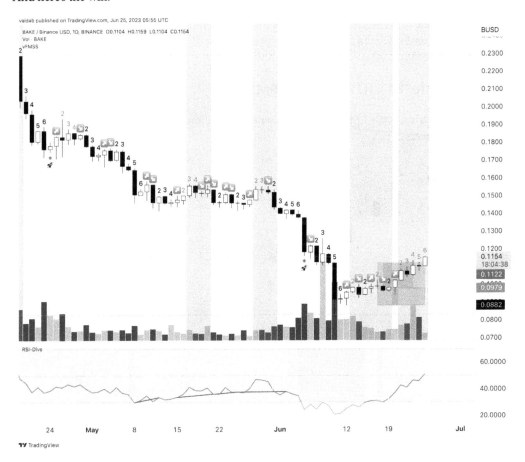

Figure B.66 – BAKE/BUSD

And here are the profits:

✔ Finished: 14.38%
Creation date 6/16/2023 8:54:51 PM

+126.64988413
+126.64$
+14.38%

Figure B.67 – The end result

> **Note**
>
> Even though using a good indicator that points to entry and exit places looks great, I would prefer that you trade with information-providing indicators, not with entry-providing ones – at least at the start, until you get a feel for how the price moves.

June, 16 – Trade 13 VIDT/BUSD (vFMSS)

This is the second trade using vFMSS. It's an easy entry on the indicator, telling me it's time for a pullback (or a price reversal):

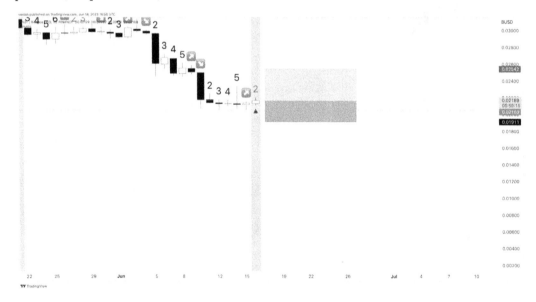

Figure B.68 – The VIDT/BUSD entry

Here's the trade confirmation:

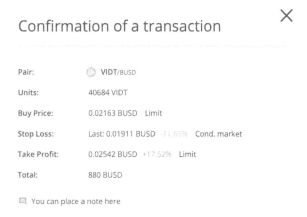

Figure B.69 – The trade confirmation

Aaand SL hunting took place. That was for shorters that followed the trend, and I actually benefited from it:

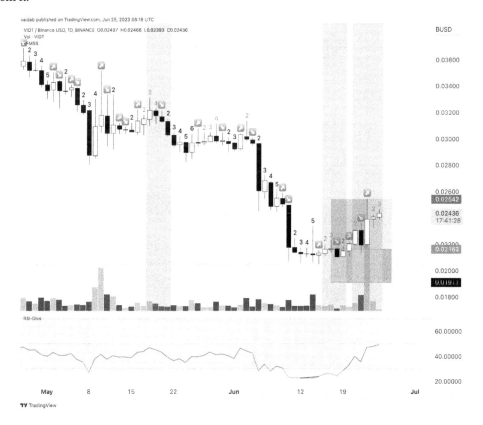

Figure B.70 – VIDT/BUSD

When the shorters got hunted, the longers took profits. When you see SL hunting happening in a market, you can take it into account when trading (using *SL timeout* or by moving your *SL higher*) or ignore it (let it be a part of statistics, as it includes situations where you benefit from it):

✔ Finished: 5.61%
Creation date 6/14/2023 5:31:22 PM

≫ +49.32209415
+49.32$
+5.61%

Figure B.71 – The end result

I successfully traded the pullback. I was actually curious whether it was a pullback (SL hunting was an additional argument for this) and followed it up later:

Figure B.72 – VIDT/BUSD later

June, 17 – Trade 14 THETA/BUSD (vFMSS)

This is the third vFMSS trade. It's an easy entry on the trade signal:

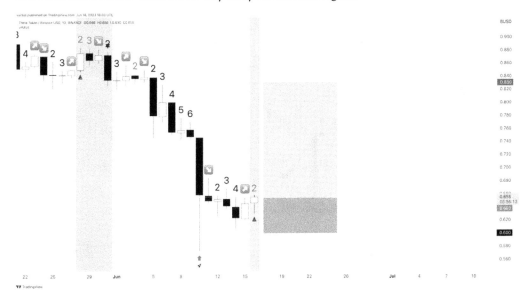

Figure B.73 – THETA/BUSD entry

Here's the trade confirmation (note that I have a SL timeout of 300 seconds):

Pair:	THETA/BUSD
Units:	1347.6 THETA
Buy Price:	0.653 BUSD Limit
Stop Loss:	Last: 0.600 BUSD -8.11% Cond. market 300 Sec
Take Profit:	0.830 BUSD +27.10% Limit
Total:	880 BUSD

Figure B.74 – The trade confirmation

The indicator shows that the trade has gone against me (the gray/orange arrow representing the entry signal disappeared – the same with the gray/green area).

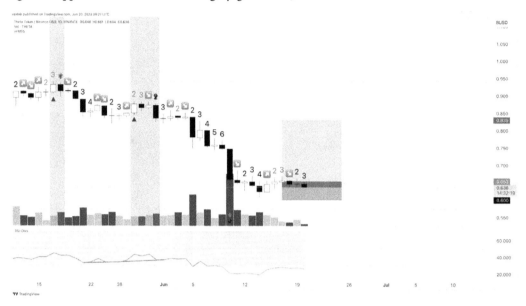

Figure B.75 – The THETA/BUSD reason to exit

I closed the trade:

❤ Closed at Market Price: -2.95%
Creation date 6/16/2023 9:04:08 PM

-25.99250880
-25.99$
-2.95%

Figure B.76 – The end result

And here's how it looks a few days after:

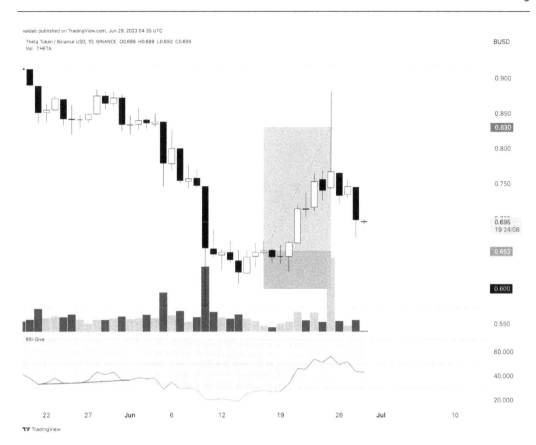

Figure B.77 – The THETA/BUSD statistics (sometimes) win

So, it was a successful pullback that I might or might not have caught (depending on the wick). Was the indicator wrong? Not necessarily. It is possible that the conditions for this situation are similar enough to loss scenarios (where the trade went the other way) that it's better to close quickly. If I developed this strategy now and I saw more than one such situation, I'd definitely check what's happening under the hood. Technically, I'd do this by adding a filter to my indicator to highlight the trades that fit this scenario and see whether I can increase my profits by slightly adjusting the conditions (and retesting everything), or just leave them be.

June, 17 – Trade 15 STG/BUSD (vFMSS)

I was expecting to be with all of my capital in trade for today and to just take a break, but some of my trades ended, so I found myself with money to trade. 😄

If the preceding statement triggers any alarms, your instincts are spot on. Under normal circumstances, you wouldn't put all of your capital into trades to protect it from unexpected market shifts. However, for the sake of illustrating more trades, I'm putting aside typical trading wisdom and adopting a writer's prerogative. So, let's proceed...

Here's the fourth vFMSS trade. We start on a signal, as usual:

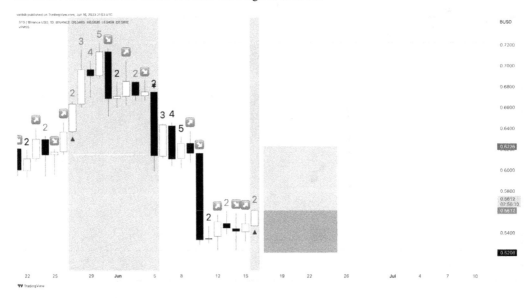

Figure B.78 – The STG/BUSD entry

Let's confirm the transaction:

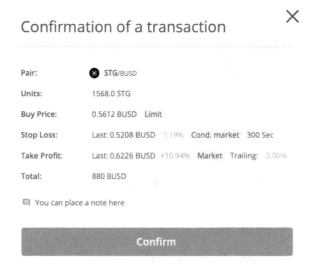

Figure B.79 – The trade confirmation

And this is what happens:

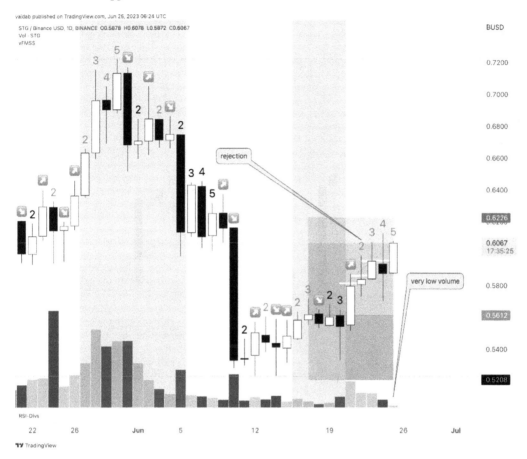

Figure B.80 – Are we continuing?

Here, we see a lot of rejected candles. I thought the last bullish candle had "*very low volume*," but I didn't look at the candle's duration. It was a daily candle after 6 hours and 30 minutes, so it still had volumes to go. 😄 My bad there. Still, seeing those rejection candles, I've decided to close:

✔ Closed at Market Price: 7.87%
Creation date 6/17/2023 12:05:36 AM

+69.35608960
+69.34$
+7.87%

Figure B.81 – The end result

I actually closed on the wick:

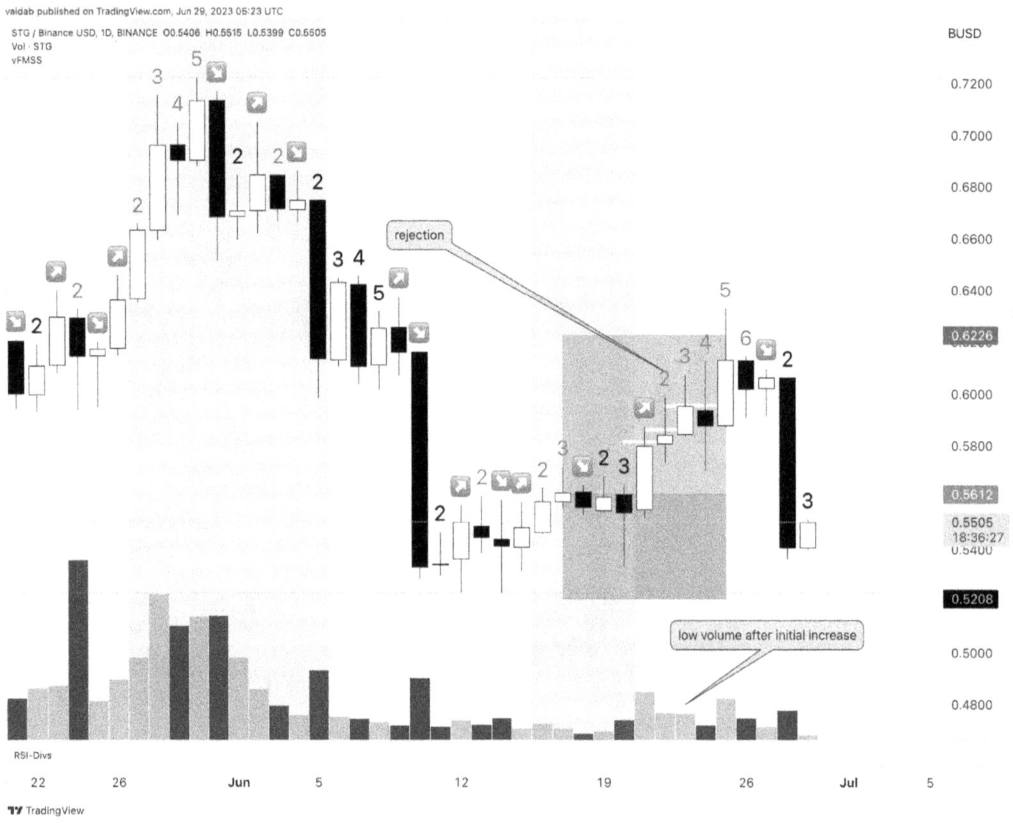

Figure B.82 – After a while

Now, I have an issue with my explanations so far. I talked to you about statistics and losses, and here, I have more wins than losses. I confront myself with this conundrum – should I leave this chapter in the book? Does it have teaching material in it? I had more luck than I normally have and wasn't expecting these results...

Trading higher timeframes is actually easier, at least for me. It eliminates a lot of noise, and the trend is clearer.

So, I'm going to switch to a **lower timeframe (LTF)** and see what happens.

> **Note**
>
> I don't usually trade LTFs due to time constraints. I prefer to have time for myself and not be stuck to the screen all day, so I usually check my trades two times a day at most.

June, 18 – Trade 16 GLMR/BUSD (the Crypto Pairs Screener)

Now, I will introduce to you a tool that I use to quickly find interesting markets to trade. It's called the **Crypto Pairs Screener**:

Figure B.83 – The Crypto Pairs Screener

You can use it to filter through the list of crypto tokens for specific conditions. For example, I'm looking for Binance spot tokens that trade against BUSD and are outside the 20–80 RSI 14 range – basically, oversold or overbought tokens:

Figure B.84 – Tokens found

I found two (you can usually find more when BTC is also in this position, but then you're trading tokens that mirror BTC, which means you're multiplying the investment and the risk based on the same pattern):

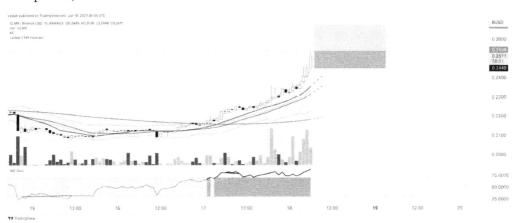

Figure B.85 – The GLMR/BUSD entry

I enter the trade:

Figure B.86 – The trade

And here's the result:

Figure B.87 – GLMR/BUSD

You'd think we won this trade, right?

No, we didn't:

✔ Stop Loss finished: -0.72%
Creation date 6/18/2023 9:03:55 AM

-6.27588555
-6.27$
-0.72%

Figure B.88 – The end result

The trade idea was good, but the candle that we actually entered triggered the SL, and we exited with a very small loss. We didn't catch the ride.

Using SLs

A word about SLs – there are multiple ways to set an SL, which I already explained in *Chapter 7*. You choose them based on what worked during your backtesting period. And, if you're not applying a particular strategy, SLs are discretionary. People usually put them under a local support line (for longs) or resistance line (for shorts), and that's a safe enough bet (except when there's SL hunting).

However, what do you do in the previous scenario, in *Figure B.85*, when the price runs in an uptrend and you want to join the ride?

Here, people usually wait for a pullback before entering into an area where the price retraces, before pushing the trend again.

That's the proper way to enter – and then there's the quick way.

My particular preference when trading is to have very tight SLs and big TPs. I want to quickly quit a losing trade, even if this makes me lose more opportunities. This also allows me to re-enter the trade at a better price, without having lost much during the fall. It's a riskier bet than having a larger SL, but I usually take it. (This is also the reason my risk-reward ratio, **R**, is usually greater than 1.5–2.)

June, 18 – Trade 17 ACH/BUSD (vFMSS)

Same intro, we enter on a signal:

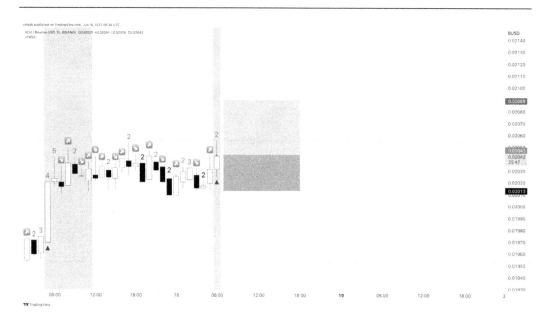

Figure B.89 – The ACH/BUSD entry

Here's the trade confirmation:

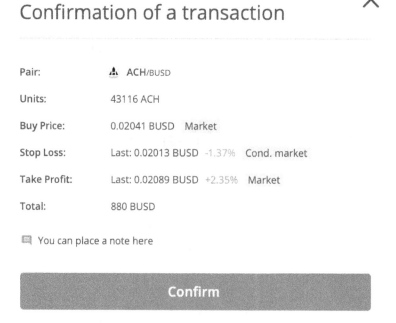

Confirmation of a transaction   ✕

Pair: ⚛ ACH/BUSD

Units: 43116 ACH

Buy Price: 0.02041 BUSD   Market

Stop Loss: Last: 0.02013 BUSD -1.37%   Cond. market

Take Profit: Last: 0.02089 BUSD +2.35%   Market

Total: 880 BUSD

🗨 You can place a note here

Confirm

Figure B.90 – The trade confirmation

And we've lost; the trend changed direction:

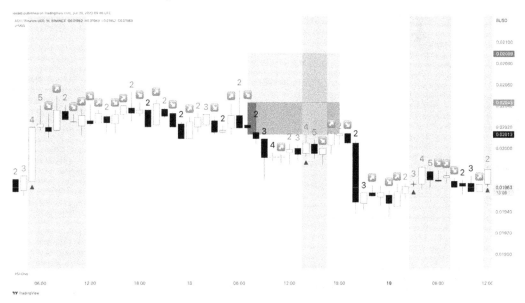

Figure B.91 – ACH/BUSD

Here's the result:

Figure B.92 – The end result

There's only one thing to note here. As seen in *Figure B.89*, the price wasn't actually trending when I tried to use the indicator; it wasn't going anywhere, and I searched for a pullback. Remember the **confirmation bias** we talked about in *Chapter 1*? I'm taking that into account when making this statement. And you should always check for it when reading this or any other book. I could be making assumptions after the fact, but on a day when my mind is 100% clear and I take my time, I wouldn't make the trade.

However, we do make mistakes, and we promise that we won't make them again. And then we make the same mistakes again. This is *discretionary trading* at its best.

June, 18 – Trade 18 KAVA/BUSD (vFMSS)

We're shorting on the signal. This is not a pullback but a trend continuation signal (as the algorithm considers the trend has changed direction downward and the previous candles as having been the pullback):

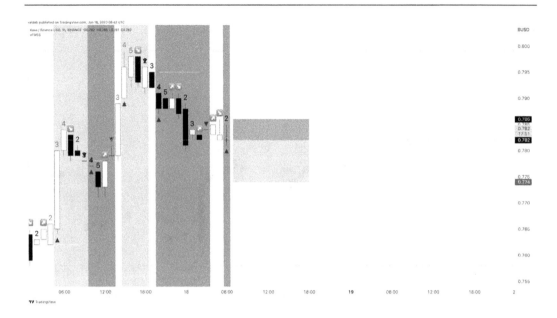

Figure B.93 – The KAVA/BUSD entry

Here's the trade confirmation:

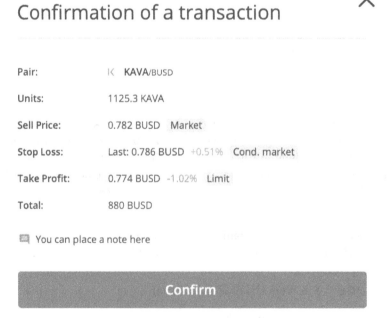

Confirmation of a transaction   ✕

Pair:	K **KAVA**/BUSD
Units:	1125.3 KAVA
Sell Price:	0.782 BUSD Market
Stop Loss:	Last: 0.786 BUSD +0.51% Cond. market
Take Profit:	0.774 BUSD -1.02% Limit
Total:	880 BUSD

📧 You can place a note here

Confirm

Figure B.94 – The trade confirmation

It seems that what we expected to be a trend change was actually just a longer pullback, and the trend continues upward.

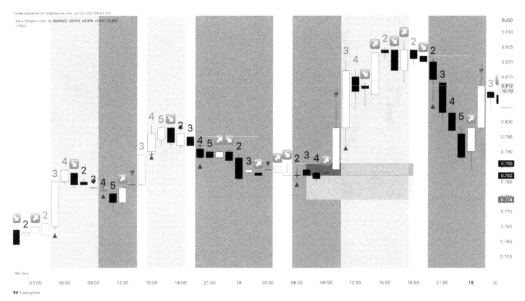

Figure B.95 – KAVA/BUSD

The result is a loss:

✔ Stop Loss finished: -0.71%
Creation date 6/18/2023 9:42:02 AM

-6.26567040
-6.26$
-0.71%

Figure B.96 – The end result

June, 18 – Trade 19 HOOK/BUSD (vFMSS)

Start of trade on the signal:

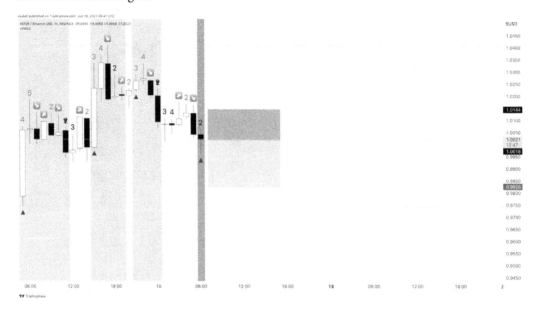

Figure B.97 – The HOOK/BUSD entry

Here's the confirmation:

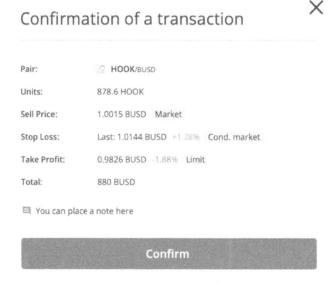

Figure B.98 – The trade confirmation

The result is a trend reversal that hit the SL:

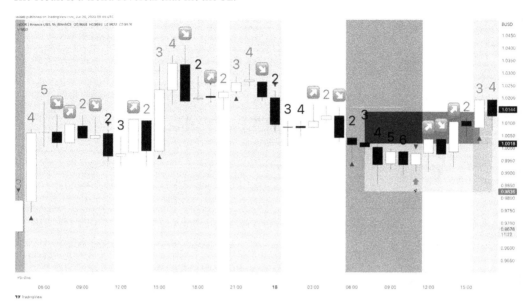

Figure B.99 – HOOK/BUSD

It's another loss:

Stop Loss finished: -1.46%
Creation date 6/18/2023 9:47:13 AM

-12.84247737
-12.84$
-1.46%

Figure B.100 – The end result

June, 18 – Trade 20 GFT/BUSD (vFMSS)

We have a signal for a long:

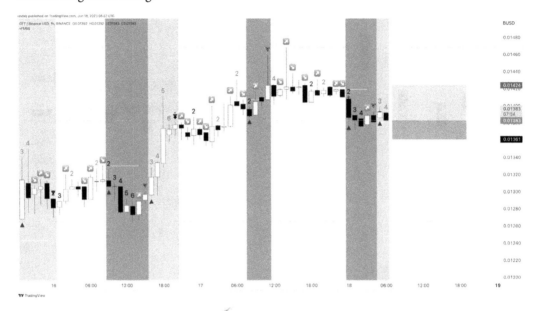

Figure B.101 – The GFT/BUSD entry

Which we take:

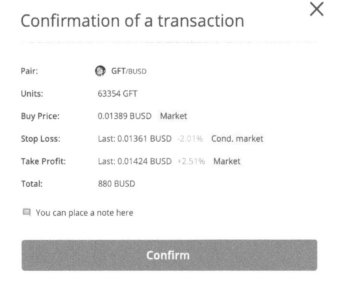

Figure B.102 – The trade confirmation

The indicator gave a stop signal at 8 a.m. UTC, which I missed, so the trade went on until it caught my SL.

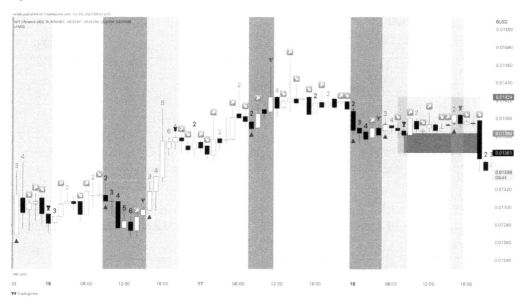

Figure B.103 – GFT/BUSD

And here's the result:

✔ Stop Loss finished: -3.72%
Creation date 6/18/2023 9:52:24 AM

-32.77239066
-32.76$
-3.72%

Figure B.104 – The end result

June, 22 – Trade 21 KEY/BUSD (the Crypto Pairs Screener)

I'm taking this trade by filtering through the Crypto Pairs Screener for tokens that rise quickly.

The question I explore here is whether the movement of the token is driven by the overall market direction or whether there is a specific catalyst influencing its price.

If I was a fundamental trader, I'd research what was happening there, but being a technical one, I can only think to either scalp the spike or long it. Here are the settings to find these spiky moments:

Symbol Type	Spot ⌄	↻	Exchange	BINANCE ⌄		↻
Exchange type	CEX ⌄	↻	Change 15m, %	Above ⌄	Value 3	↻
Change 1h, %	Above⌄ Value 2	↻	Change 4h, %	Above ⌄	Value 1	↻
Quote currency	BUSD ⌄	↻	Market Capitalization	< 10k ●————————● > 100B		

Figure B.105 – The Crypto Pairs Screener

> ### Using the Crypto Pairs Screener
> You can set the Crypto Pairs Screener to find specific trading scenarios or to filter tokens that you wouldn't trade in your strategies. It's a good way to pinpoint interesting setups.

I've found KEY/BUSD, which seems to grow out of a triangle pattern. Note that there are two local resistance lines at 0.0095 and 0.008. Because I'm unsure of the power of the move, I take partial profits before each one:

Figure B.106 – The KEY/BUSD entry

Here's the trade confirmation:

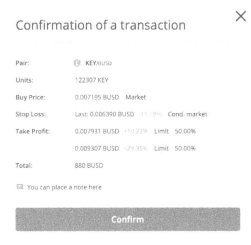

Figure B.107 – The trade confirmation

And we've been stopped:

Figure B.108 – KEY/BUSD

I love having high R ratios. This trade was 2.79. I risked a 10.74% loss for a 30% gain. I know most traders take 1.5–2 Rs, but that's just a psychological factor. Your strategy and the market dictate where you put your SLs and TPs, not a pre-defined risk/reward ratio. Think of it like this – it's OK to lose $1 10 times and win $30 the 11th:

✔ Stop Loss finished: -12.13%
Creation date 6/22/2023 7:55:15 AM

-107.36027627
-107.32$
-12.13%

Figure B.109 – The end result

This trade was a high-risk one and it went the other way. It's down to statistics (and probably a lack of thorough planning).

Things to think about

An SL is effective for a trending system in a trending market, but it may not be suitable for a non-trending market or a mean-reversion system. Conversely, profit-taking is beneficial for a mean-reversion or short-term strategy, but it may not be as effective in a trending market or with a long-term approach. For educational purposes, I put SLs in all my trades in this book, but when trading the market, I don't always do that. It's good practice, but it doesn't apply in all situations.

June, 23 – Trade 22 AGLD/BUSD

I noticed a parallel channel on AGLD/BUSD that syncs with RSI overbought/oversold signals, making it extremely easy to trade.

I see that the price has spiked up and is prepped for a short, so I quickly get in:

Figure B.110 – The AGLD/BUSD entry

Here's the trade confirmation:

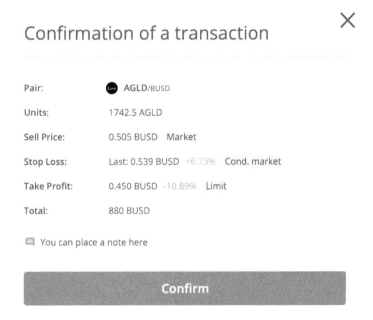

Figure B.111 – The trade confirmation

Here's the result:

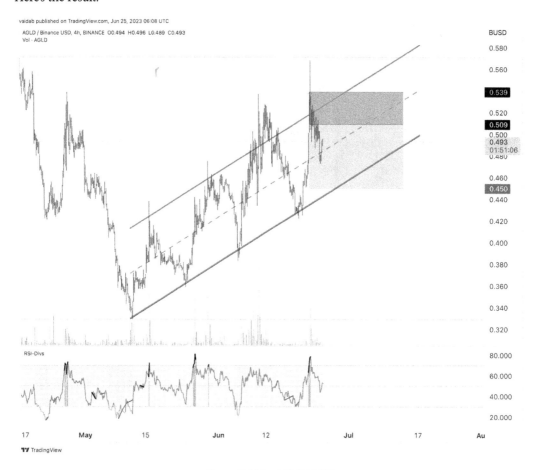

Figure B.112 – AGLD/BUSD

And the trade would've/should've/could've worked, except for the spike that hits my SL. I could've expected it, by looking at the spikes of the other highs, but I didn't. Another loss.

Figure B.113 – The end result

It's intriguing how my trading results follow a pattern of consecutive wins and losses. Interestingly, I had concerns about experiencing an unusually profitable month. However, it appears that my luck has now turned, and I'm facing a period of losses. These strings of wins followed by strings of losses are part of the expected dynamics of the market.

June, 22 – Trade 23 GLM/BUSD

I've entered this trade on 1R (risking the same amount as the potential reward). Here are the reasons for the entry – a strong overextension (I was expecting a retracement), the RSI is overbought, indecision dojis, resistance around 0.1898 (before the SL), and a potential return to the support line at 0.1734:

Figure B.114 – The GLM/BUSD entry

Here's the transaction confirmation:

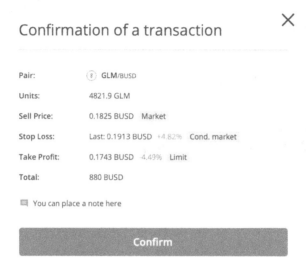

Figure B.115 – The trade confirmation

And here's the result:

Figure B.116 – GLM/BUSD

Note that my trade was caught before the big black (red) candle around June, 23, but that drop didn't catch my TP. This is not seen in the figure, as I've put the long icon further to the right, even though I entered the trade during the candles shown in *Figure B.114*. The low of that candle was 0.1748, while my TP was at 0.1743. Sometimes, you miss them by a thread, and it's a normal part of trading. You can't predict these differences.

Then, the price went the other way, broke through the first resistance at 0.1898 like a knife through butter, and stopped at around 0.2, with spikes over that value, trying to go even further.

Figure B.117 – The end result

June, 24 – Trade 24 OMG/BUSD (the Crypto Pairs Screener)

Here, I use the same settings in the Crypto Pairs Screener as before – basically, I'm looking for a token that grows quickly on three timeframes – 15m, 1H, and 4H.

I found OMG/BUSD and shorted it before the local resistance:

Figure B.118 – The OMG/BUSD entry

Here's the confirmation:

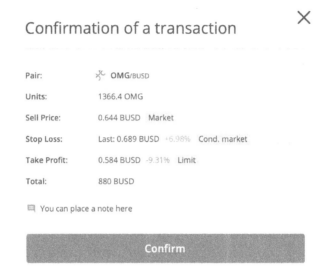

Confirmation of a transaction   ✕

Pair:	⚘ OMG/BUSD
Units:	1366.4 OMG
Sell Price:	0.644 BUSD Market
Stop Loss:	Last: 0.689 BUSD +6.98% Cond. market
Take Profit:	0.584 BUSD -9.31% Limit
Total:	880 BUSD

🖾 You can place a note here

Confirm

Figure B.119 – The trade confirmation

And it went through the resistance:

Figure B.120 – OMG/BUSD

What happened?

Well... I didn't seek any confirmation for a potential retracement besides the resistance. Basically, the token was in a spike, and I didn't look at anything that would stop its growth (except the resistance). I was expecting some kind of reaction there, but... it didn't react:

✔ Stop Loss finished: -7.06%
Creation date 6/24/2023 12:42:15 PM

-62.21715640
-62.19$
-7.06%

Figure B.121 – The end result

A note on strings having consecutive losses

Now, I have a string of losses. Quite a lot of them actually. And some are related to my emotions. I think I'm trying to prove things for this book and actually entering risky trades, ignoring common sense. My normal trading behavior is a very boring one and I can't write about it; you'd just have endless sections of the same two or three patterns. I'm also falling into **attribution bias** (see *Chapter 1*) – basically, reasoning out my losses. I'm writing this because it was a thought process that I had during my trading, and I wanted you to know about it. These things will happen inside your head too, and you'll need to process them and understand why they happen so that you don't fall prey to them. I'm also taking a break from trading to clear my head (*Editor's note – he really did take a break* 😊), and I highly recommend that you do the same. Taking a step back allows me to gain perspective and come back with a fresh mindset.

June, 25 – Taking a break

Zzz...

June, 26 – BTC analysis

I'm not going to make a full analysis today. I just want to update the BTC/BUSD chart.

Figure B.122 – A BTC/BUSD update

The channel that we identified previously worked well, and its identified support and resistance areas were places where the price reacted as expected.

On June, 20, BTC rallied through its monthly support, probably due to Deutsche Bank, Germany's largest bank, applying for a crypto license.

This surge happens in response to increased attention from institutional investors. In the wake of BlackRock, both Invesco and WisdomTree have lodged applications for spot Bitcoin ETFs. In another development, Deutsche Bank proclaimed its application for a digital asset custody license in Germany.

Where are some new SR levels?

- We have weekly support in the 30k area
- Then, we ignore (hide or delete) any SR line under 25k (for now)
- We have a weaker weekly support at 25.9k (which wasn't confirmed)
- Then, we have a 32,290 resistance area since January 2021 that we can move a bit lower to 31,791 (because of July 2021)
- 30,000 is a round number, so there is fighting in that area by default

The updated volume profile fits with our SR lines.

I also added a parallel channel on the ascending trend line that began at the start of the year.

I also noticed that the volume is very low compared to the start of the year. So, the move was not fought by the bears; it was an easy win, and it has a big risk of falling soon:

Figure B.123 – BTC/BUSD update 2

Here are the conclusions we can draw from this:

- BTC has been on an ascending trend since the start of the year.

- The trend has lost its volume, so its rise is very risky.

- The bulls are winning the 30k now because the bears took a break.

- There's a high risk of a fall. Even if it doesn't fall, I expect a pullback on the lower channel support/trendline.

- I'm short-biased for the last week of June and the start of July.

June, 28 – PUNDIX/BUSD (a new trick for you)

I used the Crypto Pairs Screener and looked for a new one-month high when I saw this situation:

Figure B.124 – A unique chart for PUNDIX/BUSD

There were a lot of wicks that I wanted to zoom in on:

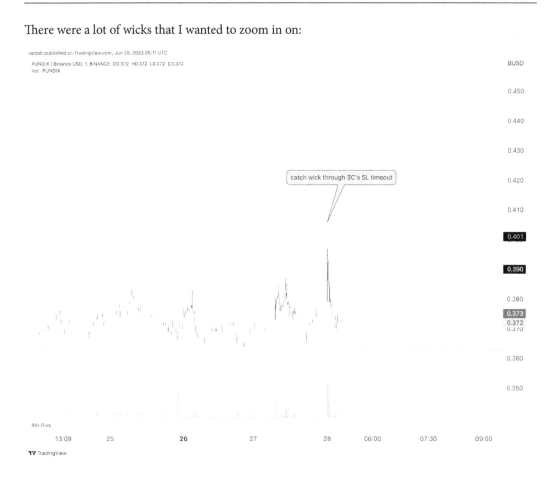

Figure B.125 – PUNDIX/BUSD zoomed in

There are a lot of wicks on this token that happen on very low timeframes. When I first encountered this situation, I had an idea – why not use 3Commas' timeout feature to prevent those spikes from being caught and short the token when it's high enough?

This is hard to do on other platforms because the SL is put on the exchange, and it's caught by the wick. However, on 3C, I add a 300-second timeout, so it doesn't happen.

Confirmation of a transaction   ✕

Pair:	✕ PUNDIX/BUSD
Units:	2273.9 PUNDIX
Conditional price:	0.387 BUSD Cond. market
Stop Loss:	Last: 0.401 BUSD +3.61% Cond. market 300 Sec
Take Profit:	0.373 BUSD -3.61% Limit
Total:	880 BUSD

If the last price rises to or above 0.387 BUSD, an order to sell 2273.9 PUNDIX at a price of 0.387 BUSD will be placed.

Figure B.126 – The trade confirmation

I've traded quite a lot of similar scenarios, and this is the result:

Figure B.127 – PUNDIX/BUSD

It's one of the few easy wins in crypto.

✔ Finished: 3.42%
Creation date 6/28/2023 8:14:52 AM

+30.10643600
+30.11$
+3.42%

Figure B.128 – The end result

June, 28 – XLM/BUSD

I've used the Crypto Pairs Screener with the **New 1-Month High** setting again:

Figure B.129 – XLM/BUSD

The only thing I was scared of was that the price went a bit further than the weekly resistance. However, the steady rise of 13 candles on the daily timeframe and the overextended RSI gave a strong enough reason for a retracement when the price hit the resistance.

So, I've added my short on a LTF, just to make sure everything was in order there:

Figure B.130 – The XLM/BUSD entry

Here's the trade confirmation (making sure I've added a 300-second timeout).

Confirmation of a transaction

Pair:	 XLM/BUSD
Units:	8477 XLM
Sell Price:	0.1038 BUSD Market
Stop Loss:	Last: 0.1081 BUSD +4.14% Cond. market 300 Sec
Take Profit:	0.0970 BUSD -6.55% Limit
Total:	880 BUSD

🖼 You can place a note here

Confirm

Figure B.131 – The trade confirmation

Here's the end result:

Figure B.132 – XLM/BUSD

I've lost because the price tested the resistance past my SL. Also, an SL hunt followed that test. Still, I think the scenario was good.

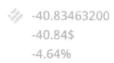

✔ Stop Loss finished: -4.64%
Creation date 6/28/2023 8:22:26 AM

Figure B.133 – The end result

Final results

The total profit was **$202.48** (8.03+59.83+149.62+99.78-34.41+49.32+67.07-4.44-17.40-32.65+126.64+49.32-25.99+69.34-6.27-14.25-6.26-12.84-32.76-107.32-62.8-46.16-62.19+30.11-40.84).

The win rate was **38.46%** (10 won, 15 lost, and I didn't catch a trade).

We began with an initial capital of $10,000, and over the course of 21 days of trading, we achieved a **2%** increase in our overall capital.

Here are some final notes regarding my month of trading:

- I haven't used leverage here, and I also didn't use compounding. I also had only 24 trades, even though I usually have around 67 trades a month. The added trades, the leverage, and the compounding would increase the wins (as well as the risk).

- Regarding the low win rate, it's worth mentioning that I intentionally opted for riskier trades in this chapter to showcase different perspectives and angles. I believe that taking calculated risks can provide valuable learning experiences, even if it means a lower win rate. Trading solely based on the safest strategy for optimal results can be monotonous and limit the depth of lessons learned.

- I've also presented a lot of discretionary trading. I usually trade using my own indicators that identify trends and pullback areas or just give me a (well-tested) signal to enter and exit a trade. I showed you vFMSS, which is one of those indicators, but I usually trade with two more, in parallel, by filtering the market for situations when the indicator almost gives a signal and adding alerts for that specific signal. And, if the indicator is good enough, I automate it.

Index

packtpub.com

Subscribe to our online digital library for full access to over 7,000 books and videos, as well as industry leading tools to help you plan your personal development and advance your career. For more information, please visit our website.

Why subscribe?

- Spend less time learning and more time coding with practical eBooks and Videos from over 4,000 industry professionals
- Improve your learning with Skill Plans built especially for you
- Get a free eBook or video every month
- Fully searchable for easy access to vital information
- Copy and paste, print, and bookmark content

Did you know that Packt offers eBook versions of every book published, with PDF and ePub files available? You can upgrade to the eBook version at packtpub.com and as a print book customer, you are entitled to a discount on the eBook copy. Get in touch with us at customercare@packtpub.com for more details.

At www.packtpub.com, you can also read a collection of free technical articles, sign up for a range of free newsletters, and receive exclusive discounts and offers on Packt books and eBooks.

Other Books You May Enjoy

If you enjoyed this book, you may be interested in these other books by Packt:

Getting Started with Forex Trading Using Python

Alex Krishtop

ISBN: 978-1-80461-685-7

- Explore the forex market organization and operations
- Understand the sources of alpha and the concept of algo trading
- Get a grasp on typical risks and ways to mitigate them
- Understand fundamental and technical analysis
- Connect to data sources and check the integrity of market data
- Use API and FIX protocol to send orders
- Translate trading ideas into code
- Run reliable backtesting emulating real-world market conditions

Hands-On Financial Trading with Python

Jiri Pik, Sourav Ghosh

ISBN: 978-1-83898-288-1

- Discover how quantitative analysis works by covering financial statistics and ARIMA
- Use core Python libraries to perform quantitative research and strategy development using real datasets
- Understand how to access financial and economic data in Python
- Implement effective data visualization with Matplotlib
- Apply scientific computing and data visualization with popular Python libraries
- Build and deploy backtesting algorithmic trading strategies

Packt is searching for authors like you

If you're interested in becoming an author for Packt, please visit `authors.packtpub.com` and apply today. We have worked with thousands of developers and tech professionals, just like you, to help them share their insight with the global tech community. You can make a general application, apply for a specific hot topic that we are recruiting an author for, or submit your own idea.

Share Your Thoughts

Now you've finished *Zero to Hero in Cryptocurrency Trading*, we'd love to hear your thoughts! Scan the QR code below to go straight to the Amazon review page for this book and share your feedback or leave a review on the site that you purchased it from.

`https://packt.link/r/1-837-63128-X`

Your review is important to us and the tech community and will help us make sure we're delivering excellent quality content.

Download a free PDF copy of this book

Thanks for purchasing this book!

Do you like to read on the go but are unable to carry your print books everywhere? Is your eBook purchase not compatible with the device of your choice?

Don't worry, now with every Packt book you get a DRM-free PDF version of that book at no cost.

Read anywhere, any place, on any device. Search, copy, and paste code from your favorite technical books directly into your application.

The perks don't stop there, you can get exclusive access to discounts, newsletters, and great free content in your inbox daily

Follow these simple steps to get the benefits:

1. Scan the QR code or visit the link below

https://packt.link/free-ebook/978-1-83763-128-5

2. Submit your proof of purchase
3. That's it! We'll send your free PDF and other benefits to your email directly